Diversified Urbanization

DIRECTIONS IN DEVELOPMENT
Countries and Regions

Diversified Urbanization

The Case of Côte d'Ivoire

Madio Fall and Souleymane Coulibaly, Editors

 **WORLD BANK GROUP**

Contents

Boxes

Figures

Maps

Tables

Acknowledgments

The study for this book was conducted by a team led by Madio Fall (Senior Water Specialist, GWADR) and Souleymane Coulibaly (Program Leader and Lead Economist for Central Africa, AFCC1) that included Andrea Betancourt (Consultant, GWADR), Annie Bidgood (Consultant, GSURR), Dina Ranarifidy (Urban Specialist, GSURR), and Alexandra Le Courtois (Urban Specialist, GSURR) for the Planning Cities chapter; Tuo Shi (Urban Economist, GSURR) and Ibou Diouf (Senior Transport Specialist, GTIDR) for the Connecting Cities chapter; Nancy Lozano-Gracia (Senior Economist, GSURR) and Alexandra Panman (Consultant, GWADR) for the Greening Cities chapter; and Jonas Ingemann Parby (Urban Specialist, GSURR), Jean-Noel Amantchi Gogoua (Senior Operation Officer, AFCF2), and Gyongshim An (Senior Urban Specialist, GSURR) for the Financing Cities chapter, with the active support of Nabil Chaherli (Program Leader, AFCF2), Lorenzo Bertollini (Senior Private Sector Development Specialist, GTCDR), Saidou Diop (Senior Financial Management Specialist, GTCDR), and Robert Yungu (Senior Public Sector Specialist, GGODR). The study draws on background consultant reports prepared by Jacques Esso, Charles Fe Doukoure, Desire Kanga, and Hugues Kouadio (ENSEA), Yeo Homiegnon (University of Bouaké), Gofaga Coulibaly (BEPU), and Emmanuel Atta (University of Nantes). The team benefited from the excellent support of Haoua Diallo and Mariame Bamba-Coulibaly (Program Assistants, AFCF2) and Nohme Sylvette Akpro (Temporary, AFCF2). The book was edited by Communications Development Incorporated.

The study was carried out with the active involvement of government counterparts led by Jules Attingbre Kouame (Adviser to the Prime Minister), Mathieu N'Guessan Seguy (Director General of Territorial Management and Regional Development, Ministry of Planning and Economic Development), Kra Kouman (Director of Urbanism, Ministry of Construction, Housing, Sanitation, and Urbanism), and many other directors from various ministries who attended the technical seminar of Bassam in June 2014 and the technical seminar of Abidjan in December 2014 to fine-tune the storyline and the analyses of this study. These seminars were designed to refine the presentation and analysis of the study. The contributions of participants and moderators of the validation workshop organized July 9, 2015, have helped to identify the recommendations of the study.

The team benefited from many brainstorming sessions with Patrick Achi (Minister of Economic Infrastructure), Kafana Kone (Chairman of UVICOCI), Dagobert Banzio (Secretary General of the Association of Region and Districts [ARDCI]), and Marie-Gabrielle Boka-Varlet (Director General of the Chamber of Commerce of Côte d'Ivoire). The proactive support of these officials is gratefully acknowledged.

The team received valuable support and contributions from Somik Lall (Lead Urban Economist, GSURR) and comments from the following peer reviewers at concept and Quality Enhancement Review (QER) stages: Christine Kessides Fallert (Manager, LLI), Roland White (Lead Urban Specialist, GSURR), Dean Cira (Lead Urban Economist, AFTU1), Catherine Farvacque-Vitkovic (Lead Urban Specialist, GSURR), Gylfi Palsson (Lead Transport Specialist, GTIDR), and Javier Sanchez-Reaza (Senior Urban Specialist, GSURR).

The team is grateful for the support received from the World Bank Management, particularly Ousmane Diagana (Country Director for Côte d'Ivoire), Sameh Wahba (Practice Manager, GSURR), and Alexander Bakalian (Practice Manager, GWADR). The study received generous financial support from the State Secretariat for Economic Cooperation (SECO) of the Government of Switzerland as part of the World Bank Multi-Donor Trust Fund on Sustainable Urbanization, which was critical for the completion of the study.

Finally, the team especially thanks His Excellency the Prime Minister of Côte d'Ivoire Daniel Kablan Duncan for his guidance and personal involvement in the launch workshops and validation of the study.

Executive Summary

Well-managed urbanization can accelerate Côte d'Ivoire's ascent to middle-income status. With an urban population share of 50 percent in 2014, Côte d'Ivoire's gross national income (GNI) per capita is $1,450 (in 2013). Georgia, Guatemala, and Indonesia, three countries located in three different continents and with urban population shares close to that of Côte d'Ivoire, have GNI per capita of $3,570, $3,340, and $3,580, respectively. Such a large gap in GNI per capita means that the underlining economic drivers of urbanization are not being fully harnessed in Côte d'Ivoire. Better managing urbanization can nurture activities that generate higher returns in economic growth and job creation.

Urbanization is not just about development of a single city within a country. In fact, a country's cities can be treated as a portfolio of assets, each differentiated by characteristics that include size, location, and density of settlement (World Bank 2009). Small cities at low urbanization level facilitate internal scale economies, such as hosting a large firm transforming local agricultural products. Secondary cities at intermediate urbanization level facilitate localization economies by enabling links between firms operating in the same sector. Large cities at advanced urbanization level facilitate urbanization economies through a diverse economic base nurturing innovation.

Côte d'Ivoire has a portfolio of places made up of a combination of three types of cities. Drawing on the findings of the World Bank's *World Development Report 2009: Reshaping Economic Geography* applied to the Ivorian context, we identify three types of cities in the country: *Global Connector* cities generating urbanization economies needed for innovation, increasing return-to-scale activities and global competitiveness; *Regional Connector* cities generating localization economies needed for efficient regional trade and transport; and *Domestic Connector* cities generating internal scale economies needed to unleash the agricultural potential of their regions (box ES.1).

Abidjan, San-Pédro, and Yamoussoukro are Côte d'Ivoire's natural Global Connectors. The Greater Abidjan area dominates with 20 percent of the population, 80 percent of formal employment, and 90 percent of formal enterprises. It is an advanced urban area facing challenges of metropolitan areas around the world. The port of San-Pédro—built from scratch under the first development plan—is the main export gateway for agricultural products and was planned to be connected by rail to the mineral heart of the west (Man and its surroundings).

Box ES.1 The Typology of Global, Regional, and Domestic Connectors Can Form the Basis for a Territorial Development Strategy

The typology of cities proposed here can provide some guiding principles for the Territorial Development Master Plan. The government is preparing an Orientation Law on Territorial Development that will lay the groundwork for the development of a Territorial Development Master Plan. The draft law is broad and highlights the government's mandate to ensure balanced territorial development by facilitating development of economic activities across all regions through the establishment of growth poles. Global experience on such balancing has had mixed results: although it makes sense to support development of economic activities in regions with endowments or economic potential, doing so at the expense of primary cities that are the country's engines of growth can retard growth. Anchoring the Territorial Development Master Plan on the typology of cities proposed here would allow tapping into the comparative advantage of various Ivorian cities.

Yamoussoukro has been the capital since the 1980s, although national public administration is still in Abidjan. The city has one of the most reputable polytechnic engineering schools in francophone Africa, offering the potential to build bridges to technology companies if information and communications technology (ICT) infrastructure is scaled up to global standards.

The Regional Connectors of Côte d'Ivoire are connected to the West African region through five corridors. The northern corridor connects Abidjan with Ouagadougou through a road and rail link that passes through Bouaké (the country's second-largest city), Korhogo (the capital of the Northern region with nearly 200,000 inhabitants), and Ferkessédougou (a secondary city of 75,000 inhabitants). Eastward, Côte d'Ivoire is connected to Lagos, Nigeria, via a road running through Aboisso and Noe on the Ivorian side and through three capital cities in West Africa (Accra in Ghana, Lomé in Togo, and Cotonou in Benin). Another eastward connection to Ghana (via Kumassi and Tamale) runs through Adzopé, Abengourou, and Bondoukou. Abidjan is connected to Nzérékoré in Guinea via a road through Yamoussoukro, Daloa, and Man, each of which has more than 150,000 inhabitants and is in a region rich in agriculture, minerals, or tourism. Another westward connection to Monrovia in Liberia goes through Grand Lahou, Sassandra, San-Pédro, and Tabou along the Gulf of Guinea. If we consider the threshold of 100,000 inhabitants, the following secondary cities along the three regional corridors are the main Regional Connectors: Adzopé and Abengourou (east corridor), Bouaké and Korhogo (north corridor), and Daloa and Man (west corridor).

Côte d'Ivoire's small cities and market towns could be anchors generating scale economies for agribusiness. Whereas southwest regions strongly contribute to the production and export of cash crops, savanna areas can help scale up food and cereal production to supply urban centers domestically and regionally. In the long term, with the movement of the cocoa belt from eastern and central regions to the south (with an eye on the port of San-Pédro), climate change and international economic conditions might once more shift the heart of these cash-crop production areas. Given increasing regional disparities in Côte d'Ivoire, good connections between the agricultural hinterlands of secondary cities and strategic regional capital cities may help smallholders to modernize into agribusiness chains.

To achieve diversified urbanization, Ivorian policy makers need to act urgently along four dimensions:

1. *Planning*—charting a course for cities by setting the terms of urbanization, especially policies for using urban land, enabling housing markets, and expanding basic infrastructure and public services.
2. *Connecting*—making a city's markets accessible (labor, goods, and services) to other cities and to other neighborhoods in the city, as well as to export markets.
3. *Greening*—enhancing livability of cities by reducing pollution and emissions and conserving scarce environmental and financial resources.
4. *Financing*—finding sources for large capital outlays needed to provide infrastructure and services as cities grow and urbanization picks up speed.

This framework reflects the principles identified by stakeholders from national and subnational governments and the private sector, which helped to formulate a shared vision of urbanization in Côte d'Ivoire. These stakeholders believe that successful urbanization should lead to "cities that are planned, structured, competitive, attractive, inclusive, and organized around development poles."

The analysis and recommendations presented in this report benefited greatly from stakeholders' inputs, through a validation workshop held in Abidjan in July 2015. A summary of the main findings along each of the four dimensions are summarized below (see boxes ES.2–ES.5).

Box ES.2 Main Points on Planning from the Validation Workshop

Three areas were identified concerning decentralization:

- Review the institutional framework for relations between the State and local communities through "decentralizing decentralization." Emphasis was placed on clarifying the roles and responsibilities between the prefects, trustees, and district leaders.
- Better distribute the support schemes between municipalities in the form of three options, aid, guidance and intermunicipal cooperation.
- Capitalize on best practices among municipalities by promoting intermunicipal exchanges.

Several interventions addressed land management as follows:

- Develop a national land use plan and to organize actors and activities based on a shared vision.
- Define a tool or a formal framework allowing all stakeholders to undertake coordinated actions.

box continues next page

Box ES.2 Main Points on Planning from the Validation Workshop *(continued)*

- Establish a policy paper with a long-term perspective.
- Reinforce the land-use planning framework, determining public policy based on the question "What do we want with our land?" particularly in urban areas.
- Take the Regional Development Plan into account, going beyond a strategic plan, which will follow from the national land use plan to ensure consistency among different plans.
- Take sustainable development dimensions into account, (for example, the eco-center at Marcory) and integrate those principles into the planning process.

Reinforcement of human capital:

- Reinforce technical competencies, review human resources, and place qualified personnel in municipalities
- Establish a budget for training in communes
- Encourage meaningful citizen engagement through training

Planning documents

- Enforce planning documents that have already been created
- Update outdated master plans
- Address parallel land tenure systems, including customary and statutory rights
- Establish a coherent system for land subdivision
- Integrate basic socioeconomic activities for local residents, solid waste management, and basic social services (health, water, energy)

Source: Validation workshop for the Urbanization Review.[1]

Reform priorities in planning.

- Improve land market fluidity. A constrained land market limits private investment. Improving the fluidity of the market will help increase the investments in industrial and residential development. This will require increasing the supply of usable land in three clear steps:
  - First, tenure security should be improved through simpler, shorter, and cheaper procedures.
  - Second, trunk infrastructure should be expanded in a timely manner, especially for new urban extensions not yet connected to urban services (in particular roads, electricity, and water) and before these are settled.
  - Third, land for different investment activities should be identified, planned, and allocated efficiently to enable meeting increasing demand for land.
- Expand service delivery. Besides creating functioning land markets, policy makers must also ensure that most basic infrastructure services reach all city residents—urban and peri-urban—alike. There are two key priorities:
  - First, step up efforts to develop serviced land.
  - Second, implement financially sustainable service delivery models and strengthen regulation to increase cost recovery and, accordingly, investment and service coverage.

- Simplify planning regulations. Land use plans can ensure that public and private developments in various zones are developed harmoniously, and that developments provide mixed economic and residential activities as well as green and protected areas. There are three key issues:
  - First, improve coordination in allocation of responsibilities governing urban areas.
  - Second, align land use policies and planning standards with infrastructure availability and plans.
  - Third, simplify and relax regulations on land use and zoning, to increase housing affordability.

Box ES.3 Main Points on Connecting from the Validation Workshop

The workshop acknowledged the quality of the report, and endorsed the proposed recommendations for connecting cities. However, the following points, grouped into three categories, were also proposed:

Planning and connecting:

- Take connectivity into account during the planning process
- Plan and organize public transport in all its dimensions
- Preserve rights-of-way of roads (many of which are currently occupied)
- Implement a policy with respect to the rule of law, and the necessary training
- Bring together relevant actors and professions and ensure proper coordination during planning phases and implementation, given that connectivity is at the center of many urban issues
- Plan urban areas so as to avoid costly trips
- Organize transportation networks to achieve higher efficiency; at present there is no single market for urban transport, and lack of coordination leads to higher costs
- Undertake an in-depth reorganization of the transport sector, especially leveraging ICT
- Expand the development of master plans to all cities, and adopt a national urban development master plan
- Integrate greening principles in transport planning

Improving connectivity through operations

- Take all forms of transport into account (ferries, rail, etc.) and plan for transfer points, feeder systems, and parking
- Take major steps to plan for future needs. For example, plan for commune-level electric-powered shuttle buses (or mobilizing renewable energies)
- Increase the number of routes dedicated to public transport
- Prioritize innovative projects to redirect demand into feeder routes
- Undertake outreach programs for transport users

Investments in connectivity

- Take decisive and ambitious investment planning decisions

Source: Validation workshop for the Urbanization Review.

Diversified Urbanization · http://dx.doi.org/10.1596/978-1-4648-0808-1

Reform priorities to enhance mobility and connectivity

- Coordinate land use and infrastructure to enhance urban mobility.
- Accelerate reforms for greater professionalization of operators in the transport sector and better access to finance.
- Better organize the freight transport sector and make it more competitive.
- Establish a market information system (MkIS) to better connect transporters with customers.
- Set up investment in strategic corridors and develop supporting plans for strengthening urban agglomerations and city development.
- Diversify the corridors connecting the domestic economy to attractive regional markets.

Box ES.4 Main Points on Greening from the Validation Workshop

The rapid expansion of cities in Côte d'Ivoire led to the degradation of biodiversity and quality of life. To rethink Ivorian cities, it's necessary to implement action programs that are mindful of the environment, favoring its conservation and improving the quality of life of the population—applying greening principles to make cities (more) attractive. These actions can focus on, among other things, mainly the efficient management of solid waste, reducing the impact of pollution, and the coherent management of natural resources (water, forests, etc.). Within this perspective, participants made the following recommendations:

- Leverage inputs from national experts who specialize in environmental issues
- Partner with NGOs in the city greening process
- Effectively apply existing legal texts on environmental topics
- Strengthen environmental taxation to facilitate financing for greening measures
- Extend the coverage of sanitation infrastructure
- Reinforce the resilience of cities to environmental shocks
- Implement effective management tools for urban waste
- Integrate greening principles in cities' strategic development plans
- Take into account the human dimension in the greening process, through outreach initiatives for behavior change

Source: Validation workshop for the Urbanization Review.

Reform priorities in greening

- Preserve and enhance environmental assets
  - Within urban planning, incorporate greening activities for arterial roads (primary and secondary)
  - Plan for the creation of small urban parks to preserve urban biodiversity, develop recreational activities, and provide a "green lung" for cities
  - Avoid or stop city expansion where it's a factor in deforestation. Promote instead vertical construction to increase urban density
- Urban sanitation
  - Plan for sanitation infrastructure such as collection points and bins, including neighborhood access routes, based on the findings of targeted studies on waste management impacts
  - Identify sites for authorized non-polluting technical landfills, including neighborhood access routes, based on the findings of targeted studies on waste management impacts
  - Plan dedicated spaces for leisure and commerce, in order to avoid unplanned land uses and obstructions
- Sustainable development
  - Plan for infrastructure dedicated to mass transit and non-motorized transit (walking, biking, etc.)
  - Establish eco-centers served by renewable energy (ex. solar energy), built with local and recycled materials, and requiring less energy
  - Develop a circular economic system based on re-employment, restoration, and waste recycling
  - Plan cities in a way that takes into account intense mixed urban uses (spaces with multiple uses—civic, leisure, sport, commercial, industrial, etc.) and mixed incomes (social housing, low-income housing, and market rate)
- Coordinate land use planning and infrastructure for reduced emission by
  - Linking people to jobs through mixed land use planning and mass transport systems when density is sufficient and
  - Linking goods to markets through improved logistics for freight.
- Coordinate land use planning and infrastructure for increased resilience by integrating the assessment of flooding and climate change risks into city planning; for example, storm water drainage and green space.

Box ES.5 Main Points on Financing from the Validation Workshop

Several recommendations were put forth by participants during the workshop on financing cities, such as:

State/Local authorities:

- Improve the legal and institutional framework for the transfer of resources to local authorities so that they can develop new sources of innovative financing
- Allocate a larger portion of the State budget to financing local authorities (at least 10 percent, instead of the current 5 percent)
- Make information on communes' revenue collections more transparent
- Organize a round-table exchange on the potential of local authorities' own-source revenues
- Allocate a portion of the property tax to finance the discharge of property rights
- Prioritize investment in communes, through the part of the budget currently allocated for operating expenditures and investments.
- Put in place a fund to finance investments in local authorities

Private sector:

- Involve the private sector in the financing of cities through public-private partnerships (PPP)
- Capture the value of ICT investments

Civil society:

- Involve civil society in the city governance through the implementation of specific activities of interest

Source: Validation workshop for the Urbanization Review.

Reform priorities in financing

- Address the inconsistencies between devolution and decentralization alignment so that delegated functions follow finance and minimum human resources capacity is in place.
- Strengthen the local finance system and revise the fiscal transfer systems in key areas, simplifying the number of transfers and supporting the expansion and improvement of own-source revenue collection and improvement of public financial management.
- Leverage collaboration among regions, municipalities, and utilities to generate economies of scale in infrastructure services delivery.
- Assess the efficiency of current transfer schemes, consolidate administrative decentralization to enable improved performance at the commune level, and consider introducing new elements to incentivize performance.
- Explore the viability of additional new sources of financing for Global Connectors and creditworthy Regional and Domestic Connectors.

For this framework to succeed, a good governance structure is a prerequisite. Policy makers, at all government levels, will have to work together. Currently, institutional fragmentation prevails with a multiplicity of policy-making institutions involved in urbanization with overlaps, unclear mandates, and a dearth of coordination. The Ministry of Planning and Economic Development is a key stakeholder because it oversees planning, land development, and population aspects. The Ministry of Construction, Housing, Sanitation, and Urbanism develops and implements urban master plans. The Ministry of the Interior and Security hosts the directorate (Direction Générale de la Décentralisation et des Collectivités Locales, or General Directorate for Decentralization and Local Communities [DGDCL]) that assures oversight of municipalities and regions. The Ministry of Economic Infrastructure is responsible for building and maintaining the infrastructure connecting domestic economic centers with each other and with regional and global centers. The Ministry of Transport is in charge of intra- and interurban transportation, as well as international transportation. Municipalities and regions are represented by two associations: the UVICOCI (Union des Villes et Communes de Côte d'Ivoire, or Association of Cities and Communes of Côte d'Ivoire) and the ARDCI (Assemblée des Régions et Districts de Côte d'Ivoire, or Association of Regions and Districts of Côte d'Ivoire) that are bottom-up consultative bodies of elected officials and urban and regional development specialists. The private sector remains the key player driving growth, hence the need to involve all active business associations.

Note

1. A technical seminar using the team alignment process was held on June 28–29, 2014, to identify constraints and solutions to integrated urban development. Participants were director-level staff from all ministries involved in urbanization, representatives of the chairmen of the association of municipalities and regions, representatives of the major private sector associations, and representatives of Parliament and the Economic and Social Council.

Reference

World Bank. 2009. *World Development Report 2009: Reshaping Economic Geography.* Washington, DC: World Bank.

Abbreviations

ACD	Definitive Concession Decision (Arrêté de Concession Définitive)
ACE	African Coast to Europe
AGEF	Agency for Land Development (Agence de Gestion Foncière)
AGETU	Agency for Urban Transport (Agence du Transport Urbain)
ANASUR	National Agency for Urban Sanitation (Agence Nationale de Salubrité Urbaine)
ARDCI	Association of Regions and Districts (Association des Régions et Districts de Côte d'Ivoire)
BNETD	National Bureau of Technical Study and Development (Bureau National d'Étude Technique et de Développement)
CEA	Country Environment Assessment
CFAF	CFA franc
CIAPOL	Centre Ivoirien Antipollution
CIE	Ivorian Company of Electricity (Compagnie Ivoirienne d'Électricité)
CIV	Côte d'Ivoire
DALY	disability-adjusted life year
DCPP	Parastatal Accounting Directorate (Direction de la Comptabilité Parapublique)
DGDCL	General Directorate for Decentralization and Local Communities (Direction Générale de la Décentralisation et des Collectivités Locales)
DGDDL	General Directorate for Decentralization and Local Development (Direction Générale de la Décentralisation et du Développement Local)
DGF	General Financial Allocation (Dotation Globale Financière)
DGI	General Directorate of Tax (Direction Générale des Impôts)
DGTCP	General Directorate of Treasury and Public Accounting (Direction Générale du Trésor et de la Comptabilité Publique)

DHS	Demographic and Health Survey
DOCD	Directorate of Operations for Decentralized Collectivities (Direction des Opérations des Collectivités Décentralisées)
ECOWAS	Economic Community of West African States
FPCL	Municipal Credit Fund (Fonds de Prêts aux Collectivités Locales)
GIZ	German Agency for International Cooperation (Deutsche Gesellschaft für Internationale Zusammenarbeit)
GNI	gross national income
HCH	High Commission on Water (Haut Commissariat à l'Hydraulique)
ICT	information and communications technology
INS	National Institute of Statistics (Institut National de la Statistique)
JICA	Japan International Cooperation Agency
km	kilometer
MCLAU	Ministry of Construction, Housing, Sanitation, and Urbanism (Ministère de la Construction, du Logement, de l'Assainissement et de l'Urbanisme)
MICS	Multiple Indicator Cluster Survey
MkIS	market information system
MOOC	massive open online courses
ONPC	National Office of Civil Protection (l'Office National de la Protection Civile)
PLANGIRE	National Action Plan for Integrated Management of Water Resources (Gestion Intégrée des Resources en Eau)
PPP	public-private partnership
RGPH	General Population and Housing Census (Recensement Général de la Population et de l'Habitat)
SAT3/WASC	South Atlantic 3/West Africa Submarine Cable
SATCI	Land Development Corporation of Côte d'Ivoire (Société d'Aménagement de Terrains Côte d'Ivoire)
SEEA	Satellite Economic and Environmental Accounts
SETU	Company Urban Land Equipment (Société d'Equipement des Terrains Urbain)
SICOGI	Ivorian Company for Construction and Real Estate Management (Société Ivoirienne de Construction et de Gestion Immobilière)
SODECI	Company for Water in Côte d'Ivoire (Société de Distribution d'Eau de Côte Ivoire)

SOGEPHIA	Company of Management and Financing of Housing (Société de Gestion et de Financement de l'Habitat)
SOTRA	Abidjan Transport Company (Société des Transports Abidjanais)
TEOM	Fee for Removal of Household Waste (Taxe d'Enlèvement des Ordures Ménagères)
TEU	twenty-foot equivalent units
ton-km	ton-kilometer
U5MR	under-5 mortality rate
UEMOA	Union Économique et Monétaire Ouest-Africaine (or West African Economic and Monetary Union [WAEMU])
UN-Habitat	United Nations Human Settlements Programme
USAID	United States Agency for International Development
UVICOCI	Association of Municipalities (Union des Villes et Communes de Côte d'Ivoire)
WACO	West African Coastal Observatory
WACS	West African Cable System
WAEMU	West African Economic and Monetary Union (or Union Économique et Monétaire Ouest-Africaine [UEMOA])
WCCD	World Council on City Data

Overview: Rethinking Ivorian Cities

Urbanization and Economic Growth

With a gross national income (GNI) per capita of $1,450 in 2013, Côte d'Ivoire seeks a development strategy to reach middle-income status—a daunting challenge. It will take an annual growth rate of 10 percent over 13 years to reach a GNI per capita of $4,100, that of a middle-income country. Further, to report middle-income metrics—if we take the average performance of current middle-income countries—Côte d'Ivoire would have to[1]

- *Cut* extreme poverty from 24 to 17 percent;
- *Raise* the share of the population with access to electricity from 59 to 92 percent;
- *Keep* the share of the urban population with access to water at 97 percent;
- *Increase* the share of the rural population with access to water from 74 to 80 percent;
- *Nearly double* the share of the urban population with access to sanitation services from 46 to 87 percent; and
- *More than double* the share of the rural population with access to sanitation services from 29 to 65 percent.

The country needs a structural transformation seen in the increasing role of urbanization in economic performance. The experience of developed and emerging economies shows that gross domestic product (GDP) per capita has risen with increasing urbanization (figure O.1). According to the *World Development Report 2009: Reshaping Economic Geography* (World Bank 2009), growing economic concentration, diminishing distance to economic density, and lowering cross-border barriers to trade are inherent to the development process as a country moves from an economy based on agriculture to one based on industry and then on services. This spatial transformation leads to the rise of cities and towns that are the natural manifestations of agglomeration economies. This is corroborated by the fact that the top 600 cities of the world contribute just over one-fifth of its population but over half of its production (figure O.2). Obviously, some of

Figure O.1 Per Capita GDP Has Risen in Tandem with Urbanization Rates

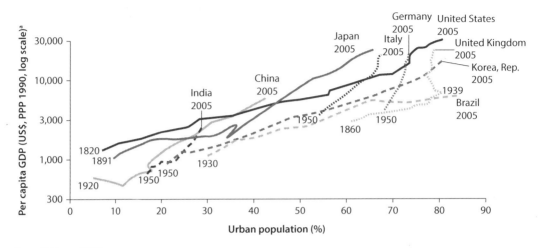

Source: Dobbs et al 2012.
Note: Definition of urbanization varies by country; pre-1950 figures for the United Kingdom are estimated. GDP = gross domestic product.
a. Historical per capita GDP series expressed in 1990 Geary-Khamis dollars, which reflect PPP.

Figure O.2 The Top 600 Cities Account for 22 Percent of Population, 54 Percent of Income

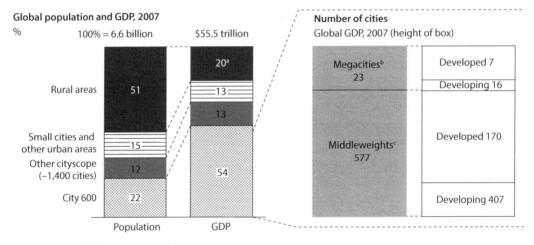

Source: McKinsey Global Institute Cityscope 1.0.
Note: GDP = gross domestic product.
a. Estimate based on global GDP not including agriculture and mining and on GDP contribution of smaller Cityscope cities.
b. Megacities include cities with over 10 million inhabitants in 2007.
c. Middleweight cities have a current population between 150,000 and 10 million.

these cities are in Sub-Saharan Africa. However, aggregate numbers indicate that the correlation between urbanization and per capita GDP in Africa is weak (figure O.3). Additionally, whereas countries in other continents passed the 40 percent urbanization marker with GDP per capita above $1,800, Sub-Saharan African countries, including Côte d'Ivoire, passed it at just $1,000 (figure O.4).

Figure O.3 Sub-Saharan African Countries Are Urbanizing

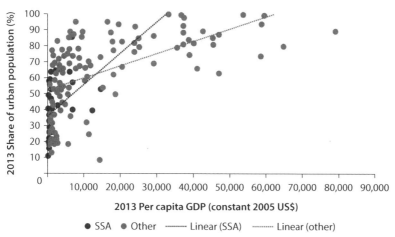

Sources: World Development Indicators; World Bank staff calculations.
Note: GDP = gross domestic product; SSA = Sub-Saharan Africa.

Figure O.4 Despite Urbanization, Incomes of Sub-Saharan Countries Remain below Those of Other Regions

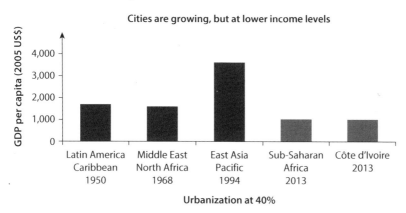

Sources: World Development Indicators; World Bank staff calculations.
Note: GDP = gross domestic product.

This highlights the limited fiscal and associated administrative capabilities of governments to lay in the investments in housing, infrastructure, and services in tandem with growth of urban settlements. This also makes the case for greater efficiency in public resource allocation to make "every franc count."

Economic theory suggests that the link between urbanization and economic performance is through the interaction between three forces: scale economies, factor mobility, and reduction in transport costs. Scale economies encourage firms, cities, or countries to produce more of some goods and services and thus reduce unit production costs and make them more productive and competitive. The mobility of factors allows their use in the most productive firm, city, or country. Decreasing transport costs allows the specialization of firms, cities, and countries, which fosters trade according to comparative advantage. At country level, these three forces interact to foster the emergence of a diversified urbanization with places at incipient, intermediate, or advanced stages of urbanization.

Urbanization is not just about development of a single city within a country. In fact, a country's cities can be treated as a portfolio of assets, each differentiated by characteristics that include size, location, and density of settlement. Three decades of research worldwide highlight that businesses and people can exploit economies of scale and agglomeration if their urban settlements perform their intended functions (World Bank 2009). Small cities at incipient urbanization level facilitate internal scale economies, such as hosting a large firm transforming local agricultural products. Secondary cities at intermediate urbanization level facilitate localization economies through competition between firms operating in the same sector. Large cities at advanced urbanization level facilitate urbanization economies through a diverse economic base favoring innovation.

Côte d'Ivoire has a portfolio of places made up of a combination of three types of cities. Drawing on the findings of the *World Development Report 2009* applied to the Ivorian context, we identify three types of cities in the country: *Global Connector* cities generating urbanization economies needed for innovation, increasing return-to-scale activities and global competitiveness; *Regional Connector* cities generating localization economies needed for efficient regional trade and transport; and *Domestic Connector* cities generating internal scale economies needed to unleash the agricultural potential of their regions. We then make the case that, to support growth and job creation, policy makers at the central, regional, and municipal levels need to coordinate their actions so as to promote a diversified urbanization through better planning, better connecting, greening, and finding ways to finance the growing development needs of these cities.

Cities, Growth, and Productivity in Côte d'Ivoire

Managing urbanization well is critical for meeting the challenges of moving to middle-income-country status. With an urban population at 50 percent,[2] Côte d'Ivoire's economy is underperforming urbanization: GNI per capita should be about $2,700 if urbanization economies worked as economic geography theory predicted (figure O.5). Georgia, Guatemala, and Indonesia, for example—countries on three different continents and with urban population shares close to that of Côte d'Ivoire—have GNI per capita of $3,570, $3,340, and $3,580, respectively. Some other Sub-Saharan African countries such as Cameroon and Ghana share the same fate. This seems to corroborate the theory of "consumption cities" versus "production cities" developed by Glaeser, Kolko, and Saiz (2001) and Jedwab (2013), among others. By this theory, urbanization in countries with consumption cities is not paced by a structural transformation of the economy because the rent generated by the resource-intensive sector is consumed in cities by workers involved in nontradable service sectors (typically in the informal sector).

Figure O.5 The Ivorian Economy Is Underperforming Urbanization

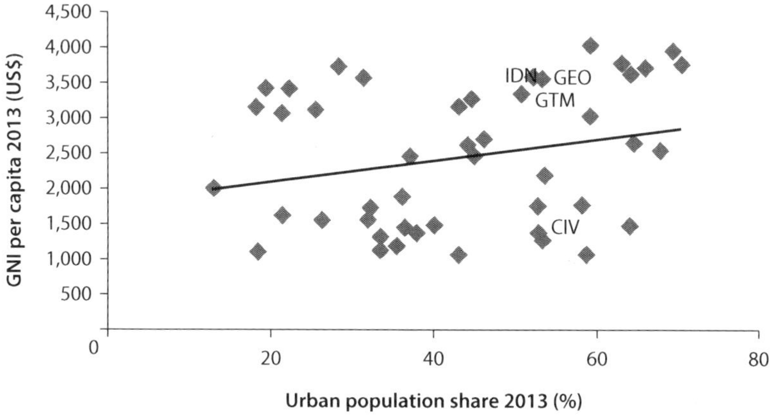

Sources: World Development Indicators; World Bank staff calculations.
Note: CIV = Côte d'Ivoire; GEO = Georgia; GNI = gross national income; GTM = Guatemala; IDN = Indonesia.

Although lagging on aggregate income per capita, manufacturing appears to be correlated with urbanization in Côte d'Ivoire. Globally, manufacturing is the engine of growth for large to medium cities with good access to markets. As countries urbanize, their manufacturing sectors tend to grow as a share of GDP until urbanization reaches 60 percent, with manufacturing as a share of GDP generally peaking at over 15 percent. The correlation between manufacturing and urbanization in Côte d'Ivoire appears to be above this trend, even if manufacturing as a share of GDP consistently declined from a peak of 17.7 percent in 2000 to 12.7 percent in 2013 (figure O.6). The decline started after the first military coup in December 1999, which was followed by a series of sociopolitical tensions that reached a culminating point after the runoff of the presidential election in November 2010. This instability might explain the deteriorating performance of manufacturing—because investment in growth-sustaining infrastructure abruptly stopped during that period.

Urbanization economies in Côte d'Ivoire have been negatively affected by the predominance of Abidjan and the limited economic activities in secondary cities, as well as a succession of crises. Urban primacy is defined as the share of the largest city in total urban population. In Côte d'Ivoire, Abidjan's primacy varied from 24 percent in 1975 to 49 percent in 1988, to 44 percent in 1998, and to 40 percent in 2014 (figure O.7). In 2013, the average and median values of urban primacy for Sub-Saharan African countries were 37 and 38 percent, respectively. Although declining, urban primacy in Côte d'Ivoire is still high.[3] Using firm-level data (Banque de Données Financiers, BDF), Coulibaly et al. (2014) found that for 2010 the location quotient (a proxy measure of urbanization economies) had a positive and statistically significant impact on firms' sales: a 10 percent increase in the location coefficient of a sector in a region would lead to a 2 percent increase in sales of firms operating in that sector and

Figure O.6 Manufacturing Is Better Correlated with Urbanization

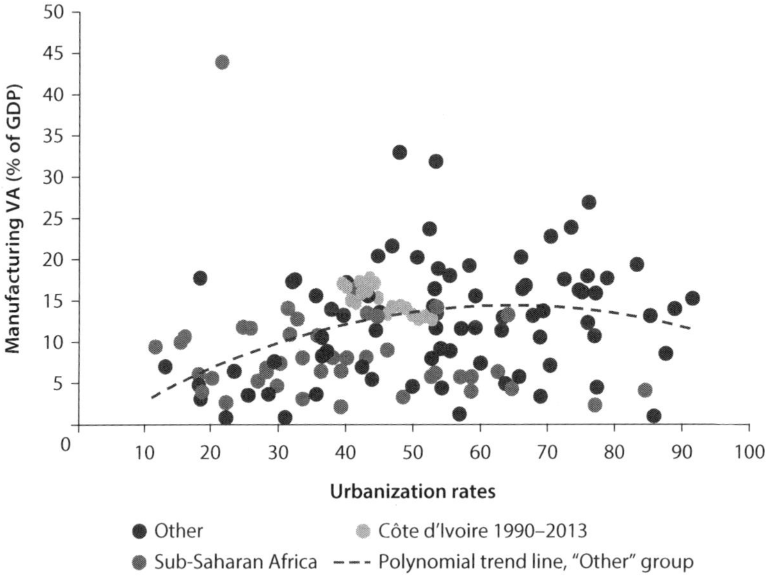

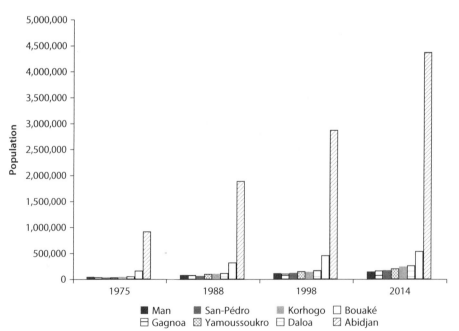

Sources: World Development Indicators; World Bank staff calculations.
Note: GDP = gross domestic product; Other = all other countries excluding Sub-Saharan African countries.

Figure O.7 The Population Gap between Abidjan and Other Ivorian Cities Has Widened since 1975

Sources: World Development Indicators; World Bank staff calculations.

Figure O.8 Economic Concentration Seems to Negatively Impact Firms' Sales in Abidjan

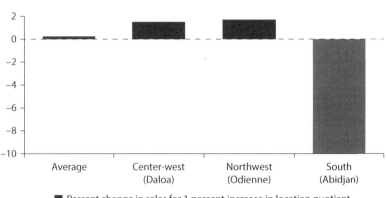

■ Percent change in sales for 1 percent increase in location quotient

Source: Coulibaly et al. 2014, using firms' financial statement statistics 1999–2011 from the Institut National de la Statistique.

region (figure O.8). This result is stronger for the center-west (Daloa) and northwest (Odienne) regions, with a 10 percent increase in the location quotient of these regions leading to a 15 and 17 percent increase, respectively, in the sales of firms operating there. By contrast, a 1 percent increase in the location quotient of the south (Abidjan) region is associated with a decrease in sales by 10 percent, indicating that congestion costs are prevailing in this city of 4 million inhabitants.

Abidjan's primacy is corroborated by freight flows between Ivorian cities, which are heavily tilted toward Abidjan from small and secondary cities (figure O.9). Four decades of successive economic and sociopolitical crises constraining investment and maintenance of urban infrastructure seem to have taken a toll on Abidjan's capacity to generate urbanization economies.

Urbanization has been negatively correlated with per capita income since 1978. Constraints such as limited access to land, housing, transport, and infrastructure slow urbanization, whereas growth in the number of people with secondary education appears to accelerate it. Indeed, Coulibaly, Esso, and Kanga (2014) find that secondary schools are concentrated in regional capital cities; this explains the elevated population with a high school education in secondary cities. The population with a secondary education is more likely to migrate than one with a primary or tertiary education. Students completing primary education move to secondary cities to complete their studies and remain if they do not pursue higher education. This finding should guide initiatives to diversify the economy of secondary cities, and reverse the declining trend in correlation between urbanization and per capita income (figure O.10).

Most firms are in a few southern cities, encouraging migration to these cities and their hinterlands. Between 1999 and 2011, 89–96 percent of registered firms

Figure O.9 The Main Economic Flows from Ivorian Cities Are toward Abidjan

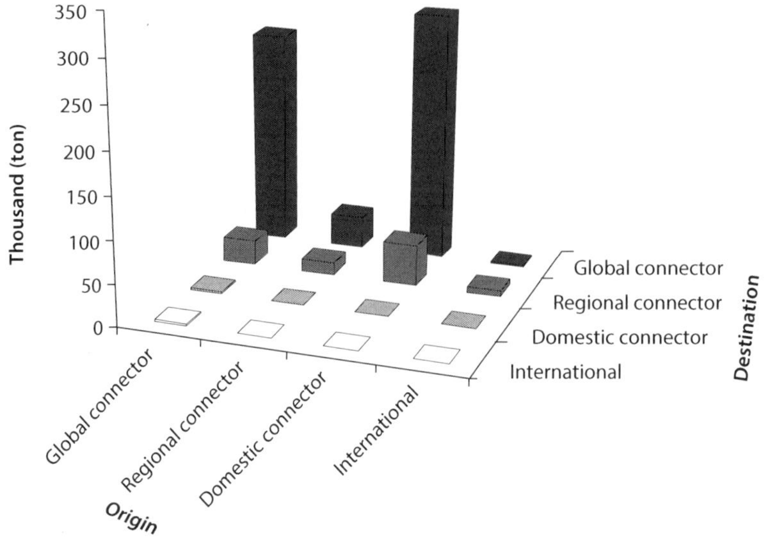

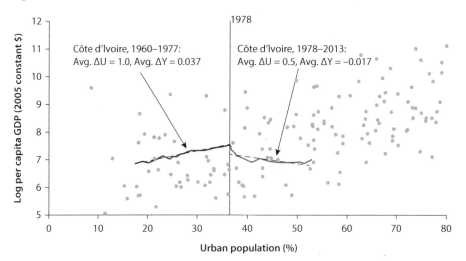

Source: ENSEA 2014.

Figure O.10 The Correlation between Urbanization and Income Shifted after 1978

Côte d'Ivoire, 1960–1977:
Avg. ΔU = 1.0, Avg. ΔY = 0.037

Côte d'Ivoire, 1978–2013:
Avg. ΔU = 0.5, Avg. ΔY = −0.017

Sources: World Development Indicators; World Bank staff calculations.
Note: GDP = gross domestic product; ΔU = change in urban population (%), year-over-year; ΔY = log change in per capita GDP (2005 constant $).

were in the South (mostly in the Greater Abidjan area). This area also has 80 percent of formal jobs, and is the main employment zone for sectors such as services to households and industries, transport, telecommunications, wholesale and retail, and food and agriculture (Coulibaly et al. 2014). The concentration of companies in the South is due to Abidjan's position as the country's main economic hub, having one of the largest ports in Sub-Saharan Africa—the

Autonomous Port of Abidjan—as well as a deep-sea port at San-Pédro. The rest of the country subsists mainly by growing cash or food crops.

This concentration calls for rethinking Ivorian cities. As Côte d'Ivoire moves from lower- to upper-middle-income-country status, its urban centers are expected to play a key role in its economic recovery as centers for economic activity and trade, for basic services (health and education), and as centers for job opportunities (informal and formal). This key role of cities has been seen in East Asian countries like Indonesia, Malaysia, the Philippines, and Thailand where urban primacy was estimated in 2003 at 12, 14, 21, and 32 percent, respectively (World Bank 2007). Although the military conflict, political unrest, and decades of underinvestments in key infrastructure have kept several cities and urban areas less efficient and less prosperous, urban areas remain critical in propelling sustainable economic growth by becoming effective production centers for the core economic drivers, such as agriculture, mining and energy, and services. Better management of urbanization—prioritizing backbone infrastructure and services able to sustain manufacturing and tradable services—could both attract activities needing increasing returns to scale in cities and boost growth and job creation. Such management should also improve the delivery of public services such as water, sanitation, waste management; other public amenities such as electricity and urban transport; and social services, helping the country deliver on the twin goals of poverty reduction and shared prosperity.

Urbanization: Dynamics and Policy Responses

Côte d'Ivoire is one of the most urbanized countries in Sub-Saharan Africa. A dozen African countries, including Côte d'Ivoire, have an urban population larger than the rural population. The share of employment in agriculture in these countries is estimated to have been declining over 2005–15, indicating that a structural transformation is underway (figure O.11). The Côte d'Ivoire 2014 population census puts urbanization at close to 50 percent, with estimated average annual growth of 3.8 percent. That share is set to rise to 60 percent by 2025 and to exceed 70 percent by 2050 (UN World Urban Population 2011). The urban system is characterized by a primary city of nearly 4.5 million (Abidjan), a city of about 500,000 (Bouaké), three cities of more than 200,000 (Daloa, Korhogo, and Yamoussoukro, the capital), and other secondary cities of more than 100,000 inhabitants (table O.1).

Urbanization in Côte d'Ivoire has been gradual. The urban population was estimated at less than 20 percent in the 1960s, with Abidjan and Bouaké hosting a large share of urban dwellers. Urbanization then accelerated because many small towns emerged in cash crop areas. Urban population growth gradually declined from about 8 percent in 1960 to 0.57 percent in 1985 at the nadir of an economic crisis because of a major terms-of-trade shock, before stabilizing at around 1.5 percent in the early 2000s. It took Côte d'Ivoire 18 years to move from 40 percent urbanization to 50 percent, against 17 years in Cameroon, 14 in Ghana, and only 9 in Gabon (figure O.12)—a relatively gradual process.

Figure O.11 Agriculture's Share in Employment Is Decreasing in Sub-Saharan African Urbanized Countries

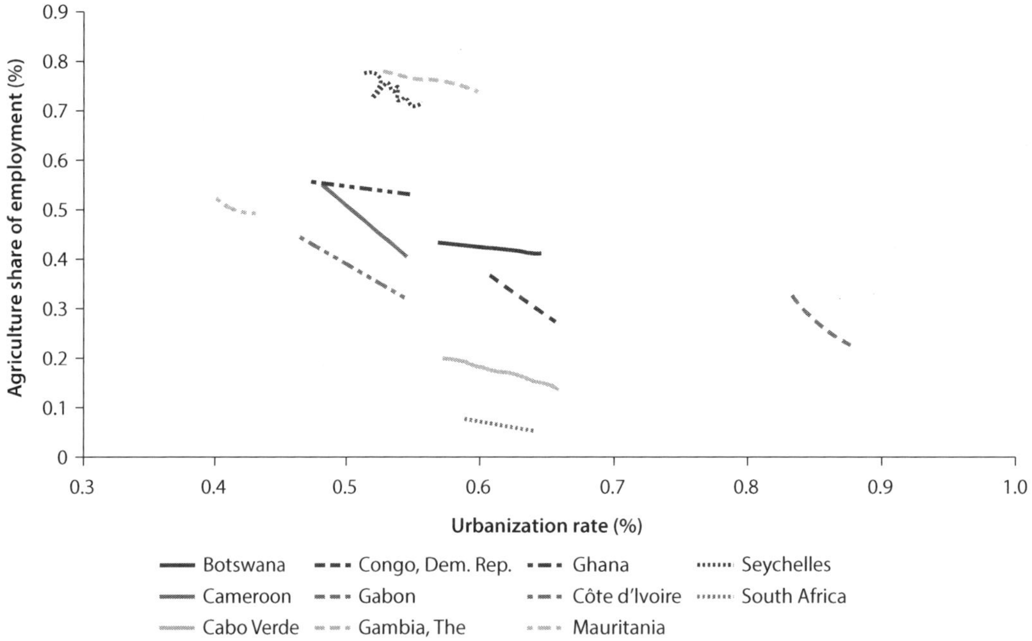

Sources: Food and Agriculture Organization of the United Nations Statistics Division (http://faostat3.fao.org/download/O/OA/E) and World Bank staff calculations.

Table O.1 Population of Cities with More than 100,000 Inhabitants, 1975–2014

	1975	1988	1998	2014
Abidjan	951,216	1,929,076	2,877,948	4,395,243
Bouaké	175,264	329,850	461,618	542,082
Daloa	60,837	121,842	173,107	266,324
Korhogo	45,250	109,445	142,039	245,239
Yamoussoukro	37,257	106,786	155,803	207,412
San-Pédro	31,606	70,611	121,800	174,287
Gagnoa	42,285	85,563	107,244	167,900
Man	50,288	89,575	116,657	148,171

Source: Institut National de la Statistique, population censuses of 1975, 1988, 1998, and 2014.

Various econometric specifications tested by Coulibaly, Esso, and Kanga (2014) show that the urbanization process in Côte d'Ivoire obeys Zipf's Law (with a 5 percent error margin)[4]—that is, that the cities (Abidjan aside) expand at similar rates, with none of them growing significantly faster than the others.

As urbanization has been negatively correlated with income per capita since the late 1970s, poverty has also been increasing. Household surveys conducted by the National Institute of Statistics (Institut National de la Statistique, or INS) indicate that income poverty has been rising since the mid-1980s, starting from

Figure O.12 Number of Years to Move from 40 to 50 Percent Urbanization: Côte d'Ivoire and Other Select Countries

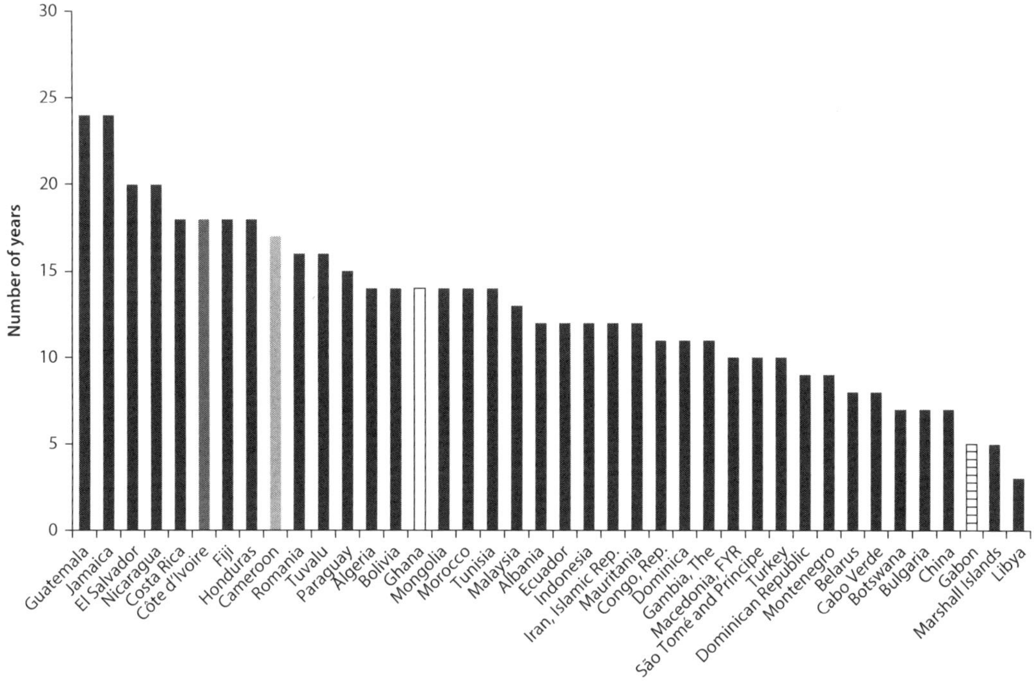

Sources: World Development Indicators; World Bank staff calculations.

a low 10 percent in 1985 to cross the 40 percent threshold by 2008 (figure O.13). A slight inflexion was observed in 1998 with the poverty rate decreasing from 36.8 percent in 1995 to 33.6 percent, but the military coup of 1999 followed by armed conflict in 2002 took the poverty rate to nearly 50 percent by 2008.

Urban areas have fared a bit better than the whole country. Urban poverty shot up from 5 percent in 1985 to 29.5 percent in 2008 (see figure O.13). Abidjan was slightly better off: its poverty rate went from under 1 percent in 1985 to 20.2 percent in 1995, then down to 11 percent in 1998 and 15 percent in 2002 before climbing back to 21 percent in 2008. Urbanization seems to have provided a little more resilience to the population over the long period of economic and then sociopolitical crises, with regional variations: over 2002–08, poverty was higher in the north (Korhogo), center-west (Daloa) and west (Man), but lower in the southern regions (Abidjan) and southwest (San-Pédro).

Poverty and basic infrastructure are worse in rural areas. In 2008 the poverty rate in rural areas was double that in urban areas (62.5 percent as opposed to 29.5 percent), with the lowest rate in Abidjan (see figure O.13). But the urban population in slums is rising steadily: only 27 percent of urban dwellers had access to adequate housing in 2008. And almost half the inhabitants still have no access to the electrical grid (concentrated in urban areas) or to clean water (improving somewhat in rural areas). Solid waste management for households

Figure O.13 Côte d'Ivoire: Urbanization and Poverty, 1985–2008

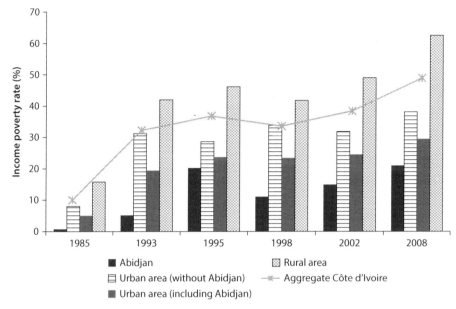

Sources: INS 2008 and World Bank staff calculations.

is poor: informal disposal prevails in rural areas, and few urban dwellers have access to an adequate system.

The stark urban-rural poverty difference causes heavy migration to urban areas. In line with the spatial transformation accompanying the structural transformation of countries, rural urban migration occurs for economic reasons as migrants leave rural areas (where modernizing agriculture has less demand for labor) toward urban centers providing jobs in manufacturing and services. In Côte d'Ivoire, the leading reason for internal migration appears to be for family reasons, with women showing a high propensity to migrate so they can reunite with their families or marry in more prosperous places (Coulibaly, Esso, and Kanga 2014). Migrants also move to find jobs and go to school. Between 2002 and 2008, some migratory flows were prompted by the sociopolitical crises, although the reasons for migration did not fundamentally change. For host areas, internal migration is beneficial (Coulibaly, Esso, and Kanga 2014). In 2008, high migration was associated with improved access to certain elements of basic infrastructure, such as decent housing and toilets, although heavy migration induces problems for waste management and access to power (figure O.14).

Earlier policy efforts at spatial integration have failed to counter market forces. Over the years (at least until 1985), the Ivorian government deployed a battery of interventions to combat the increasing spatial concentration around the three poles (or centers) of Abidjan, Bouaké, and San-Pédro. The first development plan (1960–70) identified agriculture, agribusiness, and the construction of backbone infrastructure as economic pillars and proposed a special

Figure O.14 Service Provision Is Deficient in Secondary Cities

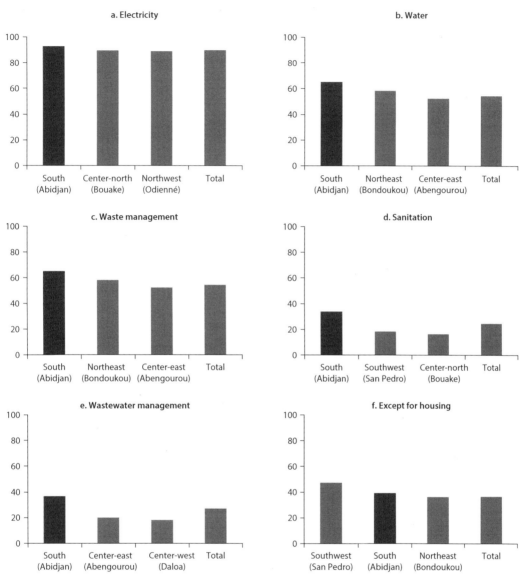

Sources: INS 2008; World Bank staff calculations.

budget for investment. The second plan (1970–75) took a more interventionist stance to address emerging spatial disparities. Three development poles were established in the southwest (deep-sea port of San-Pédro), the center (agropastoral activities), and the north (agroindustrial state-owned enterprises, or SOEs). The third plan (1975–80) continued spatial interventions and created new financial instruments, such as a rural development fund. Yet market forces still prevailed, and the disparity between the three poles and the rest of the country widened (Ministry of Economic Planning and Development 2006).

A decentralization process was initiated in 1980, enabling municipalities to take over direct government interventions.[5] Law No. 2001–476 of August 9, 2001, established five levels of decentralized entities: (i) municipalities, (ii) cities, (iii) departments, (iv) districts, and (v) regions. In 2012, however, the government reverted to a simpler structure: 197 municipalities (*communes*) and 31 regions. Fourteen supraregions have been formed; of these, two are autonomous districts—Abidjan and Yamoussoukro—whereas the other 12 supraregions are not formal decentralized entities (map O.1).

In 2006 the government adopted a new territorial development policy framework. It is anchored on five key actions: (i) adopting a territorial development law to set the legal framework for central and local government interventions; (ii) forming an interministerial committee to ensure coherence among country, urban, and sector infrastructure development plans; (iii) establishing regional councils to promote a participatory development process at the regional level; (iv) linking national development objectives to regional development plans; and (v) establishing a national observatory of spatial dynamics within the Ministry of Planning and Development to collect, analyze, and disseminate spatial information (Ministry of Economic Planning and Development 2006).

The government is preparing an Orientation Law on Territorial Development that will lay the groundwork for the development of a Territorial Development Master Plan. The draft law has been discussed by a technical working group chaired by the Ministry of Planning and Development and involving the various sector ministries such as the Ministry of Construction, Housing, Sanitation, and Urbanism; the Ministry of Economic Infrastructure; and the Ministry of Transport. The draft law is broad and highlights the government's mandate to ensure balanced territorial development by facilitating development of economic activities across all regions by establishing growth poles. Global experience on such balancing has had mixed results: although it makes sense to support development of economic activities in regions with endowments or economic potential, doing so at the expense of primary cities that are the country's engines of growth can retard growth.

Yet new efforts are needed to reap the benefits of economic agglomeration. The *World Development Report 2009* provides an intuitive framework based on three spatial dimensions (density, distance, and division), three market forces (scale economies, labor mobility, and low transport and communication costs), and three policy constructs (institutions, infrastructure, and interventions) that address policy challenges. The policy debates generally overemphasize the most spatially explicit government actions, but successful integration of every nation's network of cities requires all three instruments. The typology of cities proposed in this study could provide some guiding principles for the Territorial Development Master Plan to be developed, anchoring it on diversified urbanization and tapping into the different agglomeration economies generated by Ivorian cities.

Map O.1 Supraregions, Regions, and Autonomous Districts in Côte d'Ivoire, 2012

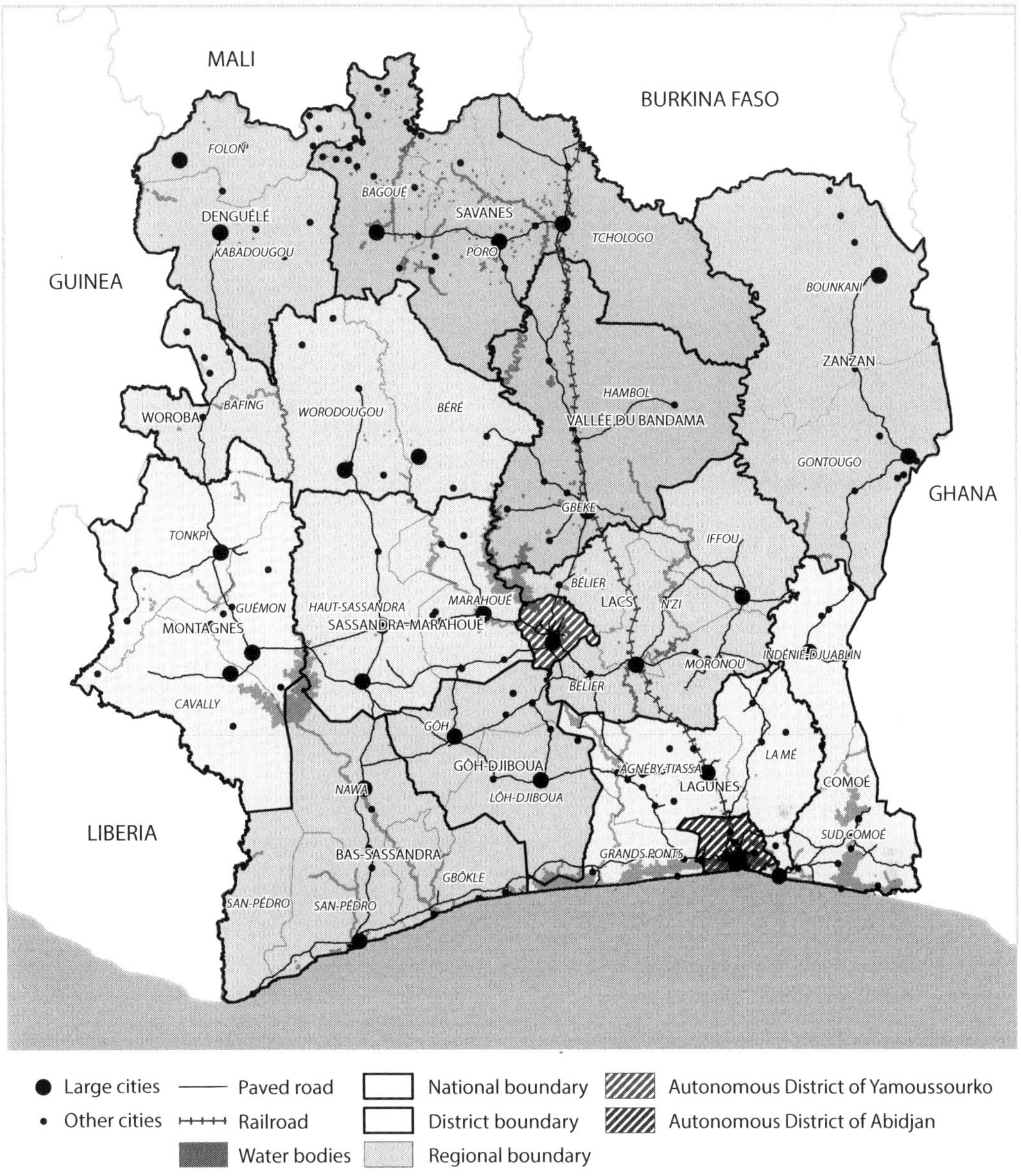

Legend:
- ● Large cities
- • Other cities
- —— Paved road
- ┼┼┼┼ Railroad
- ▨ Water bodies
- ☐ National boundary
- ☐ District boundary
- ☐ Regional boundary
- ▨ Autonomous District of Yamoussourko
- ▨ Autonomous District of Abidjan

Source: National Institute of Statistics (Institut National de la Statistique) 1998.

A Typology of Ivorian Cities: Global, Regional, and Domestic Connectors

The population distribution of Ivorian cities hints at three types of cities: cities on, above, and below the Zipf curve. Over several censuses, Bouaké has remained on the Zipf curve whereas Abidjan has remained above it (figure O.15). Several cities have also remained below the curve, although changing ranks among

Figure O.15 Côte d'Ivoire Experienced Gradual Urban Population Growth

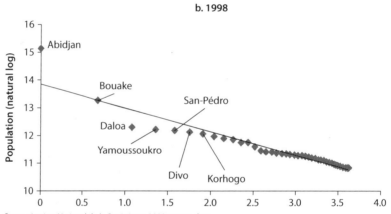

themselves: Daloa, Divo, Gagnoa, Korhogo, Man, San-Pédro, and Yamoussoukro. The preliminary results of the 2014 population census indicate that these nine cities are still among the top 10 largest Ivorian cities.

Natural endowment and connectivity also hint at three types of cities: cities located at international gateways, cities in regional transport corridors, and cities along domestic integrator roads. Among these 10 cities Abidjan, San-Pédro, and Yamoussoukro have some distinctive characteristics. Abidjan is the largest city and the economic capital, with Félix Houphouët-Boigny International Airport and the Autonomous Port of Abidjan, which are among the busiest in West Africa (map O.2). Abidjan also has the largest concentration of urban population, jobs, and private firms. Yamoussoukro is the political capital and hosts the Polytechnic Engineering School that has students from many French-speaking African countries, as well as an international airport. San-Pédro hosts the country's second port, a deep-sea port. These three cities have a basic backbone infrastructure that gives them an advantage over other cities and a role beyond local or regional characteristics, with Abidjan the best positioned relative to global cities. Bouaké and Korhogo are on the North–South regional corridor linking Abidjan to Ouagadougou (the capital of Burkina Faso—see map O.2 below). Daloa and Man are along the western regional corridor linking Abidjan to Conakry. The other secondary cities, particularly those in the poorest areas, are all in regions with potential for producing staple foods that provide other domestic and regional urban centers with food as their populations keep growing (map O.3).

The typology distinguishes the cities' contribution to growth and job creation through agglomeration economies. Global Connectors generate *urbanization economies* needed for innovation and competitiveness, Regional Connectors generate *localization economies* needed for efficient regional trade and transport, and Domestic Connectors generate *localization economies* needed to release agricultural potential.[6] Map O.4 illustrates the spatial interaction of some Ivorian cities with domestic (via internal road and rail

Map O.2 Major Production Zones in Côte d'Ivoire

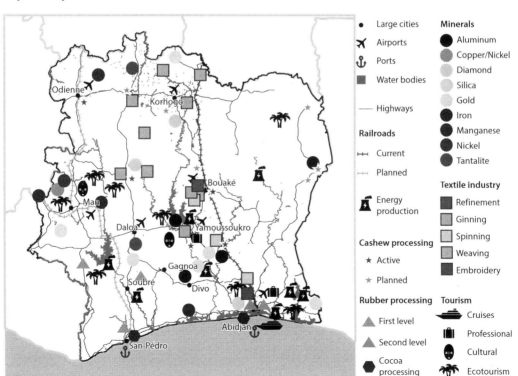

Source: Ministry of Industry and Mining, Côte d'Ivoire.

Diversified Urbanization • http://dx.doi.org/10.1596/978-1-4648-0808-1

Map O.3 Côte d'Ivoire: Areas of Staple Food Cultivation

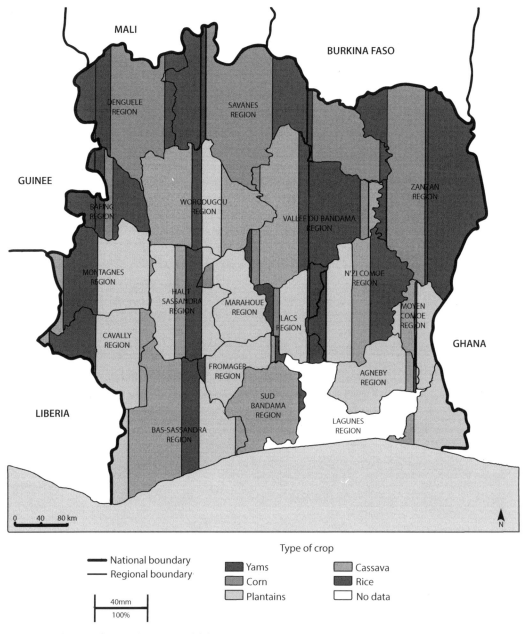

Source: National Institute of Statistics (Institut National de la Statistique) 1998.

connections), regional (via land to neighboring countries), and global markets (via the sea). A few cities stand out as strategic nodes (Abidjan, San-Pédro, Bouaké, Yamoussoukro, Man, and Korhogo), but most are administrative centers whose economies function only through the larger geographic regions to which they belong.

Map O.4 Ivorian Cities as Domestic, Regional, and Global Connectors

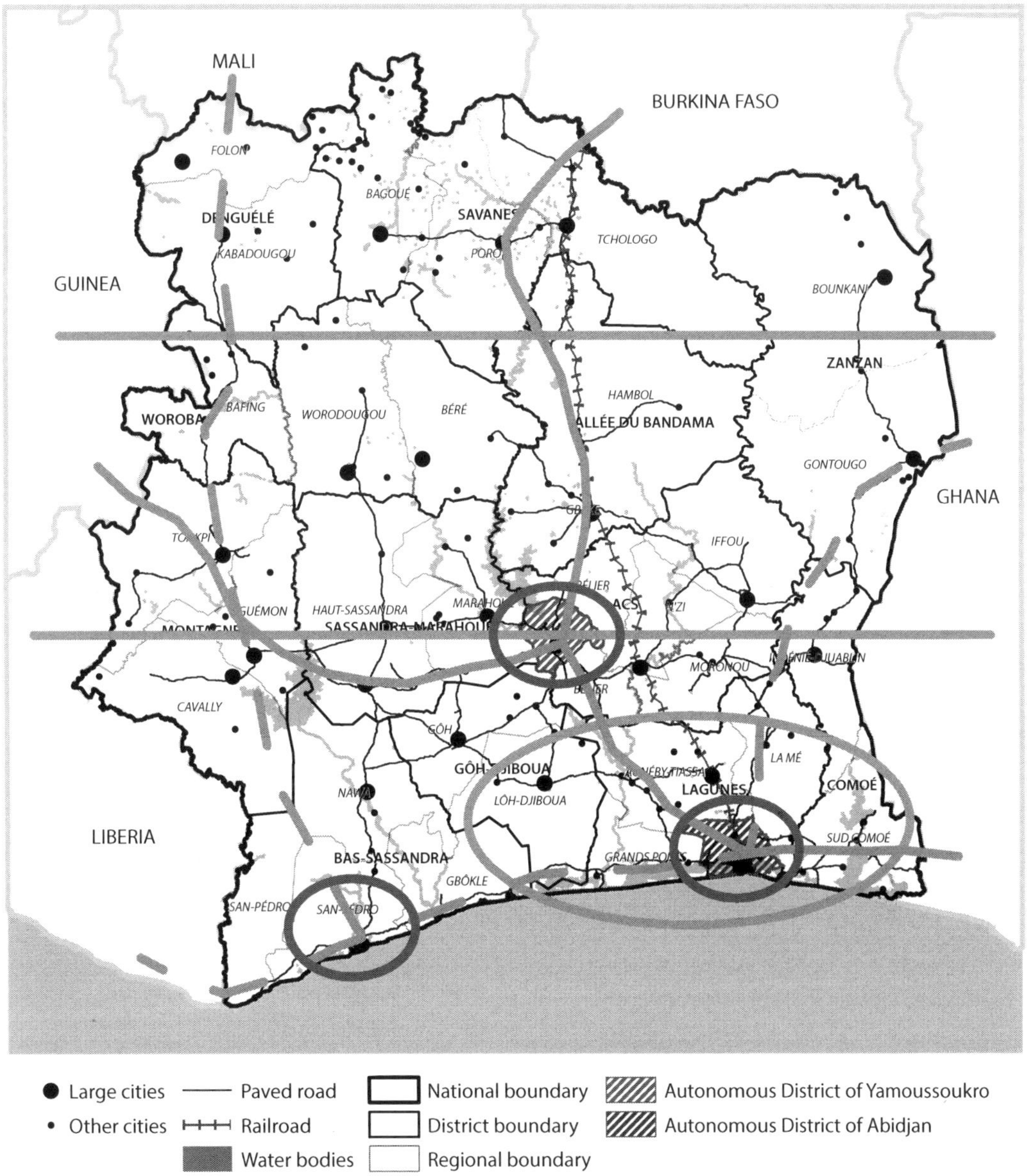

● Large cities   —— Paved road   ☐ National boundary   ▨ Autonomous District of Yamoussoukro

• Other cities   ⊢⊢⊢⊣ Railroad   ☐ District boundary   ▨ Autonomous District of Abidjan

         ▨ Water bodies   ☐ Regional boundary

Sources: Direction Generale de la Decentralisation et des Collectivites Locales, Ministry of the Interior and Security, and AGEROUTE.
Note: Global Connectors are circled in red. Regional Connectors are along the orange lines. Domestic Connectors are along the green lines and within the green oval.

Global Connectors

Abidjan, San-Pédro, and Yamoussoukro are Côte d'Ivoire's natural Global Connectors. The Greater Abidjan area dominates the country in all ways, with about 20 percent of the population, 80 percent of formal employment, and 90 percent of formal enterprises. It is an advanced urban area facing the challenges of metropolitan areas around the world. The port of San-Pédro—built from scratch under the first development plan—is the main export gateway for agricultural products, and was planned to connect by rail to the mineral heart of the west (Man and its surroundings). Yamoussoukro has been the capital since the 1980s, although national public administration is still in Abidjan. Transferring at least part of the administration to Yamoussoukro will boost its local economy and trigger a spatial transformation. The city also has one of the most reputable polytechnic engineering schools in francophone Africa, offering the potential to build bridges to technology companies if information and communications technology (ICT) infrastructure is scaled up to global standards.

Regional Connectors

The Regional Connectors of Côte d'Ivoire are connected to the West African region through five corridors. The northern corridor connects Abidjan with Ouagadougou through a road and rail link that passes through Bouaké (the country's second-largest city), Korhogo (the capital of the northern region with nearly 200,000 inhabitants), and Ferkessédougou (a secondary city of 75,000 inhabitants). Eastward, Côte d'Ivoire is connected to Lagos, Nigeria, via a road running through Aboisso and Noe on the Ivorian side and through three capital cities in West Africa (Accra in Ghana, Lomé in Togo, and Cotonou in Benin). Another eastward connection to Ghana (via Kumassi and Tamale) runs through Adzopé, Abengourou, and Bondoukou. Abidjan is connected to Nzérékoré in Guinea via a road through Yamoussoukro, Daloa, and Man, each of which has more than 150,000 inhabitants and is in a region rich in agriculture, minerals, or tourism. Another westward connection to Monrovia in Liberia goes through Grand Lahou, Sassandra, San-Pédro, and Tabou along the Gulf of Guinea. If we consider the threshold of 100,000 inhabitants, the following secondary cities along the three regional corridors are the main Regional Connectors: Adzopé and Abengourou (east corridor), Bouaké and Korhogo (north corridor), and Daloa and Man (west corridor).

Domestic Connectors

Côte d'Ivoire's small cities and market towns could be anchors generating localization economies for agribusiness. While southwest regions strongly contribute to the production and export of cash crops, savanna areas can help scale up food and cereal production to supply urban centers domestically and regionally (Yeo 2014). In the long term, with the movement of the cocoa belt from eastern and central regions to the south (with an eye on the port of San-Pédro), climate change and international economic conditions might once more shift the heart of these cash crop production areas. Given increasing regional disparities in Côte d'Ivoire, good connections between the agricultural hinterlands of secondary cities with strategic regional capital cities may help smallholders to modernize into agribusiness chains (see map O.4).

The following are Domestic Connectors:

- The hinterland of the metropolis, consisting of the remaining secondary cities in the supraregions of Goh-Djiboua (such as Divo and Gagnoa) and Grands Ponts (such as Agboville and Dabou)
- The central integrator, consisting of the remaining secondary cities in the supraregions of Lacs (such as Bongouanou, Daoukro, Dimbokro, and Toumodi), Sassandra-Marahoue (such as Bouafle), Montagnes (such as Duekoue and Guiglo), and Bas-Sassandra (such as Soubre)
- The northern integrator, consisting of the remaining secondary cities in the supraregions of Zanzan (such as Bouna), Vallée du Bandama (Katiola), Savanes (such as Boundiali), Woroba (such as Mankono, Seguela, and Touba), and Denguele (such as Odienné and Minignan)

Rethinking Ivorian Cities: Better Planning, Connecting, Greening, and Financing

To achieve diversified urbanization, Ivorian policy makers need to act urgently along four dimensions:

1. *Planning*—charting a course for cities by setting the terms of urbanization, especially policies for using urban land, enabling housing markets, and expanding basic infrastructure and public services
2. *Connecting*—making a city's markets accessible (labor, goods, and services) to other cities and to other neighborhoods in the city, as well as to export markets
3. *Greening*—enhancing livability of cities by reducing pollution and emissions and conserving scarce environmental and financial resources
4. *Financing*—finding sources for large capital outlays needed to provide infrastructure and services as cities grow and urbanization picks up speed

This framework reflects the principles identified by stakeholders from national and subnational government and the private sector, which helped to formulate a shared vision of urbanization in Côte d'Ivoire.[7] These stakeholders believe that successful urbanization should lead to "cities that are planned, structured, competitive, attractive, inclusive, and organized around development poles."

For this framework to succeed, a good governance structure is a prerequisite. Policy makers, at all government levels, will have to work together. Currently, institutional fragmentation prevails with a multiplicity of policymaking institutions involved in urbanization with overlaps, unclear mandates, and a dearth of coordination. The Ministry of Planning and Economic Development is a key stakeholder because it oversees planning, land development, and population aspects. The Ministry of Construction, Housing, Sanitation, and Urbanism develops and implements urban master plans.

The Ministry of the Interior and Security hosts the directorate (Direction Générale de la Décentralisation et des Collectivités Locales, or General Directorate for Decentralization and Local Communities [DGDCL]) that assures oversight of municipalities and regions. The Ministry of Economic Infrastructure is responsible for building and maintaining the infrastructure connecting domestic economic centers with each other and with regional and global centers. The Ministry of Transport is in charge of intra- and interurban transportation, as well as international transportation. Municipalities and regions are represented by two associations: the UVICOCI (Union de Villes et Communes de Côte d'Ivoire, or Association of Cities and Communes of Côte d'Ivoire) and the ARDCI (Assemblée des Régions et Districts de Côte d'Ivoire, or Association of Regions and Districts of Côte d'Ivoire) that are bottom-up consultative bodies of elected officials and urban and regional development specialists. The private sector remains the key player driving growth, hence the need to involve all active business associations; it is represented by the Chamber of Commerce and Industry of Côte d'Ivoire.

Planning

Planning is fundamental to agglomeration economies in four ways. First, land use planning requires effective systems for land valuation to allocate land to its most viable uses, as well as a sound understanding of demand by different market segments. Second, land use planning must ensure integration with infrastructure and especially transport. Third, affordable and well-sited housing reduces the trade-off between urban density and livability. Fourth, the most basic infrastructure services—water, energy, sanitation, and solid waste management—need to be provided for all residents, urban and peri-urban alike.

The main challenge is that the densification of Ivorian cities has not been matched by improved livability. Core issues include access to adequate, affordable housing and the provision of basic services and infrastructure. Households face the hard choice of high rents in well-connected areas versus high transport costs in areas on the periphery, and often live in overcrowded conditions to avoid costly commutes from peri-urban areas. More than 50 percent of Abidjan's residents live in overcrowded homes, sharing a room with two or more people.

Following the government's withdrawal from land development and housing production in the early 1980s, the country entered a housing crisis exacerbated by the sociopolitical crises of the late 1990s and 2000s. The total housing deficit is estimated at 400,000–600,000 units, and is widening. The deficit is concentrated in cities, half in Abidjan. But the qualitative deficit is worse: lack of access to basic services and weak tenure security usually affect households' confidence in the future and reduce their willingness to invest in the house, such that a large part of the housing stock lacks access to basic services and is built of temporary material. About two-thirds of the stock of primary housing has permanent walls but less than 4 percent has a permanent roof (Lozano-Gracia and Young 2014). Investment in sanitation (primarily by households) is also limited: just 27 percent of households in 2008 had access to flush or improved toilets, down from 35 percent in 2002 (INS 2008). Little investment in housing reflects a fundamental land-access problem, which precludes a large share of urban households from accessing affordable housing.

Despite efforts introduced in the 1998 Rural Land Law to promote transparent land markets, land registration and titling remain problematic. The state continues to face difficulties accessing land, and uncertainty persists over demarcation between rural and urban areas (Legendre 2014). The state must deal not only with a dominant customary system of land ownership and tenure and only sporadic use of the Rural Land Law, but also with lengthy, expensive, and bureaucratic processes to register land and obtain title. Registration costs—estimated at 10.8 percent of a property's value—are high and above the Sub-Saharan Africa average (CAHF 2014), discouraging people from going down this path. Other disincentives are the likelihood of taxes being levied on registered land (USAID 2013). Demand for land titles remains low, and its value added—relative to the process of land security based on local consensus—is uncertain.[8] About 98 percent of the country's land is still governed by customary practices, despite the statutory system.

Regional and Global Connector cities suffer greatly from a lack of housing with basic services, contributing to the qualitative housing deficit. While access to electricity is almost 90 percent in urban areas, piped water connection is 72 percent, down 7 points between 1998 and 2011 (INS and ICF 2012), essentially in secondary cities. In several cities, the proportion of formal/organized neighborhoods[9] is significant, but housing is severely underprovisioned and underserviced, and is deteriorating. Organized and provisioned neighborhoods occupy from 20 percent in communes of Abidjan to 50 percent in the residential sector in San-Pédro and Bouaké. In smaller cities, the share of formal/provisioned housing tends to be much lower, with only 3 percent in Korhogo, concentrated in the city center's individual homes and buildings.

Informal housing in irregular settlements is expanding, especially in large cities (Global Connectors). Informal settlements are common in urban and peri-urban areas of Côte d'Ivoire and are usually situated on publicly owned land. These neighborhoods follow no urban guidelines, often lack land title and building permits, and suffer serious sanitation problems as well as little or no access to other basic services. Most houses are built of wood and zinc, and resemble huts. Irregular settlements are a common feature in the urban areas of large cities, such as San-Pédro and Abidjan (Koumassi, Port Bouet, Attecoube, and Yopougon). Informal housing accounts for more than 6 percent of all urban dwellings in Côte d'Ivoire, housing 15–17 percent of the urban population. In Abidjan, it is estimated that roughly 15–17 percent of settlements are illegal because of their location, absence of basic services, or substandard construction (USAID 2013). As evidenced in the cities that were audited, informal or irregular neighborhoods are not as common as formal underprovisioned neighborhoods at a national level; nonetheless, they are expanding on the periphery of cities as urban populations grow and find no access to affordable formal housing.

Diversified Urbanization • http://dx.doi.org/10.1596/978-1-4648-0808-1

The challenge of the urban housing deficit is exacerbated by low affordability and limited mobility. For the region more widely, housing expenditure—relatively constant among all quintiles at 17–18 percent of total spending—is high with only three Sub-Saharan African countries (Angola, Malawi, and Rwanda) of a sample of 20 showing higher average rates. When adding transport, however, Abidjan has the highest share of expenditures of all urban areas across the region, at 26.6 percent (figure O.16). Transport accounts for more than a third of those financial outlays, and is steeper in higher-population quintiles. The rental market in central areas is therefore under severe pressure as the large housing deficit creates speculation on rents. In Abidjan, the monthly rent of a studio can range from CFAF 100,000 to CFAF 150,000 (US$189–283), which is affordable for only 20 percent of the population, based on a household size of three (CAHF 2014).[10] Moreover, the barriers to land development in peri-urban areas (including costs of registration, development, and unclear tenure), as well as lack of clarity on urban reserves, have contributed to land scarcity and high prices in urban areas, making formal and decent housing expensive, and restricting it to middle- and higher-income groups.

Mobility and access to services are hindered by poor street coverage. A dense and well-connected street grid is essential for connectivity, productivity, quality of life, and social inclusion. Because streets often function as a public right-of-way for other systems, their coverage also serves as a proxy for access to basic services like water and sanitation, solid waste collection, and storm water drainage to prevent flooding. In a global study, the United Nations Human Settlements

Figure O.16 Housing and Transport Expenditures by Country

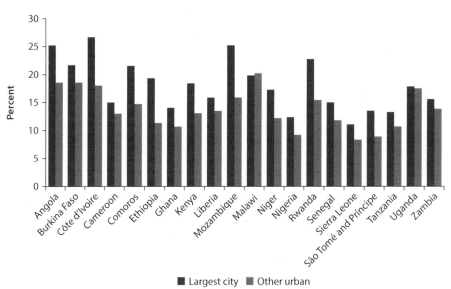

Source: Lozano-Gracia and Young 2014.

Programme (UN-Habitat) determined that livable and competitive cities are those with at least 20 kilometers of paved road per square kilometer of land area (UN-Habitat 2013a; UN-Habitat 2013b). By contrast, the largest cities in Côte d'Ivoire have street densities of between 2.1 and 10.5 kilometers per square kilometer.[11]

The infrastructure in cities, already deficient, has deteriorated greatly and requires urgent investment. The physical infrastructure for most basic services (potable water, sanitation, waste collection, and electricity) was heavily damaged during the civil war and has not been maintained or improved in the past 10–15 years. Such pressures contributed to fast-deteriorating infrastructure. From small towns (Domestic Connectors), to regional cities (Regional Connectors), and the communes of metropolitan Abidjan (Global Connector), most infrastructure was built before the military crisis, with little maintenance investment since 2009. In Abidjan, for instance, before the 2002 civil war, water coverage was estimated at 75 percent. After 2002, coverage went down to 56 percent as the city struggled to provide 1 million displaced Ivorians with basic services. The electricity networks that serve up to half the urban population are deficient, forcing dwellers to rely on informal and illegal connections, risking the safety of their neighborhoods. In San-Pédro, electricity covers less than half the commune's neighborhoods; in Korhogo, public lighting covers only a quarter of the city. In the communes of Abidjan, the deficits are related mainly to drainage and sanitation. Waste management also suffers from severe deficits and underperformance across cities.

Reform Priorities in Planning

The above issues point to a kernel of reform priorities. Ivorian cities need to be urgently planned, and box O.1 suggests initial steps in this huge undertaking.

Connecting

Connections—between cities and within cities—benefit producers and consumers. They give producers access to input (including labor) and output markets. They give consumers options and, in many cases, better prices. Furthermore connections expose cities to new economic opportunities. The connections between and within Ivorian cities are being severed along three dimensions:

- First, low mobility within cities is fragmenting urban labor markets and creating a wedge between people and jobs.
- Second, high transport costs across cities are dampening economic gains from market access and specialization.
- Third, lack of intermodal infrastructure is another factor hindering economic growth.

Across cities, this lack of connection limits economic gains that specialization and market access can bring; within cities, it limits the matching of the skills of job seekers with employment opportunities.

Diversified Urbanization • http://dx.doi.org/10.1596/978-1-4648-0808-1

Box O.1 Planning for Ivorian Cities Should Start Now

Improving land market fluidity. A constrained land market limits private investment. Improving the fluidity of the market will help increase the investments in industrial and residential development. This will require increasing the production of usable land in three clear steps (chapter 1 provides detail):

- First, tenure security should be improved through simpler, shorter, and cheaper procedures.
- Second, trunk infrastructure should be provided in a timely manner, especially for new urban extensions not yet connected to urban services (in particular roads, electricity, and water) and before these are settled.
- Third, land for different investment activities should also be identified, planned, and allocated efficiently to enable meeting increasing demand for land.

Expanding service delivery. Besides creating functioning land markets, policy makers must also ensure that most basic infrastructure services reach all city residents—urban and peri-urban—because existing Global and Regional Connectors will continue to grow and new Domestic Connectors will demand basic services. Investing in infrastructure will require that local and national authorities work together to prioritize needs and design sustainable financing models. There are two key priorities:

- First, step up efforts to develop serviced land.
- Second, implement financially sustainable service delivery models and strengthen regulation to increase cost recovery and, accordingly, investment and service coverage.

Simplify planning regulations. Land use plans help city authorities ensure compliance with planning guidelines and building codes, guide development by allocating budgets to different zones, and develop zoning regulations. These plans can ensure that public and private developments in various zones are developed harmoniously, and that developments provide mixed economic and residential activities as well as green and protected areas. There are three key issues:

- First, improve coordination in allocation of responsibilities governing urban areas. For example, the structural decisions of city planning in Abidjan (and other cities) are in the hands of the Ministry of Construction, Housing, Sanitation, and Urbanism (MCLAU), rather than with mayors and the chairmen of regional councils. But it is these latter groups that, with local governments, have wide knowledge of their commune's needs, as well as experience in providing facilities and amenities and delivery of services.
- Second, align land use policies and planning standards with infrastructure availability and plans.
- Third, simplify and relax regulations on land use and zoning, to increase housing affordability.

Urban mobility. More than 50 percent of trips to work in Abidjan are on foot or on a bicycle. Public transport is not used by most people in Abidjan even though this would be expected for such a large city (figure O.17). This constrains access to employment opportunities for workers. In Abidjan, work and business activities are concentrated in the center of the city, with far fewer jobs in the periphery. Mobility is worse for the poor, who have access only to a small share of the labor market because the average distance they can reasonably travel for work is less than 5 km. The consequence: Abidjan is losing out on the potential agglomeration benefits that come from a unified labor market. International evidence shows that as incomes rise people travel farther and faster and transport modes change. There is an increased use of buses, cars, trains, and planes relative to walking and cycling, the transport modes of the poor (Schafer 1998; WBCSD 2001). And international research shows a strong correlation between under-five mortality (as a proxy for income or poverty) and the proportion of people traveling to work by foot or bike in cities of Africa.

Figure O.17 In Abidjan, Most People Walk or Bike, Limiting Job Opportunities

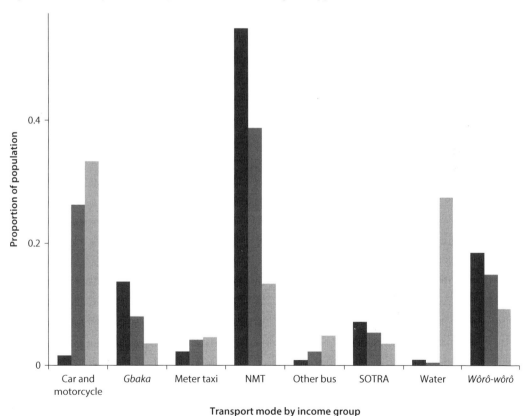

Source: JICA 2014.
Note: NMT = nonmotorized transport; SOTRA = Société des Transports Abidjanais (Abidjan Transport Company).

Diversified Urbanization • http://dx.doi.org/10.1596/978-1-4648-0808-1

In the Greater Abidjan area, the informal sector—*gbaka*, meter taxis, *wôrô-wôrô*, and intercommunal taxis—accounts for 85 percent of public transport trips and has grown at the expense of the formal sector. Unqualified actors operate with obsolete vehicles that pose safety, reliability, and pollution problems. Bus services are concentrated on routes originating from suburban areas and ending in several city terminals such as Adjame or the Plateau. Public transportation modes are not diversified despite a navigable lagoon and are not commensurate for a metropolis of more than 4 million.

Regional connectivity. Across cities, transport costs are an implicit trade barrier. Global evidence shows that falling transport costs caused by large infrastructure investments and breakthroughs brought closer economic integration and specialization within countries. The main Ivorian cities are linked by an extensive road network, with four main axes starting from Abidjan.

However, domestic transport costs in Côte d'Ivoire are among the highest in the world. A trucking survey conducted for this study highlights that the average freight transport cost is $0.35 per ton-kilometer, which is much higher than in other developing countries such as India and Vietnam and considerably higher than in the United States, where labor costs and overheads are much greater.

Transporters who serve Domestic Connectors face the highest costs. The transport costs (per ton-kilometer) are highest along routes connecting Regional and Domestic Connectors ($0.47 per ton-kilometer) and those connecting Domestic and Global connectors ($0.39 per ton-kilometer). In comparison, transport costs within Global Connectors are more in line with national average ($0.32 per ton-kilometer) and routes connecting Global and Regional Connectors have lower transport costs ($0.17 per ton-kilometer).

High transport costs are detrimental to growth of secondary cities and reduce connectivity for economically lagging areas with higher poverty incidence. The routes connecting Domestic and Global Connectors carry considerable freight and serve as integrators between the domestic and global economy. Further, the routes along the Domestic and Regional Connectors link the country's lagging areas with markets. Disproportionately high costs of connections are hurting national economic competitiveness as well as the development potential of cities in lagging areas (figure O.9).

Global connectivity. Infrastructure for transport and ICT is vital to boosting the economic efficiency of the Global, Regional, and Domestic Connectors. Policy makers need to treat their cities as an interlinked portfolio of assets—each differentiated by size, location, density of settlement, and function—that connect their economy to local, regional, and global markets. Worldwide evidence highlights that businesses and people can exploit economies of scale and agglomeration if their settlements perform their intended functions. This is very much dependent on a city's connections—external and internal. External connectivity of a country passes through node cities at or along international transport and communication infrastructure: ports, airports, railways, and ICT backbone.

Abidjan and San-Pédro are world-class ports. The Autonomous Port of Abidjan (with one container terminal and another under construction) and the deep-sea port of San-Pédro provide maritime transport for Côte d'Ivoire and landlocked countries such as Burkina Faso, Mali, and Niger. Abidjan's port is the country's main port, accommodating 80 percent of maritime traffic in the country. Abidjan handles larger freight volumes than most ports in West Africa and has a capacity of around 650,000 twenty-foot equivalent units (TEUs) per year. It was, however, one of the most expensive in 2009. Limited competition among actors operating at the port is also keeping prices high. The San-Pédro port is dedicated mainly to timber traffic and part of the export of agricultural products (like coffee and cocoa).

Abidjan port's operation was seriously interrupted by the sociopolitical crises between 1999 and 2011. After the end of the postelection crisis of 2011, it has been slowly regaining its place among the most important ports of Africa, although its container traffic is still low (about 700,000 TEUs in 2013) compared with South Africa (over 4 million TEUs in 2013). Traffic in transit toward hinterland countries experienced a resurgence of activity (for example, Burkina Faso and Mali) after the end of the sociopolitical crises. In 2013, the volume of traffic in transit toward the hinterland was double that in 2011 (1.76 million tons versus 0.76 million tons).

Connectivity through ICT is relatively developed compared with regional peers. Mobile phone coverage is above the average for the Economic Community of West African States (ECOWAS)—95 percent against 78 percent. In Abidjan, as with other cities, most citizens live within reach of a 3G-enabled mobile telephone network, and access to the Internet is relatively good through Wi-Fi and 3G. Furthermore, three major fiber optic cables land in Abidjan: the West African Cable System (WACS), the ACE (African Coast to Europe), and the SAT3/WASC (South Atlantic 3/West Africa Submarine Cable) (map O.5). This fosters competition among three major Internet service providers (MTN, Orange, and Côte d'Ivoire Telecom), which has driven Internet connection costs down a little, although connectivity charges remain high compared with countries like Ghana and South Africa and access outside urban centers is relatively low. Advanced 4G technology is also being introduced. However, much more investment is needed. High speed Internet is generally lacking. According to the United Nations E-Government Survey 2014, Côte d'Ivoire is currently 171st (out of 193 countries) in the world, near the average of ECOWAS countries, but significantly behind Ghana (123rd) and Senegal (151st). Mobile broadband is also relatively low with only about 6.8 percent penetration (end 2013), which is on par with Senegal and Nigeria, but significantly lower than Ghana (28.2 per 100 inhabitants).

Reform Priorities to Enhance Mobility and Connectivity

To address these challenges, policy makers need to coordinate land use and infrastructure to enhance urban mobility. To enhance mobility within cities, land use planning and urban transport need to be better integrated. Transport and

Map O.5 Submarine Cables Landing in Abidjan

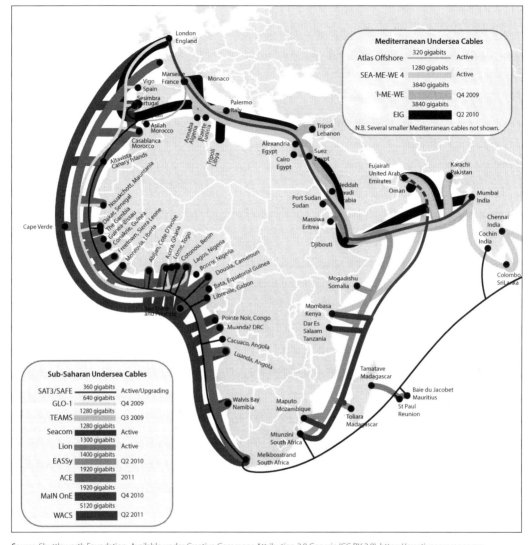

Note: ACE = Africa Coast to Europe; EASSY = Eastern Africa Submarine Cable System; EIG = Europe India Gateway; GLO-1 = Globacom-1;
I-ME-WE = India-Middle East-Western Europe; LION = Lower Indian Ocean Network; SAT3/SAFE = South Atlantic 3-South Africa Far East;
SEA-ME-WE 4 = South East Asia–Middle East–Western Europe 4; TEAMS = The East African Marine System; WACS = West Africa Cable System.

mobility are best addressed as part of an integrated urban strategy that can cater
to various user groups and anticipate long-term needs. Ivorian cities need an
urban transport master plan that promotes a reliable, safe, modern, and sustainable multimodal transport system accessible to all urban dwellers. There is no
national transport master plan,[12] and the national road master plan needs to be
updated to reflect the government's spatial development strategy.

    It is also important to accelerate reforms for greater professionalization of
operators in the transport sector and better access to finance. Policy makers need

to give priority to more efficient transport services through deep reforms that promote professionalism and foster market competition. In this regard, introduction of qualitative criteria for access to the transport sector profession will have significant positive impact. This will result in lower prices and more efficient logistics and transport services. As far as urban transport services are concerned, measures to enhance the attractiveness of public transport are equally important for improving the overall efficiency of the system. As a matter of fact, upgrading traffic signal control, implementing traffic information systems and traffic management on highways, and better enforcing traffic regulation will definitely improve urban transport services. Restrictive parking management combined with priority treatment for public transports are also important measures that could be considered to improve urban mobility. Finally, putting in place an enabling environment for transporters to access finance to renew their fleet is also key to unleashing the sector's potential.

The freight transport sector needs to be better organized and be more competitive. Until the new legislative framework enters into force, entry into the transport sector is quite easy, leading to a fragmented market dominated by informal and small players relying on obsolete trucks and overage vehicles. As a result, they are vulnerable to informal payments because many of them do not comply with regulations. Multiple local trade unions translate into "vested interests poles" that fragment the market and distort prices. Indeed, practices such as freight repartition and *tour de rôle* (assigning freight loads to transport operators in a rotating manner) have negative impact on the quantity, quality, and prices of transport services. Therefore, greater efficiency of transport services will imply new measures and mechanisms to improve transparency of transport prices. In this regard, the establishment of a robust and transparent market information system will be instrumental.

Establishment of a market information system (MkIS) can better connect transporters with customers. For both freight and passengers' transports, the queuing system (*tour de rôle*) and the oligopolistic behavior of unions and professional associations are long-standing practices that jeopardize market efficiency. Promoting an MkIS can help better coordinate the supply and demand side of transport services. The system would provide a platform where information could formally be centralized, analyzed, treated, and made accessible to all market players. The MkIS could build upon the ICTs with two legs: a virtual freight exchange and customer management applications for passengers.

Policy makers also need to step up investment in strategic corridors and develop supporting plans for strengthening urban agglomerations and city development. For the Abidjan–Ouagadougou regional corridor, an extension of the highway beyond Yamoussoukro to connect Bouaké and Korhogo should be a strong leverage to amplify the benefits expected from the regional trade facilitation operation, which aims at boosting trade between the two countries and increasing competitiveness of the two countries. As a matter of fact, it would definitely increase volume and speed up exchanges (for both freight and passenger traffic) between the four big cities mentioned above—which account for nearly a quarter of the country's total population—and open up trade and transport opportunities for the Sikasso–Bobodioulasso–Korhogo border region.

To support diversified urbanization, it is important to diversify the corridors connecting the domestic economy to attractive regional markets. The Abidjan–Lagos corridor offers denser market potential, and extending the Grand-Bassam–Aboisso highway to the Ghana border should be assessed because it would allow a seamless connection between six major African cities along the Gulf coast: Abidjan, Accra, Lomé, Cotonou, and Lagos. An alternative eastward corridor goes through Adzopé, Abengourou, Agnibilékro, and Bondoukou to connect with inland secondary cities in Ghana such as Kumassi and Tamale. A third corridor going to the west and linking Abidjan to Nzérékoré could be considered, with a highway connecting Yamoussoukro to Daloa and Man to unleash domestic and regional trade along this direction and provide enticing regional trade opportunities to Daloa and Man. As these regional corridors develop, a focus should be on providing efficient logistics, distribution infrastructure, and institutions in the Regional Connector cities.

Cities need to be spatially connected in a way that supports their particular agglomeration economies. Global Connectors must have world-class infrastructure facilitating international connectivity (ports, airports, and ICT) and good interurban infrastructure to link industrial zones with domestic raw material sources. These goals are in line with the country's ambition to become a transport hub for West Africa. The livability of these cities is also essential, underscoring the central role of efficient public urban transport. The most needed inputs for Regional Connectors are trade and transport that seamlessly connect the domestic economy to regional markets, with lower transport costs. Because most Domestic Connectors are in predominantly agriculture- or resource-based regions of emerging urbanization with low economic density, agglomeration forces need to be reinforced via market institutions to regulate land use and transactions and delivery of basic services.

There is an opportunity to make Yamoussoukro a technology hub in West Africa. Because the government's growth pole initiative for Abidjan, Bouaké, and San-Pédro is integral to its growth and employment strategy, it is important to back it up by establishing a technology hub in Yamoussoukro based in the Polytechnic Engineering School. Domestic technology firms (wherever they are) and external private partners could form a cluster around the polytechnic school to tap the numerous and low-wage skilled workers graduating every year. This would mean securing world-class ICT connectivity to at least the three Global Connectors (Abidjan, San-Pédro, and Yamoussoukro) to take advantage of recent ICT innovations—such as MOOCs (massive open online courses) that could be developed in partnership with the Polytechnic Engineering School—and technology-oriented city redevelopment as New York is currently experimenting with in partnership with Cornell University to catalyze spinoff companies and increase the probability that the next high growth company—a Google, Amazon, or Facebook—will emerge in New York City (http://www.nycedc.com/project /applied-sciences-nyc).

Greening

As our discussions on planning and connecting show, infrastructure and land use decisions determine the form and growth patterns of urban areas, but their environmental cost is rarely considered. These costs can be steep: in China, for example, the health costs of air pollution in cities have been estimated at 3.8 percent of GDP (World Bank 2007). Other costs can include knock-on effects for economic development of a city as a whole because health problems undermine worker productivity, pollution makes a city unattractive to families, and climate-related extreme weather events disrupt businesses and destroy infrastructure.

As urbanization intensifies and wealth grows, environmental externalities are likely to be amplified. As cities grow, negative externalities of congestion and air pollution generally rise, adversely affecting well-being and the environment (Whitehead et al. 2010). In addition, as Ivorian cities become wealthier, the consumption and waste associated with each urban resident is also likely to grow, straining solid waste services and, unless managed properly, raising pollution and health risks (Hoornweg and Bhada-Tata 2012). Making a city greener requires thinking about the externalities that planning and management decisions may bring. If these challenges are ignored, they could undermine hard-won gains in quality of life.

But today, failures in infrastructure and land use coordination deepen Côte d'Ivoire's urban pollution and its vulnerability to natural disasters. The cities severely lack basic sanitation, solid waste management, and storm water infrastructure, so untreated water from industry and households is disposed directly into urban water bodies and the Atlantic Ocean, exacerbating problems from extreme weather events and washing additional pollutants into lakes, lagoons, and the ocean. In Abidjan more than 20 people died in flood-related incidents in June 2014 alone. Poor coordination has led to urban mobility trends that point to increasing reliance on environmentally inefficient forms of transport (figure O.18). As motorization increases, there will be rising emissions, while green spaces in and around cities—which help filter pollutants and absorb flood water—are disappearing through lack of green management.

Air and water pollution come at a steep cost. Air pollution has been linked to lower respiratory tract diseases such as asthma and pneumonia,[13] with lower respiratory tract diseases accounting for 6,417 years of life lost per 100,000 due to disability or death.[14] Polluted water is associated with the spread of waterborne diseases such as diarrhea and cholera, which are among the communicable diseases accounting for more than 50 percent of adult deaths and about 80 percent of deaths among children under five (WHO 2012). The number of disability-adjusted life years (DALYs) lost because of diarrhea alone are 7,897 per 100,000. And pollution can also affect productivity and constrain economic activity. Water pollution hurts tourism, property values, fishing, and other sectors that depend on clean water.

Figure O.18 Energy Consumption and Pollution Emissions per Passenger, Abidjan (gram/trip)

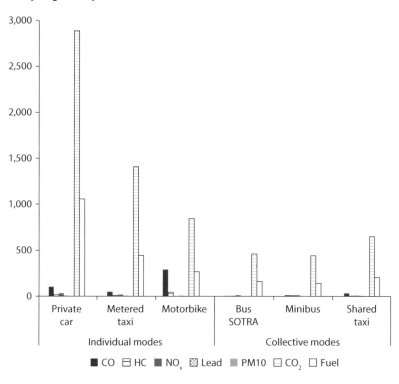

Source: Certu 2002 as quoted in UN-Habitat 2012.
Note: CO = carbon monoxide; CO_2 = carbon dioxide; HC = hydrocarbon; PM10 = particulate matter under 10 micrometers in diameter; NO_x = nitrogen oxide; SOTRA = Société des Transports Abidjanais (Abidjan Transport Company).

Reform Priorities in Greening

The impacts of pollution and environmental degradation can be mitigated with coordinated, forward-looking, and context-specific decisions. Greening cities does not require a new paradigm. In Côte d'Ivoire, priority greening initiatives are those that help address key development challenges throughout the system of cities. They are initiatives that will help cities, individually, anticipate future costs of today's decisions, leading to efficiency gains and building resilience to environmental risks.

For Global Connector cities, greening can improve competitiveness and productivity. The economy of Abidjan and other Global Connectors is based on international trade, innovation, and productivity. High rates of urban pollution threaten their quality of life, making them unattractive to high-skilled labor and their families, undermining productivity and livability. While estimates do not exist for Ivorian cities, World Bank studies find that the costs of environmental degradation are steep in Nigeria (about 9 percent of GDP) and Ghana (about 10 percent of GDP) (Bromhead 2012). Coastal cities are also particularly vulnerable to natural disasters, such as flooding associated with sea-level rise. Two-thirds of the country's coast is exposed to erosion, with records showing loss of land of one to two meters a year but sometimes up to 20 meters. Greening initiatives potentially offer myriad solutions to these challenges. Integrated planning to upgrade basic infrastructure in Abidjan's 144 precarious settlements can result in a triple win of social, economic, and environmental benefits. Protection of green and open spaces along the waterfront can make the city more attractive and livable while providing a vital buffer against climate change–related risks. Further, coordinated efforts to provide a system of public transport can help stem rising congestion and air pollution while providing a wide range of social and economic advantages.

For Regional Connectors, green policies can be aligned with the bigger priority to support growth through regional trade and transport. The economy of the Regional Connectors is grounded in regional trade related to extractive industries and small manufacturing. A fuller understanding of the environmental costs and trade-offs associated with these activities is important to ensure more efficient use of resources, which will help cities plan ahead. It will also help cities save in the long run by building, into infrastructure investment, resilience to environmental risks: for example, roads should be designed to withstand landslides, coastal erosion, and heavy rains to prevent waste of public investment.

International experience indicates that there are opportunities to reduce the environmental footprint and improve the economic efficiency of light manufacturing, often at industrial zones where economies of scale can be attained in pollution-treatment infrastructure. The government has already identified the economic and social gains of better-regulated and modernized freight transport, which could help minimize the environmental costs of trucking. The natural beauty and ecological uniqueness of regions such as Man present underexploited economic opportunities, in a context where ecotourism is the fastest-growing area of the tourism industry (TEEB 2010) and is an important area for growth in green jobs (OECD 2013).

For Domestic Connector cities, establishing greener growth patterns will stimulate localization economies. Domestic Connector cities are important in the system of cities and national economy because they connect agricultural inputs and outputs to markets. These cities need to get basic services right from the outset to support more sustainable growth patterns. Planning can greatly reduce the long-term costs of urban development by laying the foundation for basic service infrastructure such as sewage systems and roads (chapter 1). This can help insulate small cities from unnecessary future costs, such as those now faced by larger cities like Abidjan, where, for example, solid-waste collection trucks cannot reach 40 percent of houses because of the physical layout of the city. Domestic Connector cities can also explore alternative technologies to potentially reduce costs for basic services, as smaller cities in Kenya are doing, by exploring off-grid photovoltaic street lighting.

The national government also has a vital role to play in enabling greener urban development across cities: this is too great a burden for city governments alone. The central authorities can provide information and create incentives to change behavior and support more efficient, sustainable development. Policy makers and consumers require better information on the environmental costs of their decisions. The government can ensure that this information is collected and disseminated, for example by establishing reporting standards for firms, monitoring national data on water and air quality, and supporting cities in measuring urban indicators that help urban households, businesses, and policy makers better consider future costs and challenges in their decision making today. It can also educate through schools. It can provide incentives by creating regulations and using price instruments to stimulate behavior change among firms and households. Although the effect of such measures is hard to predict, international experience with fuel standards and vehicle-upgrading programs suggests that important transformations can occur through a well-designed and integrated system.

Financing

Ivorian policy makers need to find sources for large capital outlays needed to provide infrastructure and services as cities grow and urbanization picks up speed. Côte d'Ivoire has committed itself to an ambitious decentralization plan following the passing of the Decentralization Law in 2012, indicating the will to bring communes to the forefront in local economic development and the provision of local and urban services. But implementing the reforms is still slow. While the current legal framework sets out regulations governing municipal financing and financial management, funding options for municipalities, and financial management oversight bodies, several key gaps remain, including that many key laws have yet to be adopted, including implementation decrees on devolving functions and finances and establishing a basic and reliable framework for staffing of local governments. There is also widespread noncompliance with laws.

The fiscal autonomy of Ivorian municipalities is undermined by inconsistencies in the revenue regime, affecting both the predictability and the volume of resources. Over the last decade, government resources transferred to local governments have diminished, the application of criteria for allocation of resources from central transfers and shared revenues is not applied consistently, and transfers are mostly untimely and unpredictable, reducing the ability of communes to develop and implement their budgets.

The failure to fully transfer financial resources is seen in limited financing for capital and operational spending, and insufficient mobilization of their own resources, even in larger cities. Local governments remain highly dependent on shared revenues as well as on grants and transfers from central government. Their investment budget for development is too small for their needs, which is challenging for Global and Regional Connector cities. For example, total revenues assigned directly to the 197 municipalities between 2007 and 2013 amounted to CFAF 374.6 billion (about US$750 million; figure O.19), an average of only 0.44 percent of GDP (in Ghana, total revenues amounted to about 0.9 percent of GDP in 2012).

Figure O.19 Local Government Revenues, 2007–13 (CFAF million)

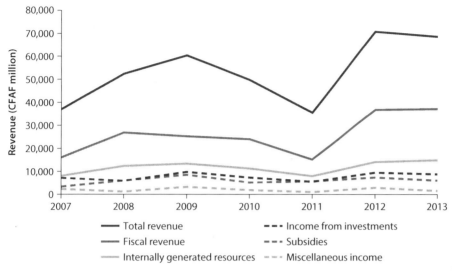

Source: Direction de la Comptabilité Parapublique (Parastatal Accounting Directorate).

Central government financing of communes has decreased and the provision of staffing to communes has diminished, rendering most communes in significant difficulties to manage and deliver on their core functions in accord with the law. In 2014, there were only 348 formal civil servants to serve 197 communes of the country, and the share of the government budget allocated to local governments was cut by half from 3.6 percent in 2003 to 1.27 percent in 2014. The majority of communes remain incapable of providing the basic management of the overall programming, budgeting, and budget execution process.

Municipal finances are inadequate for investment. One of the major obstacles to funding investment is the difficulty in mobilizing own-resource or central government resources and the high allocation for operational expenditures. For every dollar of municipal spending between 2007 and 2013, irrespective of location 82 cents went on operations—with about 40 cents of that going to staff costs—and only 18 cents to investment. Operational spending also covers facilities, supplies, and financial charges. Surprisingly, Regional and Domestic Connectors spend more on infrastructure than the municipalities of Abidjan surveyed. Between 2007 and 2013, operating and investment expenditures were estimated at 83 percent and 17 percent for Regional and Domestic Connector municipalities against 94 percent and 6 percent for municipalities in Abidjan, which undermines its role as a Global Connector. The average rate of income recovery from investments is 71.7 percent. The difficulty in mobilizing resources is one of the reasons for the gap between projections and actual infrastructure development. Donor assistance helps fill the gap. After years of crisis and a dearth of public funding, the government is now seeking to mobilize external resources to finance local infrastructure, including grants and soft loans.

Reform Priorities in Financing

Inconsistencies in the legal and institutional framework and its rollout—especially relative to the government's 2003 decentralization policy—need to be reconciled urgently. Devolution has not been accompanied by a transfer of financial and human resources. Law No. 2003–208 of July 7, 2003, on the transfer and distribution of responsibilities of the state to local authorities, specifies 16 areas of expertise for transfer. But this division of powers is based on the old organization of local government with five levels of decentralization. Another impediment is that the implementation of the power transfer sometimes leads to conflicts of responsibility between decentralized entities and other public bodies.

The systemic gaps in financing across Global, Regional, and Domestic Connectors require immediate attention to address the issues of the regulatory framework, volume, and predictability of financing. Local finances and public financial management need improvement for cities to meet their growing needs for financing infrastructure and services.

Three policy actions need to be taken together as a package:

- First, address the inconsistencies between devolution and decentralization alignment so that delegated functions follow finance and minimum human resources capacity is in place.
- Second, strengthen the local finance system and revise the fiscal transfer systems in key areas, simplifying the number of transfers and supporting the expansion and improvement of own-source revenue collection and improvement of public financial management. This entails registering all taxpayers, expanding street addressing and basic measures to consolidate the tax base and upgrade cadastral registers, and revising formulas for the allocation of shared revenues.
- Third, leverage collaboration among regions, municipalities, and utilities to generate economies of scale in infrastructure services delivery.

Complementing these interventions, the government should assess the efficiency of current transfer schemes, consolidate administrative decentralization to enable improved performance at the commune level, and consider introducing new elements to incentivize performance. Such measures could include (i) assessing the performance of General Financial Allocation (Dotation Globale Financière [DGF]) and its efficiency in absorbing and using these resources; (ii) introducing other targeted development grants for urban areas with an emphasis on introducing conditions for performance (as in revenue collection, budgeting, planning, and implementation, asset management, and financial management); (iii) using a fixed percentage of national budget or national revenues as allocations for municipalities through DGF, to ensure predictable funding; (iv) reviewing the performance of the Municipal Credit Fund (Fonds de Prêts aux Collectivités Locales) and its relevance for the financing of local governments going forward, including addressing the issues of existing municipal debts; and (v) introducing minimum standards across all municipalities with an emphasis on large urban areas.

In the medium to long term, the government could usefully explore the viability of additional new sources of financing for Global Connectors and creditworthy Regional and Domestic Connectors. This would include (i) assessing the sustainability of the current municipal borrowing scheme to see whether or not it would be a credible instrument given the current low repayment rates; (ii) investigating to what extent municipalities in Abidjan could become sufficiently creditworthy to become eligible for the International Finance Corporation subnational finance; (iii) exploring the opportunity to amend and update the legislation on public-private partnerships (PPPs) to allow municipalities to further engage in PPPs;[15] (iv) investigating opportunities for land financing; and (v) expanding, deepening, and institutionalizing existing mechanisms for inter-municipal collaboration. Of these potential new sources, (iii) and (v) will be the most promising options in the short to medium term.

These innovative financing instruments call for sound fiscal policy at the central level to mitigate risks. For instance, with debt comes the risk of insolvency, and so the country's fiscal risk management should be strengthened before it takes further steps with these instruments. Likewise, fiscal rules on borrowing by subnational governments would help ensure that debt finances capital expenditure and that repayment capacity is sufficient to service the debt. And, most important, cities need to fix their local finances and get the basics right from the onset before embarking.

Notes

1. Excluding small islands.

2. Preliminary results of the 2014 population census.

3. Ades and Glaeser (1995) offer an empirical analysis that shows that high tariffs, high costs of internal trade, and low level of international trade increase the degree of urban concentration. The degree of instability also tends to favor urban primacy. A very good predictor is a political variable: dictatorships have central cities that are, on average, 50 percent larger than their democratic counterparts. Their evidence suggests that the causation goes from political factors to urban concentration rather than the opposite. In the case of Côte d'Ivoire high internal trade costs and political instability since the mid-1990s might explain Abidjan's primacy.

4. The Zipf Law in urban economics states that the size of a city is inversely proportionate to its rank.

5. Laws No. 80–1180 of 1980 on municipal organization, No. 80–1181 on the municipal electoral system, and No. 80–1182 on the status of Abidjan and subsequent laws formally launched decentralization, with municipalities as the key players.

6. It may help if readers visualize the three shapes of a geographic system: *points* (the three cities of Abidjan, San-Pédro, and Yamoussoukro); *lines* (the three corridors connecting some cities to regional markets in the north, east, and west); and *polygons* (the super-regions that are development poles structuring a network of secondary cities around food and cash crops).

7. A technical seminar using the team alignment process was held on June 28–29, 2014, to identify constraints and solutions to integrated urban development. Participants

were director-level staff from all ministries involved in urbanization, representatives of the chairmen of the association of municipalities and regions, representatives of the major private sector associations, and representatives of Parliament and the Economic and Social Council.

8. Aide-memoire mission, World Bank 2014.

9. In contrast to informal or spontaneous settlements, like slums.

10. The access rate is calculated based on the national daily revenues per person and taking a household of three persons for a studio. With a lower rent of $189 and a maximum outlay of 40 percent, only a small proportion at the top of the pyramid earning more than $4 per day can afford this rent.

11. World Bank staff calculations based on OpenStreetMap and European Commission, *Global Human Settlements Layer*. See www.openstreetmap.org, Measurements only included paved streets, according to the OpenStreetMap classification.

12. Although JICA is assisting the government with the Greater Abidjan Transport Master Plan.

13. As measured by the Global Burden of Disease Study, which is a collaborative project of nearly 500 researchers in 50 countries led by the Institute for Health Metrics and Evaluation at the University of Washington.

14. Disability-adjusted life years (DALYs) combine the years of life lost due to disability with the years of life lost due to death attributed to specific causes.

15. Local authorities are also increasingly turning to build–operate–transfer arrangements to make up for inadequate financing for income-generating infrastructure. This system has been used to construct markets, stalls, and kiosks. In Adjamé, a CFAF 12 billion market was built with financing provided entirely by the Société Ivoirienne de Concept et de Gestion, which will manage the market for 25 years and then return it to the municipality. Similar operations are in Treichville, Sinfra, and Daloa.

Bibliography

Ades, A., and E. Glaeser. 1995. "Trade and Circuses: Explaining Urban Giants." *Quarterly Journal of Economics* 110: 195–228.

Bromhead, Marjory-Anne. 2012. *Enhancing Competitiveness and Resilience in Africa: An Action Plan for Improved Natural Resource and Environment Management*. Washington, DC: World Bank.

CAHF (Centre for Affordable Housing Finance in Africa). 2014. *Housing Finance in Africa Yearbook 2014*. Parkville, South Africa: CAHF.

Coulibaly, Souleymane, Jacques Esso, and Desire Kanga. 2014. "Revue de l'Urbanisation: Analyse Démographique." Background paper for this review.

Coulibaly, Souleymane, Jacques Esso, Charles Fe Doukoure, and Desire Kanga. 2014. "Revue de l'Urbanisation: Analyse Économique." Background paper prepared for this report.

Dobbs, Richard, Jaana Remes, James Manyika, Charles Roxburgh, Sven Smit, and Fabian Schaer. 2012. *Urban World: Cities and the Rise of the Consuming Class*. McKinsey Global Institute Report, McKinsey & Company.

ENSEA (École Nationale Supérieure de Statistique et d'Économie Appliquée d'Abidjan). 2014. "Repositioning Cities Based on Their Comparatiive Advantage." Background paper for this review.

Glaeser, Edward L., Jed Kolko, and Albert Saiz. 2001. "Consumer City." *Journal of Economic Geography* 1 (2001): 27–50.

Hoornweg, D., and P. Bhada-Tata. 2012. *What a Waste: A Global Review of Solid Waste Management.* World Bank Urban Development Series 15. Washington, DC: World Bank.

INS (Institut National de la Statistique). 1998. *Recensement Général de la Population et de l'Habitation.* Abidjan: Institut National de la Statistique.

———. 2002. *Enquête sur le Niveau de Vie des Ménages de Côte d'Ivoire.* Abidjan: Institut National de la Statistique.

———. 2008. *Enquête sur le Niveau de Vie des Ménages.* Abidjan: Institut National de la Statistique.

INS (Institut National de la Statistique) and ICF International. 2012. Enquête Démographic et de Santé et à Indicateurs Multiples de Côte d'Ivoire 2011–2012. Calverton, MD: INS and ICF International.

Jedwab, Remi. 2013. "Urbanization without Structural Transformation: Evidence from Consumption Cities in Africa." mimeo, George Washington University.

JICA (Japan International Cooperation Agency). 2014. Background paper for the Urban Master Plan of the Greater Abidjan. JICA.

Lasset, Biko Nick. 1987. *La crise de logement à Abidjan.* Report.

Legendre, R. 2014. *Recommandations pour l'Optimisation des Modes Opératoires de Délimitation de Territoires Villageois et de Certification Foncière.* Rapport final phase 1. Washington, DC: World Bank.

Liu, L., and J. Pradelli. 2012. "Financing Infrastructure and Monitoring Fiscal Risks at the Subnational Level." Policy Research Working Paper WPS6069, World Bank, Washington, DC.

Loba, Binde Fernand. 2011. "La problématique des quartiers précaires dans la ville d'Abidjan." Master Thesis, INPHB (Institut national polytechnique Félix Houphouët-Boigny), Yamoussoukro.

Lozano-Gracia, Nancy, and Cheryl Young. 2014. "Housing Consumption and Urbanization." Policy Research Working Paper 7112, World Bank, Washington, DC.

Ministry of Economic Planning and Development, Côte d'Ivoire. 2006. "Pre-Bilan Aménagement du Territoire." Study conducted by Direction Générale du Développement Économique Régional, Abidjan.

OECD (Organisation for Economic Co-operation and Development). 2013. "Future Flood Losses in Major Coastal Cities." *Nature Climate Change Magazine.*

Peterson, G. E., and O. Kaganova. 2010. "Integrating Land Financing into Subnational Fiscal Management." Policy Research Working Paper WPS5409, World Bank, Washington, DC.

Schäfer, A. 1998. "The Global Demand for Motorized Mobility." *Transportation Research A* 32 (6): 455–77.

TEEB (The Economics of Ecosystems & Biodiversity). 2010. *The Economics of Ecosystems and Biodiversity: Mainstreaming the Economics of Nature: A Synthesis.* Geneva: TEEB.

UN-Habitat (United Nations Human Settlements Programme). 2012. *Côte d'Ivoire: Profil Urbain d'Abidjan.* UN-Habitat.

———. 2013a. *The Relevance of Street Patterns and Public Space in Urban Areas.* Working Paper. UN-Habitat.

———. 2013b. *Streets as Public Spaces and Drivers of Urban Prosperity.* UN-Habitat.

United Nations. 2011. *World Urbanization Prospects: The 2011 Revision*. New York: United Nations.

USAID (United States Agency for International Development). 2013. "Land Tenure Côte d'Ivoire Profile." USAID Land Tenure and Property Rights Portal (accessed September 3, 2014), http://usaidlandtenure.net/cote-divoire.

WBCSD (World Business Council for Sustainable Development). 2001. *Mobility 2001: World Mobility at the End of the 20th Century and Its Sustainability*. Geneva: WBCSD.

Whitehead, Christine, Rebecca L. H. Chiu, Sasha Tsenkova, and Bengt Turner. 2010. "Land Use Regulation: Transferring Lessons from Developed Economies." In *Urban Land Markets: Improving Land Management for Successful Urbanization*, edited by S. Lall, M. Freire, B. Yuen, R. Rajack, and J. Helluin, 51–70. Dordrecht, The Netherlands: Springer, World Bank.

WHO (World Health Organization). 2012. "Health Indicators of Sustainable Cities." Initial Findings from a WHO Expert Consultation, May 17–18. http://www.who.int /hia/green_economy/indicators_cities.pdf.

World Bank. 2007. *An East Asia Renaissance: Ideas for Economic Growth*. Washington, DC: World Bank.

———. 2009. *World Development Report 2009: Reshaping Economic Geography*. Washington, DC: World Bank.

———. 2015. "Program Information Document, Appraisal Stage: Regional Trade Facilitation and Competitiveness DPO, Republic of Burkina Faso and Republic of Cote d'Ivoire." Report No. 95668-AFR AB7721. World Bank, Washington, DC.

Yeo, Homiegnon. 2014. "Étude des Axes Integrateurs." Background paper prepared for this report.

CHAPTER 1

Planning Cities

Alexandra Le Courtois, Dina Ranarifidy, Andrea Betancourt, and Annie Bidgood

Introduction

Urban planning should start from a clear and articulated vision of the urban development ambitions of the country and of particular localities. The urbanization policy dialogue needs to be anchored on the country's broader development vision because development happens in specific places and not in a vacuum. Consequently, there is a need to undertake wider public debate about national, regional, and local urban goals and objectives before devising and applying implementing instruments. To partly address this imperative, this study initiated a three-part policy dialogue (government, subnational, and private) to help formulate a shared vision of urbanization in Côte d'Ivoire.[1] These stakeholders believe that successful urbanization should lead to "cities that are planned, structured, competitive, attractive, inclusive, and organized around development poles." This vision implies that, to support growth and job creation, policy makers at the central, regional, and municipal levels need to promote a diversified urbanization through better planning, better connecting, greening, and finding ways to finance the growing development needs of these cities.

Urban planning and land management impact strongly on the costs and availability of land for business and residential purposes and on the quality of life in urban areas. Competitive real estate markets are key to local socioeconomic development and to urban productivity. When done well, urban planning enables real estate markets to assess investment risk, reduces uncertainty by setting transparent rules and a level playing field, and enables the government to protect public interest without discouraging private sector investments. Effective land management by local governments is a tool to implement good urban planning by producing an efficient allocation of urban land that also favors positive externalities and public goods (for example, green space) and limits negative externalities (such as congestion). Urban planning and land management both require that central governments provide an enabling legislative framework, and delegate requisite competencies to local governments while assuring their sufficient implementation capacity.

Problems with urban planning and land management in Côte d'Ivoire stem from cities that are growing and expanding informally and unconnected to basic infrastructure and services. In the face of population growth and after a decade of internal conflict, the government needs to invest in infrastructure. It should also expand its services with the support of empowered city authorities, coordinate provision of services with urban expansion, upgrade dense neighborhoods and existing structures, and continue to work on housing programs while maintaining their connectivity to economic centers. Planning and improving services, as well as promoting access to housing for low-income populations, will require political coordination between different government levels. Stronger local authorities can enforce urban planning regulations and target the needs of their populations.

The Current State of Urban Development in Côte d'Ivoire

Ivorian cities are growing rapidly, undermining the quality of life of their inhabitants and the productivity of these urban areas. They are growing and expanding but are also developing informally, unconnected to basic infrastructure and services, for two main reasons. First, land availability is constrained by the complexity of ownership and tenure systems. Second, there is a failure to coordinate city growth with the provision of basic services and access to low-income housing. Poor planning is worsened by the absence of updated planning regulations (and their enforcement) and of widespread information for decision making as well as by poor institutional coordination and weak governance, particularly at a local level. Planning is necessary to ensure that land use is coordinated with infrastructure provision that meets current and projected needs.

Population Growth

The urban population growth rate in Côte d'Ivoire is on par with that of other countries in the region. The World Bank estimates that the urban population growth rate in 2013 was 3.8 percent (World Bank 2015a), implying that the total urban population will double every 19 years. This is as fast as, or faster than, many countries in West Africa, including Guinea (3.8 percent), Benin (3.7 percent), Cameroon (3.6 percent), Senegal (3.6 percent), Ghana (3.4 percent), and Liberia (3.2 percent). The same can be said for Côte d'Ivoire's largest city, Abidjan. The United Nations (UN) estimates Abidjan will reach 7.8 million residents by 2030, doubling in less than 25 years (figure 1.1).

Growth rates in the largest cities of Côte d'Ivoire have generally slowed somewhat since the 1970s, but to varying degrees (INS 2014). Greater Abidjan (including Anyama) grew 5.6 percent per year on average from 1975 to 1988, but only 2.7 percent per year from 1999 to 2014 (figure 1.2). Among the Regional Connectors, growth rates in Daloa have fallen from approximately 5.5 percent per year (1975–88) to 2.8 percent (1998–2014). Korhogo has actually reversed the trend: it grew at 7.0 percent from 1975 to 88, 2.6 percent from 1988 to 1998, and then 3.5 percent from 1998 to 2014. The remaining

Figure 1.1 Abidjan Is Growing Faster Than Peer Cities in West Africa

Source: United Nations Population Division.

Figure 1.2 In Most Large Cities, Annual Population Growth Outpaces Land Area Expansion, Leading to Densification

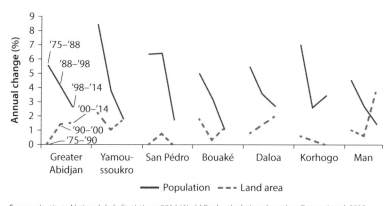

Sources: Institute National de la Statistique 2014; World Bank calculations based on Pesaresi et al. 2012. http://ghslsys.jrc.ec.europa.eu/.
Note: Gagnoa was omitted for lack of data.

Global Connectors (Yamoussoukro and San-Pédro) and Regional Connectors (Bouaké and Man), with populations over 100,000, are all currently growing at rates between 1.0 percent and 1.8 percent per year, meaning they would take more than 40 years to double.

Unlike population growth, the total built-up areas of these cities have remained stagnant or increased only slightly, leading to higher densities. Spatial expansion rates have exceeded population growth only in the cities of Bouaké and Man.[2] Indeed, in all cities except Man the rate of expansion was below 2 percent over 2000–14. Even Greater Abidjan, which is expanding at 1.6 percent per year, would take 45 years to double its built-up area. Figure 1.2 compares population growth and built-up area expansion for the following periods: 1975–90, 1990–2000, and 2000–14. As population growth continues to outpace land area expansion, these cities will become denser, presenting challenges for adequate housing provision and mobility. Although not all cities are sprawling, new development is often informal and not connected to basic infrastructure and services.

Density alone is not sufficient to reap the benefits of urbanization—agglomeration economies, lower transport costs, and higher productivity, to name a few. Density without livability can, in fact, contribute to diseconomies of scale, such as overcrowding, congestion, high living costs, inadequate urban services, and environmental degradation. The stark contrast between density and livability is highlighted by the comparison of Singapore and Lagos. They have similar populations and population densities, but lie on opposite ends of the livability spectrum (figure 1.3) (Centre for Liveable Cities and Urban Land Institute 2013). In Lagos, basic formal housing is largely unaffordable and two-thirds of the population lives in slums. These households are made even more vulnerable by regular flooding across large parts of the city.

Figure 1.3 Not All Dense Cities Are Livable

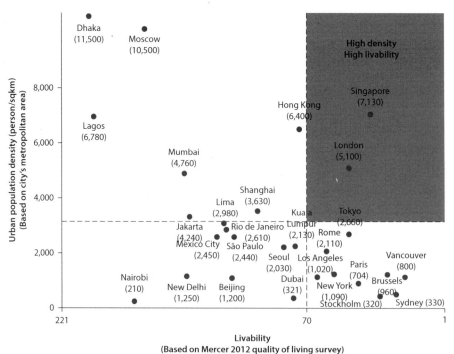

Source: Centre for Liveable Cities and Urban Land Institute 2013.
Note: CLC = Centre for Liveable Cities; sqkm = square kilometer.

Existing infrastructure has deteriorated for lack of maintenance, and current investment needs far exceed budgetary capacity of the city. By contrast, Singapore has managed to leverage its density into livability and economic prosperity through comprehensive, well-coordinated, and long-term planning. In the decades after independence the city addressed a serious housing crisis, redeveloped its waterfront, and attracted private investment to a modern, vibrant commercial center. Today, half of Singapore's land area is dedicated to green and open space. Authorities regularly invest in infrastructure improvements and maintain ample land reserves for future projects like public transportation. For these reasons among others, Singapore regularly ranks at the top of global livability surveys, whereas in Côte d'Ivoire access to urban infrastructure such as improved sanitation has been declining across urban areas, impeding further private investment in housing (figure 1.4).

Urban Infrastructure and Access to Basic Services

Growth and densification in Ivorian cities have not been accompanied by improved living standards. As cities in Côte d'Ivoire grow and densify, many struggle with key aspects of livability, particularly the provision of basic services and access to adequate, affordable housing. Households in urban areas are faced with the difficult choice between overcrowded and expensive living conditions in central areas near existing services or unserved development on the urban periphery (often informal) coupled with unaffordable transport costs.

Mobility and access to services are hindered by poor street coverage. A dense and well-connected street grid is essential for connectivity, productivity, quality

Figure 1.4 Access to Improved Sanitation, Côte d'Ivoire

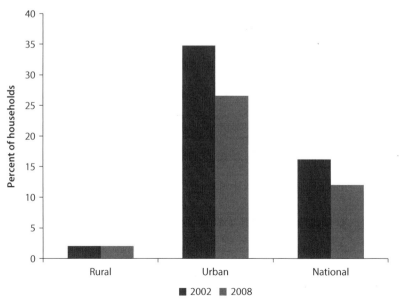

Sources: INS 2002 and 2008.

Diversified Urbanization • http://dx.doi.org/10.1596/978-1-4648-0808-1

of life, and social inclusion. Because streets often function as a public right-of-way for other systems, their coverage also serves as proxy for access to basic services like water and sanitation, solid waste collection, and adequate storm water drainage to prevent flooding. In a global study, the United Nations Human Settlements Programme (UN-Habitat) determined that livable and competitive cities are those with at least 20 kilometers of paved road per square kilometer of land area (UN-Habitat 2013a; 2013b). By contrast, the largest cities in Côte d'Ivoire have street densities between 2.1 and 10.5 kilometers per square kilometer. Some cities rank slightly better on street density relative to population: Greater Abidjan, for example, has up to 824 meters per 1,000 residents. This measure of access is above that in most large African cities (300 meters per 1,000 inhabitants on average) but still falls short of cities in Asia and in Latin America and the Caribbean (typically above 1,000 meters per 1,000 inhabitants). One benefit of the increasing density of Ivorian cities is that their street grids are usually better connected than those in low-density "modern planned cities" like Brasilia. Greater Abidjan, Yamoussoukro, and Bouaké all have more than 100 intersections per square kilometer, the threshold recommended by UN-Habitat. Figure 1.5 compares Global Connectors and Regional Connectors on measures of street coverage.

Increased pressure on safe drinking water supply has raised poor urban dwellers' vulnerability. Bouaké, for instance, has a deficit of daily potable water production (from only one source) of 3,000 cubic meters. With most taps broken in urban areas, many residents are forced to buy potable water from informal water vendors, rendering them vulnerable to price hikes and unsafe or

Figure 1.5 Many Large Cities Suffer from Poor Street Coverage

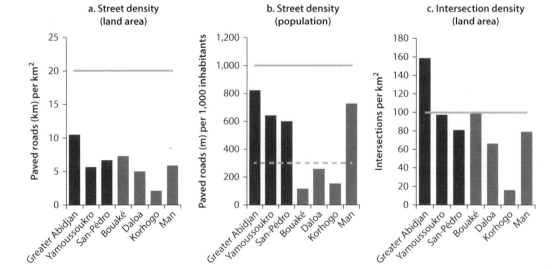

Source: Calculations based on OpenStreetMap 2015 and Pesaresi et al. 2012, http://ghslsys.jrc.ec.europa.eu/; UN-Habitat 2013a, 2013b.
Note: km = kilometer; m = meter.

illegally sourced water. The national water utility (Société de Distribution d'Eau de Côte d'Ivoire [SODECI]) has accused informal water vendors of illicitly siphoning water out of SODECI's pipes at night (Kouassi 2011, 2012).

The provision of infrastructure and basic services is unequally distributed within cities. Evidence from urban audits carried out in Ivorian cities in 2013 shows that central areas and formal neighborhoods are adequately endowed with infrastructure and public services, in sharp contrast to peri-urban and informal neighborhoods (box 1.1). These audits also noted that growth of peri-urban areas was marked by an absence of basic infrastructure. In San-Pédro, for example, 31.5 percent of the city's urban landscape is occupied by informal neighborhoods (housing), with limited access to basic services. In Bouaké, peri-urban neighborhoods are growing without access to water and electricity (although formal/central neighborhoods also have degrading infrastructure). In the communes

---

Box 1.1 Urban, Financial, and Organizational Audits of 10 Communes in Côte d'Ivoire

In 2013, the World Bank assisted the Ministry of Economic Infrastructure in carrying out audits of 10 cities to assess the urban, financial, and organizational state of municipalities (communes) and the needs in infrastructure, basic service provision, and social and recreational equipment (education, healthcare, and sports). The audited communes included San-Pédro, Bouaké, Kohogo, Divo, Yopougon, Port Bouet, Koumassi, Adjame, and Abobo (the last five are communes of the District of Abidjan).

These audits aimed to study the functioning of the communes and identify the strengths and opportunities for development, as well as to highlight the weaknesses and main dysfunctions. Each audit is extremely detailed and is organized under three main topics: urban audit, organizational audit, and financial audit. The urban section addresses demographic characteristics, employment and economic growth, spatial development patterns, access to infrastructure and basic services, as well as recent and planned investments. The second part is concerned with the organization of local government, the legal framework in place, impacts of devolution and decentralization efforts, and technical capacity to deliver services. The final section presents analysis of the financial situation of the local government, including fiscal resources, expenditures, major investments, capacity to execute budgets, and level of transparency.

This documentation is intended to help elected officials find and prioritize effective strategies for better management of local public services, and implement a policy of sustainable community development. It also provides a useful framework to gather and synthesize data in additional urban areas of Côte d'Ivoire. On the basis of these audits, the investment effort of the municipalities will be supported by partners, through the Priority Investment Program (Programme d'Investissement Prioritaire [PIP]) and the Program and Priority Maintenance (Programme d'Entretien Prioritaire [PEP]).

Source: Urban audits 2013.[a]

a. The urban audits are a series of reports that were outputs of the PUIUR project in Côte d'Ivoire (RCI-Emergency Urban Infrastructure, P110020).

(municipalities) of Abidjan included in the audits (particularly Yopougon, the largest), more than half the residential neighborhoods have limited access to public services and infrastructure.

Sociopolitical crises since the 1999 military coup have affected the provision and quality of basic services. In Abidjan, for instance, before the 2002 civil war, water coverage in the city was estimated at 75 percent. After 2002, coverage went down to 56 percent as the city struggled to provide 1 million displaced Ivorians with basic services. Such pressures contributed to fast-deteriorating infrastructure. Since 2002 waste management in cities worsened dramatically: cities increased their daily solid waste production from 2,500 tons in 2002 to 3,600 tons in 2014, but collection *rates* dropped sharply (World Bank 2015b), leading to overflowing collection centers, proliferating open dump sites, and worsening public health and safety hazards. Because of the degradation of roads, more than 40 percent of households have become difficult to access, leaving the overall collection rate in the district of Abidjan at 70 percent (World Bank 2015b). In other cities like Bouaké, precollection services performed well and were financed through monthly fees; however, existing infrastructure was insufficient and unsuitable for full garbage collection. The Akouédo landfill, which receives more than 1.2 million tons of waste yearly, does not comply with international standards and is now too small to bury Abidjan's solid waste, presenting further public health and environmental risks (World Bank 2015b; World Bank and BURGEAP 2011). The country's waste management system currently relies on government support and payments from the inhabitants of Abidjan.

The infrastructure in cities, already deficient, has deteriorated greatly and requires urgent investment. The physical infrastructure for most basic services (potable water, sanitation, waste collection, and electricity) was heavily damaged during the civil war and has not been maintained or improved in the past 10–15 years. From small towns (Domestic Connectors) to regional cities (Regional Connectors) and the communes of metropolitan Abidjan (Global Connector), infrastructure (roads, electricity, potable water, drainage, and sanitation) had been mainly built before the military crisis, with little maintenance investment since 2009. The electricity networks that serve up to half the urban population are deficient, forcing dwellers to rely on informal and illegal connections, risking the safety of their neighborhoods. In San-Pédro, electricity covers less than half the commune's neighborhoods; in Korhogo, public lighting covers only a quarter of the city. In the communes of Abidjan, the deficits are related mainly to drainage and sanitation. Waste management also suffers from severe deficits and underperformance across cities.

The Housing Challenge

After the government's withdrawal from land development and housing production in the early 1980s, the country entered a housing crisis exacerbated later by the sociopolitical crises of the late 1990s and 2000s. The housing crisis is seen in the spread of informal settlements, high-priced rents, and noncompliance with urban planning and building standards. The living environment in cities of

Côte d'Ivoire, especially Abidjan, deteriorated during the crises because of insufficient investment in urban infrastructure and to increasing poverty. The housing market in Abidjan does not meet the needs of the population and has come to a critical point. Prices, especially in the rental sector (for three-quarters of the population) are increasing rapidly, making housing affordability more challenging, pointing to a housing deficit in well-located areas.

Different sources estimate the total housing deficit to be between 400,000[3] and 600,000 units (CAHF 2014)—and increasing. The deficit is concentrated in cities, with half in Abidjan. The housing deficit is usually calculated as an accumulation of the quantitative and qualitative deficits. In light of the overcrowding in Abidjan, the quantitative deficit (making it difficult for households to split or forcing multiple households to live together) there is steep. But even more important is the qualitative deficit: lack of access to basic services and weak tenure security usually affect households' confidence in the future and reduce their willingness to invest in the structure, such that a large part of the housing stock lacks access to basic services and is built of temporary material. About two-thirds of the stock of primary housing has permanent walls, but less than 4 percent has a permanent roof (Lozano-Gracia and Young 2014). Investment in sanitation (primarily made by households) is also limited: just 27 percent of households in 2008 had access to flush or improved toilets, down from 35 percent in 2002 (INS 2008).

Regional and Global Connectors suffer from a lack of housing provisioned with basic services, contributing to the qualitative housing deficit. While access to electricity is almost 90 percent in urban areas, piped water connection is 72 percent, down 7 points between 1998 and 2011 (INS and ICF 2012), essentially in secondary cities. In several cities, the proportion of formal/organized neighborhoods is significant, but housing is severely underprovisioned and underserviced, and is deteriorating. Organized and provisioned neighborhoods occupy between 20 percent of the residential sector in the communes of Abidjan and 50 percent in San-Pédro and Bouaké (table 1.1; and see box 1.2).[4] These neighborhoods also have most of the important infrastructure facilities and roads of the city. In smaller cities, the share of formal/provisioned housing tends to be much lower, with only 3 percent in Korhogo, concentrated in the city center's individual homes and buildings. Smaller cities lack proper developers, and housing is left to municipalities or informal developers that provide only the minimum. Some other neighborhoods in large cities are fairly well structured, but their access to basic amenities and social services is greatly limited. Of greater concern, underprovisioned areas or slum-type neighborhoods (built on abandoned or customary land) already house a significant proportion of the urban population, up to one-third in large cities, and are growing more rapidly under the demographic pressure of urbanization. Those areas lack urban structuring, with almost no roads and access to basic amenities and services. This type of housing is mostly on the urban periphery or in the lowlands.

Informal housing in irregular settlements is expanding, especially in large cities (Global Connectors). Informal settlements are common in urban and peri-urban areas of Côte d'Ivoire and are usually situated on publicly owned land.

Table 1.1 Share of Housing Type in Total, by Residential Area
percent

Type	San-Pédro	Korhogo	Bouaké	Koumassi (Abidjan)	Port-Bouet (Abidjan)
Formal well provisioned	50	3	50	23.5	18.5
Formal fairly provisioned	0	0	32	0	0
Formal underprovisioned	18	96	18	39	47.5
Irregular settlements	32	1	0	37.5	34

Source: Information extracted from the urban audits 2013.

Box 1.2 The Different Types of Housing in Large Ivorian Cities

There are three main types of housing in Ivorian cities:

1. Old comfortable villas and apartments, mostly in the neighborhoods of Cocody and Marcory in Abidjan, house the high-income population.
2. Modern social housing comprises low row houses with low fences, collectively owned and managed by public or mixed real estate agencies. Most of these houses were built by the state for public officials in the 1970s and 1980s, and were later bought by their original tenants. Newer similar houses for middle-income populations were built by private developers after 1994. These first two types of housing are in limited supply and are often well provisioned and served.
3. The third type—the dominant type of housing—is an urban structure formed by a group of houses built around a central courtyard shared by residents. This type is mostly in the lower-income neighborhoods of Abidjan, such as Abobo (85 percent of the total), Attecoube, Treichville, and Yopougon. The urban environment in these areas is generally highly degraded and of poor quality, making it unattractive to private developers.

Source: Terrabo, BEPU, and PWC 2013.

These neighborhoods follow no urban guidelines, often lack land title and building permits, and suffer serious sanitation problems as well as little or no access to other basic services. Most houses are built of wood and zinc and resemble huts. Irregular settlements have a high presence in the urban towns of large cities, such as San-Pédro and Abidjan (Koumassi, Port Bouet, Attecoube, and Yopougon). Informal housing accounts for more than 6 percent of all urban dwellings in Côte d'Ivoire, housing 15–17 percent of the urban population. In Abidjan, it is estimated that roughly 15–17 percent of settlements are illegal because of their location, absence of basic services, or substandard construction (Gulyani and Connors 2002). As evidenced in the cities that were audited, informal or irregular neighborhoods are not as common as formal underprovisioned neighborhoods at a national level; nonetheless, they are expanding on the periphery of cities as urban populations grow and find no access to affordable formal housing.

In 2013 the government attempted several initiatives to relocate informal populations in risk-prone areas to new housing projects on the urban periphery. According to national authorities and urban experts,[5] relocation projects failed when informal populations were moved from central to peripheral residential areas and received compensation. Many returned shortly after, the main reasons being the centrality of their location (fairly well connected to economic centers) and familiar surroundings.

The challenge of the housing deficit in urban areas is exacerbated by low affordability and limited mobility. Households face the hard choice of high rents in well-connected areas versus high transport costs in neighborhoods on the periphery, and often live in overcrowded conditions to avoid costly commutes from peri-urban areas. For the region more widely, housing expenditures— relatively constant among all quintiles at 17–18 percent—is high with only three Sub-Saharan African countries (Angola, Malawi, and Rwanda) of a sample of 20 showing higher average rates (figure 1.6). When adding transport, though, Abidjan has the highest share of expenditures of all urban areas across the region, at 26.6 percent (figure 1.7). Transport accounts for more than a third of those financial outlays, and is steeper in higher-population quintiles. The rental market in central areas is therefore under severe pressure as the large housing deficit creates speculation on rents. In Abidjan, the monthly rent of a studio can range from CFAF 100,000 to CFAF 150,000 (US$189–283), which less than 20 percent of the population can afford on the basis of a household of three.[6]

Figure 1.6 Housing Expenditures by Country and Quintile, in Ascending Order of GDP per Capita (Urban Areas)

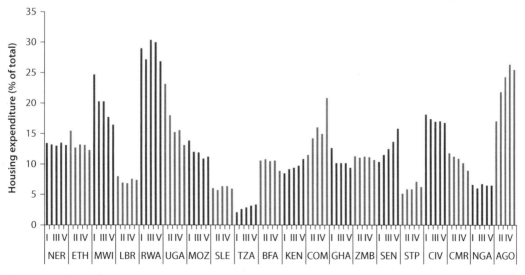

Source: Lozano-Gracia and Young 2014.
Note: GDP = gross domestic product; AGO = Angola; BFA = Burkina Faso; CIV = Côte d'Ivoire; CMR = Cameroon; COM = Comoros; ETH = Ethiopia; GHA = Ghana; KEN = Kenya; LBR = Liberia; MOZ = Mozambique; MWI = Malawi; NER = Niger; NGA = Nigeria; RWA = Rwanda; SEN = Senegal; SLE = Sierra Leone; STP = São Tomé and Príncipe; TZA = Tanzania; UGA = Uganda; ZAM = Zambia.

Figure 1.7 Housing and Transport Expenditures by Country

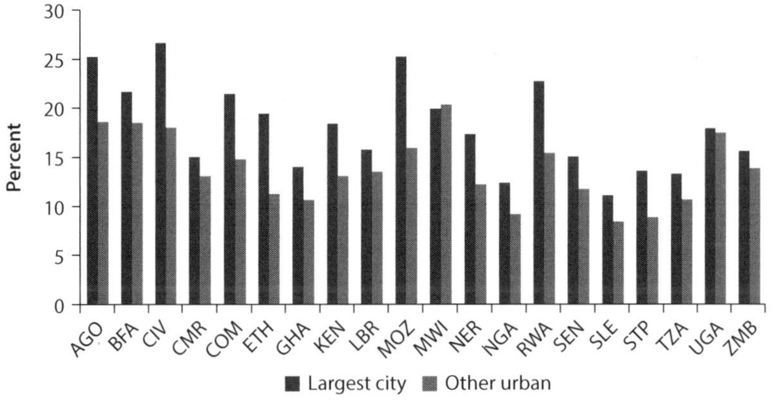

Source: Lozano-Gracia and Young 2014.

Note: GDP = gross domestic product; AGO = Angola; BFA = Burkina Faso; CIV = Côte d'Ivoire; CMR = Cameroon; COM = Comoros; ETH = Ethiopia; GHA = Ghana; KEN = Kenya; LBR = Liberia; MOZ = Mozambique; MWI = Malawi; NER = Niger; NGA = Nigeria; RWA = Rwanda; SEN = Senegal; SLE = Sierra Leone; STP = São Tomé and Príncipe; TZA = Tanzania; UGA = Uganda; ZAM = Zambia.

Moreover, the barriers to land development in peri-urban areas (including costs of registration, development, and unclear tenure), as well as lack of clarity on urban reserves, have contributed to land scarcity and high prices in urban areas, making formal and decent housing expensive and restricting it to middle- and higher-income groups.

Because of poor affordability, the housing units in Abidjan are overcrowded: over half have more than three people sleeping to a room. While overcrowding was reduced in the 1990s, the trend switched during the political crises, going up from 45 percent a decade before. Other cities are less affected by overcrowding (14 points lower) and the impact of the crises was less, just stalling the earlier rate of improvement (figure 1.8). Yet, although the household size in cities of Côte d'Ivoire (except Abidjan) is lower than in rural areas (4.7 versus 5.1 persons), it is higher in Abidjan at 5.3 (INS and ICF 2012). This trend is the opposite of what is seen in many other developing countries where household size decreases as cities become bigger, usually because of lower birth rates and other factors such as labor mobility, bringing single family members to the city for economic opportunities that will support the families remaining somewhere else. With affordability issues and high transport costs in Abidjan, family members tend to stay longer with the household (for example, young adults delay getting their own houses).

Ownership rates are very low in Ivorian cities. While a rental market is an essential factor in labor mobility, ownership helps increase the resilience of poor households to economic shocks. Therefore a balance needs to be found between the affordability of the housing rental and accessibility to housing ownership to

Figure 1.8 One to Two Persons Sleeping to a Room in Côte d'Ivoire

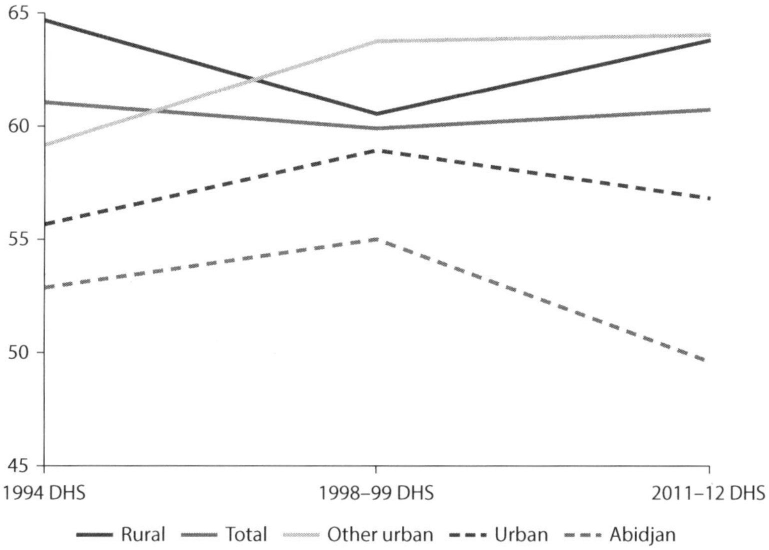

Source: ICF International 2015.
Note: DHS = Demographic and Health Survey.

increase the economic resilience of urban dwellers. Ownership in Ivorian cities is the lowest in the region (among a sample of 20 countries) at 47.4 percent (figure 1.9), dropping by 7 percentage points between 2002 and 2007 in urban areas, and affecting more the 40 percent poorest and the 20 percent richest of the population. This richest quintile, which usually has the highest ownership rate, has seen a major drop, at almost 14 points (figure 1.10). With rampant poverty during the crises, the poorest households moving to cities cannot access ownership anymore and search housing solutions instead on the rental market. The housing rental market therefore needs to be made affordable as a priority, to help urban dwellers in the short term while they look for long-term solutions of access to affordable housing finance.

Access to ownership requires different financial efforts from rental solutions. Up-front investments for ownership are heavy—to buy the land and build the first part of the house where home life will focus before further incremental investments are made—whereas spending will be low or almost nonexistent (except for utilities) later. So access to ownership, especially for poor households, requires them to have accumulated savings. When savings are not available or when they are used for other purposes (perhaps during a political crisis), the rental market offers greater flexibility. In Abidjan where urban growth is high, largely reflecting rural–urban migration, access to ownership is more difficult for new households, and the rental market covers about three-quarters of the city's population.

Figure 1.9 Ownership Rate in Côte d'Ivoire and Other Sub-Saharan African Countries

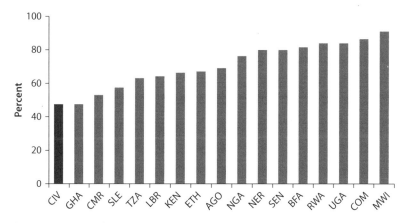

Source: Lozano-Gracia and Young 2014.
Note: AGO = Angola; BFA = Burkina Faso; CIV = Côte d'Ivoire; CMR = Cameroon; COM = Comoros;
ETH = Ethiopia; GHA = Ghana; KEN = Kenya; LBR = Liberia; MWI = Malawi; NER = Niger; NGA = Nigeria;
RWA = Rwanda; SEN = Senegal; SLE = Sierra Leone; TZA = Tanzania; UGA = Uganda.

Figure 1.10 Owner Occupancy of Urban Households per Quintile in Côte d'Ivoire

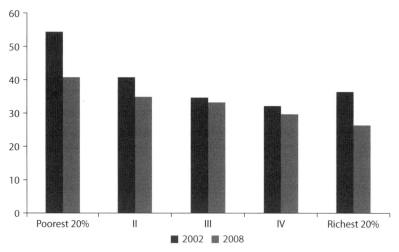

Sources: INS 2002, 2008.

The government is well aware of the challenge for poorer communities especially, and has made the sector a priority. A few years ago it launched a national program for constructing 60,000 new housing units, organized working groups to revise land regulations, and drafted a new law for the rental sector; however, many of those measures are still to be implemented. The share of public "pro-poor spending" has been fluctuating, with a growing trend: in 2013 it was 9.3 percent of gross domestic product (GDP), supporting an urban upgrading policy to help narrow the gap in access to basic services (CAHF 2014).

Main Drivers of Urbanization Challenges

The challenges of rapid urbanization in Côte d'Ivoire stem from bottlenecks in the planning and development process. The country lacks an overarching urban planning policy to guide new development. Current planning regulations are outdated, unenforced, or simply nonexistant for smaller cities. Access to serviced land is hindered by complexity and uncertainty because customary practices prevail over state-led efforts at registration and titling. Cities struggle to aggregate land on the fringes for future urban expansion. Finally, local governments lack the financial and technical capacity to expand basic services to existing and new developments, or to improve access to affordable housing.

Outdated Planning Regulations

At independence, city planning policy targeted modernization. Unlike smaller towns under local authorities, the building of Abidjan was driven by planning goals embedded in all government urban policies. Plans allowed the government to control the distribution of the main activities along the industrial–harbor axis, assisted in providing infrastructure, and defined state housing developments. Besides attempting to expropriate all vacant land (or land under customary rights), the state made property rights dependent on proper development standards to control the city's expansion (Rakodi 1997). However, the various city development plans prepared in the 1980s were unable to prevent social segregation, worsening transport problems and inequality between the central and peripheral areas.

Today, Côte d'Ivoire lacks an overarching urban planning policy to govern, regulate, and provide clear information on land use and availability. In 2012, the government committed to adopt an urban code, which is still pending. This leaves issues of urban land management unresolved and allows scattered and piecemeal expansion, while there is a need to collect information on land divisions and boundaries and on land use to better coordinate land supply for urban expansion. This lack of city planning makes it difficult to have timely information on land transactions.

Côte d'Ivoire has multiple urban plans, but few cities have adopted or kept them up to date. They range from the broad Urban Master Plan of Greater Abidjan (Schéma Directeur du Grand Abidjan) (map 1.1), to the Urban Development Plan (Plan Directeur d'Urbanisme) for Regional and Domestic Connectors, to the Detailed Urban Development Plan (Plan d'Urbanisme de Détail) and Short-Term Urban Development Program (Plan Programme à Court Terme). Despite having been mandated, most cities have failed to draft or implement such plans; and, when plans do exist, they are poorly applied, tend to be unknown by local authorities (presidents of regions, governors of districts, mayors), or have little funding. In the last two years, however, the government has taken steps to develop or update master plans for Abidjan, Bouaké, and Yamoussoukro.[7]

In the case of Greater Abidjan, the 2000 land use plan is still effective and relevant because no major urban projects altered it. An important contribution

Map 1.1 Urban Master Plan of Greater Abidjan

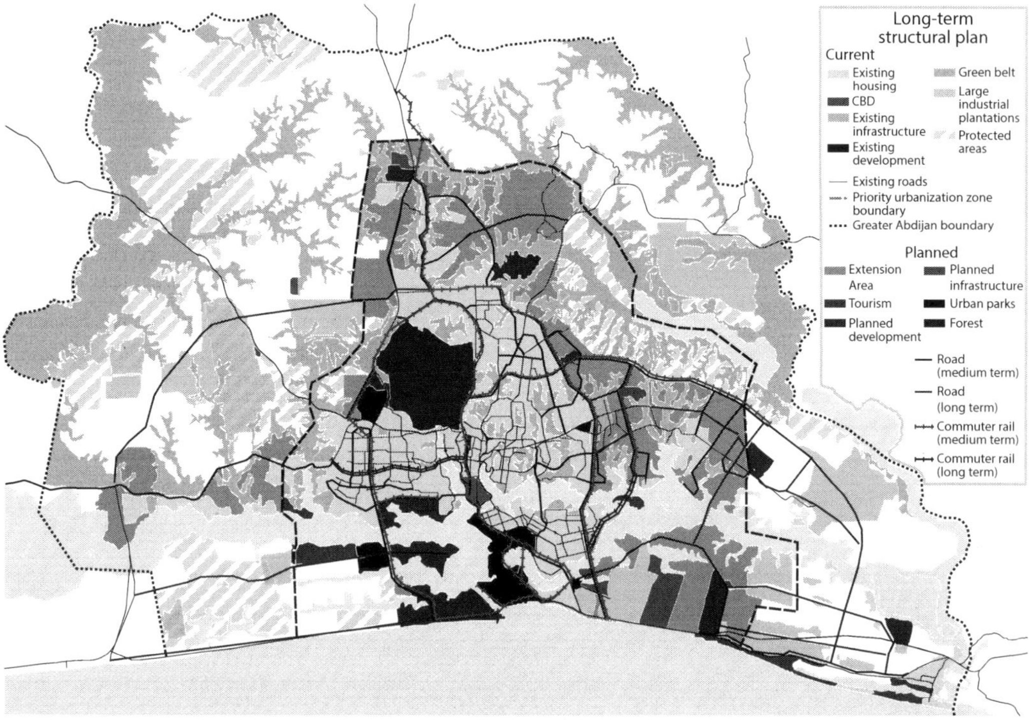

Source: Bureau National dÉtude Technique et de Développement.

of the Urban Master Plan of Greater Abidjan is the information on present and future land use, which helps with decisions about urban growth, infrastructure, and service provision. The current land use map shows a concentrated amount of residential areas of varying densities around the main urban center, where government, industrial, and port activities are concentrated.

These urban-level planning tools need to be coherent with the country's new territorial development policy framework, which the government adopted in 2006. The policy framework is anchored on five key actions: (i) adopting a territorial development law to set the legal framework for central and local government interventions; (ii) forming an inter-ministerial committee to ensure coherence among country, urban, and sector infrastructure development plans; (iii) establishing regional councils to promote a participatory development process at the regional level; (iv) linking national development objectives to regional development plans; and (v) establishing a national observatory of spatial dynamics within the Ministry of Planning and Development to collect, analyze, and disseminate spatial information (MEMPD 2006). But the Orientation Law on Territorial Development is still in draft form, and according to it a Territorial Development Master Plan needs to be developed and adopted to provide the overarching direction to urban-level planning documents. This time-inconsistent problem, with higher-level regulatory documents missing, while lower-levels documents are developed in an uncoordinated manner, will most likely end up being costlier and less effective. The government needs to provide clear guidance about the hierarchy of planning documents and to act accordingly and quickly to address any inconsistency problem.

Construction guidelines of Global Connectors are outdated, poorly enforced, and cumbersome, and most Regional and Domestic Connectors simply do not even have them. Some guidelines work against denser planning. For instance, the building code of 1952 requires that the distance between buildings does not exceed their height and that residential areas build on 60 percent maximum of the plot, which may result in low-density construction. Planning and building regulations, which must be applied by officials from the Ministry of Construction, Housing, Sanitation, and Urbanism (Ministère de la Construction, du Logement, de l'Assainissement et de l'Urbanisme [MCLAU]) and from local government officials alike, also suffer from lax implementation. Although a local government may approve construction, the MCLAU may disapprove it, and vice versa. And, after dealing with outdated documents and contesting bureaucracies, urban developers must face long procedures to acquire building permits, for which Côte d'Ivoire ranks low in the Doing Business Ranking, at 162 (out of 189). It takes 364 days to issue a permit to build a warehouse. These hurdles may lead developers to get approval from only one government entity or even skip the formal process completely, building informally. High formal costs (box 1.3) also reduce the entry of small and medium firms—limiting competition, decreasing affordability, and promoting informality. Such issues are common to many countries, however (box 1.4).

The responsibilities of municipal councils are very limited in urban planning, land management, and construction regulations. The central government—in the guise of the MCLAU—has full responsibility for issuing building permits, urban planning certificates, demolition permits, and compliance certificates. Metropolitan and local authorities are closer to their constituents, particularly in peri-urban villages, and are consulted at the application-processing phase of ownership or development documents. However, their decisions and policies are not always aligned with those of the MCLAU; individuals may receive development or construction approval at the local level but later be rejected by that ministry. Such lack of coordination discourages formal registration and development.

Parallel Tenure Systems

Ownership and tenure of land in Côte d'Ivoire is highly informal and insecure, and has been for decades. In 1998, the Rural Land Law sought to modernize ownership rights and set up a statutory legal framework for promoting land markets. Through this law, the government expected to secure ownership rights of indigenous (autochthonous) populations and use rights of foreigners (USAID 2013). But customary practices remain widely used by the population, most of whom are unfamiliar with the Rural Land Law.

Diversified Urbanization • http://dx.doi.org/10.1596/978-1-4648-0808-1

Box 1.3 The Process to Obtain Formal Land Tenure Rights in Côte d'Ivoire

The MCLAU (Ministère de la Construction, du Logement, de l'Assainissement et de l'Urbanisme controls and manages vacant government-owned land in Abidjan and the other major cities of Côte d'Ivoire. It is responsible for the distribution of urban plots. Obtaining formal land tenure rights under the 1998 law is a two-step process:

1.   Apply for a land certificate, which confers a transitory type of tenure. The applicant must demonstrate "continuous and peaceful existence of customary rights which involves an official investigation at the sub-prefecture level." An investigative commissioner is charged to rule on the veracity of the documentation, and, if this is confirmed, a land certificate is signed by the prefect, registered by the local representative of the Ministry of Agriculture, and published in the prefecture's *Official Journal*.
2.   The certificate holder may apply to obtain either a title deed or an emphyteutic lease. Although the land certificate can be issued to any individual or legal entity, the law provides that only the state, public entities, or Ivorian nationals may become owners.

All costs tied to registration of land rights, including surveying one's land and certifying one's rights, are borne by the applicant. These costs, coupled with the likelihood of taxes being levied on registered land, are disincentives to registration.

Source: USAID 2013.

Box 1.4 Inappropriate Building Regulations Hamper Affordability

Land use regulations, zoning, and building regulations are some of the most valuable tools for governments to guide development and promote livability of cities. Unfortunately, certain interventions in urban land markets can negatively impact affordability and access to serviced land, if they are not benchmarked against what the local population can afford to pay. Evidence from around the world indicates that inappropriate minimum standards actually increase informal development even on formally titled land.

Many cities in India have imposed strict limits for building heights. In Bangalore, the policy resulted in horizontal low-density expansion of built-up area, and increased housing costs by 3–6 percent of the median household income. In Mumbai, constrained by the surrounding topography, the effect was even more pronounced. Building heights were limited to less than one-tenth of those allowed in other Asian cities, and, according to Buckley and Kalarickal (2006), the restriction increased housing prices by an estimated 15–20 percent of income.

Likewise, in Dar es Salaam, inappropriate size regulations make the majority of buildings de facto illegal, regardless of formal land title or the quality of the structure (figure B1.4.1). Those developments that are out of compliance (building areas below 375 square meters) are condemned to be unplanned and excluded from water and sanitation services, making it extremely

box continues next page

Box 1.4 Inappropriate Building Regulations Hamper Affordability *(continued)*

costly and difficult to redevelop the land later, legally. A more effective approach would be to rationalize standards for development based on performance (for example, structural integrity) and affordability by the local population.

Figure B1.4.1 Compliance with Minimum Building Size Regulations in Dar es Salaam

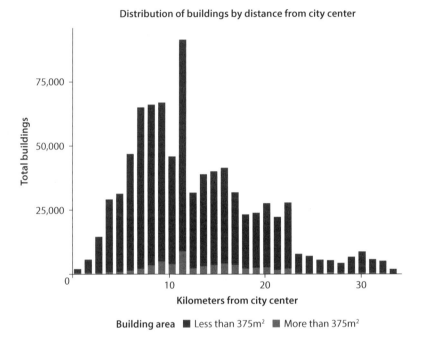

Distribution of buildings by distance from city center

Building area ■ Less than 375m² ■ More than 375m²

Sources: Buckley and Kalarickal 2006; World Bank, forthcoming.

Foreigners' rights to land were at the root of the sociopolitical conflict. Until 2007, land conflicts were widespread in Côte d'Ivoire, in particular in the south where a large number of domestic and foreign migrants moved to work on coffee and cocoa plantations. This region has seen increasingly frequent monetary transactions for land (Stamm 2007). Nonetheless, the apparent contradiction between respecting and modernizing local practices over land introduced in the 1998 Rural Land Law generated conflicts over land among Ivorian nationals and foreigners.

Even today the country's land market is characterized by informality and uncertainty. Less than 2 percent of land is held under title deed, and land transactions are seldom recorded. Because of the decade-long political crises and the complexity of the Rural Land Law (coupled with the lack of resources for implementing the law), only 1,172 title deeds and 339 emphyteutic leases (entitling holders to heritable and alienable tenure rights for varying periods) have been issued in the whole country (USAID 2013). At the end of 2013, urban areas had an estimated 1 million plots of land, against fewer than 250,000 government-processed titles for urban and rural lands.

Despite efforts introduced in the 1998 Rural Land Law to promote transparent land markets, land registration and titling remain problematic. The state continues to face difficulties accessing land, and uncertainty persists over demarcation between rural and urban areas (Legendre 2014). The state must deal not only with a dominant customary system of land ownership and tenure and only sporadic use of the Rural Land Law, but also with lengthy, expensive, and bureaucratic processes to register land and obtain title. Registration costs—estimated at 10.8 percent of a property's value—are high and above the Sub-Saharan Africa average (CAHF 2014), discouraging people from going down this path. Other disincentives are the likelihood of taxes being levied on registered land (USAID 2013). Demand for land titles remains low, and its value added—relative to the process of land security based on local consensus—is uncertain.[8] About 98 percent of the country's land is still governed by customary practices, despite the statutory system (box 1.5).

In most Sub-Saharan African countries such as Côte d'Ivoire, land is transferred and developed in a complex framework, involving several actors. Ownership and tenure are regulated by a variety of institutions—state and

---

Box 1.5 The Statutory Land System

The statutory system comes into play only when land is registered. The statutory land regime reduces flexibility and the ability to meet the needs of the population, and discourages people from following the statutory system, because it recognizes only three types of tenure rights:

1. Land certificates issued under the Rural Land Law—documents that grant a provisional form of tenure. Within three years, Ivorian certificate holders must apply for a definitive land title. In the meantime, rights under this certificate may be sold or leased, as documented by Chauveau (2007).
2. Freehold rights. Persons holding title to a parcel of land have freehold rights. Only the state, public entities, and Ivorian individuals are eligible to own rural land. A land title may be sold to Ivorians or passed on to heirs, and the property may be leased, but not sold, to non-Ivorians or private companies.
3. Emphyteutic leases, which entitle holders to heritable and alienable tenure rights for periods of 18–99 years. While leaseholders do not own the land, they own everything built and produced on it. This is the most secure form of tenure available to non-Ivorians, as documented by Chauveau (2007).

Source: Chauveau 2007.

nonstate, formal and informal—and are shaped by constitutional codes and social practices that have evolved over time (Crook et al. 2007). Questions frequently arise as to the seller's legitimacy, the contents of the rights being transferred, and the obligations of the purchaser to the seller. Despite increased demand for land throughout the country, which is fueled by the continued development of cash crops and by urban growth, the process transferring rights of land, even in urban areas, nearly always follows custom rather than law (USAID 2013). Even though the government recognizes and supports only statutory codes, traditional or customary forms of land rights are widely invoked in land management practices (Crook et al. 2007; USAID 2013).

Recently, the government has tried to speed up registration and encourage the population to formalize land holdings. In 2013, it introduced a single document—equivalent to a land title—the Decree of Definitive Concession (Arrêté de Concession Définitive), to shorten and simplify registration and titling, bypassing two intermediate steps (the Order of Provisional Concession and the Property Ownership Certificate, which have been removed). This decree provides full title and confirms that a given plot is no longer state property but governed by rules for private property. To streamline land registration, the government has set up 31 decentralized regional offices where applications under the Decree can be processed, and expects to establish 14 more.[9] These efforts seem to be paying off because Côte d'Ivoire now ranks 127th out of 189 countries for land registration as per Doing Business Indicators—a rise of 25 places from 2013.

Undeveloped Land: A Public or Private Resource?

Rules for rural land transfer into urban land are unfavorable to rural communities that prefer to develop informally. In principle, the state must acquire land from village communities and allocate it for urbanization. In exchange, it compensates villagers through a compensation schedule. The state subdivides the acquired land into plots that are, eventually after some primary infrastructure investment, sold to private developers. Although the prices of land purchased by the state from communities are administered by law, sale prices to developers are not and can be fairly high even if the land still lacks basic urban infrastructure, services, and connections to urban centers. Most community land rights holders see the compensation provided by the state as undervalued and failing to make up for the loss of existing croplands. In practice therefore, village landowners deal directly with real estate companies and individuals who are willing to pay higher land prices than those set by the state. Once this land is acquired, some developers turn to local authorities to ask for basic infrastructure, although these latter were not involved in the subdivision of land plots and the acquisition process.

Communities are more likely to embrace the law when the purpose of the transaction is for public use. In normal practice, public institutions do not justify land use when purchasing land from communities, although in the recent program for social housing the government was able to secure 500 hectares (ha) of land from communities. The transaction was made on a voluntary basis, and the argument of the public nature of the social housing program greatly encouraged communities to participate. This would not have been as easy for many other projects, especially for higher-income segments as seen with projects realized by housing developers, including public developers such as SICOGI (Ivorian Company for Construction and Real Estate Management, or Société Ivoirienne de Construction et de Gestion Immobilière) for housing or the Agency for Land Development (Agence de Gestion Foncière [AGEF]) for serviced plots.

Regulation of rural–urban conversion puts the public institutions at the core of urban land development and provision of urban services, but lacks proper instruments to implement urbanization. It leads to a mismatch between the principles and the reality of regulation. In principle, as described, public institutions must gain full control of the land—through complete ownership of the land being planned for urbanization—and then transfer the land from rural to urban purposes by a land developer. They acquire land from rural communities or other private owners, provide the primary and eventually secondary infrastructure, and subdivide for allocation and sale to developers. In reality, public institutions can meet only a small fraction of the needs. Municipal and regional governments need to be involved in the decision of rural–urban land conversion, together with village landowners and the central government to identify up front the responsibility of each public actor before private developers are brought in the process. Indeed, the private sector—sometimes the beneficiary of the public institutions' land development projects—is also active in the informal sector to provide further housing solutions, which adds to the complexity of the situation.

Preparing Land for Urban Purposes

Land at the fringes of growing cities like Abidjan is governed by the Rural Land Law, on the theory that it will be assembled to form land reserves for future urban growth. This law is linked to decrees[10] to subdivide community land into plots for urban development. But in practice the switch from village into urban land follows customary and informal processes. In the context of the Urban Master Plan of Greater Abidjan, the state established a deferred development zone to create land reserves for the district of Abidjan, including the municipalities of Dabou, Grand-Bassam, and the entire coastal strip, which is part of Jacqueville. These urban reserves are governed by the state. More widely, the management of urban land within the city falls under several state agencies, including the Cadaster Office (within the Bureau National d'Étude Technique et Développement [BNETD]), the Urban Domain (within the MCLAU), and the Land and Housing Single Window (Service du Guichet Unique du Foncier et de l'Habitat).

Such a large scope of activities allocated by regulation to public institutions is far beyond their actual capacities. For Abidjan alone, the annual need for the residential sector is at the very minimum 400 ha per year for 25,000 new households.[11] For all cities of Côte d'Ivoire, huge financial efforts for up-front investments (and technical capacities) are needed, which the single public land developer, AGEF, simply cannot meet. Private partnerships with transfer of responsibilities have also been tested, with a concession to the Land Development Corporation (Société d'Aménagement de Terrains Côte d'Ivoire [SATCI]) of 80 ha approved in 1998, but since then the area has not been fully developed yet. The length of the land development cycle borne by a single operator is too long. Further, the rules of sale of rural land to public institutions are not adapted to the role of land reserves. While the transfer from rural to urban use is meant to be coordinated by public institutions, in practice the informal market is very active, as discussed earlier. The sale of rural land by communities is in fact not mandatory (which would be a sort of expropriation otherwise), but voluntary only. Thus it raises the question of use of the land allocated by communities and the actual instruments that the government can use to purchase undeveloped land and transfer it from rural to urban purposes. It is in practice a free market where public institutions are in competition with private developers. But public institutions are not structured to bid for land. Private developers have different urban requirements and can usually deliver a higher net value from the land, even with a higher purchase price. Formally involving elected local authorities (municipal and regional counsels) in the decision-making process could help bridge the conflicting incentives among rural landowners, private developers, and the central government.

The government had earlier attempted to provide the necessary technical capacities. In 1998, backed by the World Bank, the government adopted a holistic program to support a national housing program (Programme d'Appui Institutionnel à la Politique de l'Habitat), which included a definition of developable land. Under the program, AGEF was created to guide, regulate, and support land development and engage the private sector. As the country's cities, particularly Abidjan, were under pressure to extend their boundaries, AGEF was mandated to build land reserves for public purposes, to set terms of reference for urban development contracts, and to assign concessions to private developers.

But AGEF faces major challenges in building urban land reserves and preparing land for new urban growth. First, the absence of updated planning directives for cities prohibits AGEF from identifying suitable land for urban expansion. Second, the state does not have the financial means to purchase land from private owners (or from villagers with customary rights). Third, because of its limited financial base, AGEF loses out to private developers who can afford higher land prices and who choose to negotiate directly with owners, villagers, and village chiefs, bypassing formal land transaction processes (according to an interview with an AGEF director). With AGEF's hands tied, it now mainly facilitates formal land transactions and developments for higher-income groups and for businesses—but that of course contradicts the public purpose that would justify the low price of the rural land bought from communities.

Delivering Urban Services
In the mid-1980s, administrative reform gave new power to local authorities as the main city managers. Côte d'Ivoire at that time showed political will to

implement government decentralization and strengthen locally elected officials. Local governments developed experience in planning their cities and in identifying the needs of their populations. They were engaged in coordinating and supplying their cities with infrastructure for key services and community facilities—before the 1999 military coup and its aftermath.

Now, the actions of local governments are hampered by weak finances and an inefficient structure of municipal services (BERGEC and GERAD 2013a, 2013b). Local authorities appear to be struggling to address, prioritize, and invest in infrastructure, services, and facilities, or to coordinate the expansion of urban footprints. Because of the economic slowdown during the military conflict, the capacities of local governments to manage and provide services and infrastructure deteriorated, funding and investment suffered greatly, while the needs of the growing urban population increased. Across Regional Connectors such as Korhogo and Bouaké, and Global Connectors such as San-Pédro or Abidjan, local governments experienced a shortage of finance to maintain infrastructure. Technical and human resources in municipalities are low (in terms of education, skills, and organization). Technical expertise in areas related to roads and drainage are lacking. And the management of services is weak. In particular, waste collection services have been taken over by the central government. In addition, the failure to implement decrees transferring powers and responsibilities to local governments since 2003 has exacerbated their low accountability (BERGEC and GERAD 2013a, 2013b).

These challenges impair the ability of local governments to coordinate urban expansion and to provide services within their communes and with other levels of government. Communes are growing, with their populations facing unequal access to services and amenities (schools, clinics, sports centers), making evident the need for further expansion of socioeconomic infrastructure. Despite local governments' having received government, international, and nongovernmental support to implement development projects, their needs for investment remain high. For these reasons, local authorities are not in a position to lead urban development projects, either financially or technically, nor to coordinate urban expansion and provision of infrastructure and services. This situation needs to be addressed urgently to avoid having the central government overstretch and become less effective, too.

At the national and local levels, the main actors failed to enforce regulations. Investment in access to drinking water has stayed extremely low over the last decade—averaging 0.3 percent of municipalities' investment budgets. This situation was partly reinforced by the withdrawal of development partners' investments (in the aftermath of the 2002 crisis). The inability of the government to implement clear, updated regulations for clean water provision has slowed development. In 2006, the water sector underwent an institutional reform that was left incomplete, and many of the suggested modifications to the 1998 Water Code, the Environmental Code, and the transfer of responsibilities to local communities have not been implemented.

The multitude of actors and fragmented activities has led to an uncoordinated approach in most sectors. The water management system, notably, involves many different institutions, blurring responsibilities and leading to inefficiencies in conducting reforms. In 1996, the government created the high commission on water (Haut Commissariat à l'Hydraulique [HCH]) to lead water policy reform and coordination. In June 2012, the HCH approved the National Action Plan for Integrated Management of Water Resources (the PLANGIRE), which further reforms the institutional framework for water management. The structure has proven inefficient so far; the implementation process may also be slowed by the financial costs of pushing through with the Water Code, which may cost CFAF 20 billion (about US34 million) (USAID 2013).

Financial challenges also prevent urban basic services from functioning well. The costs of providing potable water and electricity have risen in the past decade, but tariffs have not been adjusted, leading to financial shortfalls for the operator. For example, the deficit of the water sector was estimated at CFAF 41 billion (about US$82 million) by the end of 2008, and operating losses due to inadequate tariffs in urban areas amount to about CFAF 5 billion (US$10 million) every year. Likewise, the smooth running of the waste sector has been heavily constrained by municipalities' inability to pay their electricity bill to the national electricity company (Compagnie Ivoirienne d'Électricité [CIE]), preventing them from receiving their share of the fee for household garbage collection (Taxe d'Enlèvement des Ordures Ménagères [TEOM]).

Affordable Housing Delivery

The public sector set out to build subsidized housing as a first step toward modernization. Between 1960 and 1975, the government focused on modernizing Abidjan by creating (i) a subsidized public housing building mechanism, in partnership with the state-owned Housing Management and Financing Company (Société de Gestion et de Financement de l'Habitat [SOGEFIHA]) and the parastatal SICOGI through a financial mechanism (the Housing Fund); and (ii) an urban development mechanism with SETU (Société d'Équipement des Terrains Urbain), a state company responsible for building roads and other infrastructure for low-cost housing developments. At the same time, existing districts with state housing built during the colonial period or with unbuilt areas were renovated, and low-income basic housing was built on the city's outskirts. Despite these considerable efforts, the public sector urban model housed only one-fifth of Abidjan's inhabitants by 1985.

Later, the government adopted a new approach to developing the private sector in housing provision. By the end of the 1980s, "modern housing" (private houses and apartment blocks) occupied 47 percent of residential land. Nonetheless, access to modern housing for low-income populations was a problem, compounded by the discrepancy between state housing funds and a massive influx of migrants. In the early 1990s, as the state abandoned its house-building efforts in favor of services and management, the backbones of state intervention—SOGEFIHA and SETU—were discontinued, and public housing development companies were privatized. Efforts were made to facilitate tenants' access to ownership, benefiting generally higher-income tenants (Rakodi 1997). The opening of the market had a positive impact with the creation of numerous private real estate companies (sociétés civiles immobilières). But, more important, Abidjan remained a city of self-built courtyards, where only 19 percent of households owned their accommodation. Legally or illegally, land was often occupied and dwellings were constructed with minimum investment and without any services (Rakodi 1997). The creation of the Housing Bank in 1993 was another step toward privatizing housing construction, helping develop the mortgage market for private applicants.

But today's formal construction, whether public or private, ignores the urban poor. AGEF produces land plots for individual housing construction, but its output—plots of 300–600 square meters in Abidjan and 1,000–1,200 square meters in Yamoussoukro—is accessible only to middle- and higher-income segments. SICOGI builds houses and apartment buildings with housing products that sell at a minimum of US$30,000. The 2013 social housing program of 60,000 units will sell at US$7,000–15,000, which will be a huge effort (and highly subsidized through the administered price of rural land from communities that chose to participate) for helping lower-income households. But, considering the pace of the program and the annual demand of 25,000 for Abidjan alone, this program will still trail demand. More efforts for incremental serviced land subdivisions are needed to help meet the gap.

Looking Ahead: Priorities for Action

Cities are unlikely to work efficiently if left unmanaged and unregulated. Whereas some costs generated by urban density are internalized by households and firms (including construction costs), other costs (including air pollution and congestion) and benefits (agglomeration economies for firms and greater work opportunities) are not. Thus, if left to "free will," urban development is likely to be dysfunctional. Preventing unbalanced population density through coordinated policies on land use and infrastructure is essential given that a city's physical structures, once established, may remain in place for a century or more. Greater density must be supported by primary infrastructure, alongside policing, waste disposal, and other social amenities. Policies to manage density must therefore be coordinated with those that define investment in infrastructure and its location.

Improving Land Market Fluidity

A constrained land market is a land market that limits private investments. Improving the fluidity of the market will help increase the investments in the various segments of urban development, from industrial to residential. Getting the land market to work more efficiently will bring better returns to dynamic and productive cities in Côte d'Ivoire. Often one hears that too little land is available. In fact, there is land everywhere; but that land is inappropriate for urban use because it is designated for rural activities or tenure is insecure, or the land is not serviced. Getting there—increasing the production of usable land—requires improving the environment at three levels. First, tenure security should be improved through simpler, shorter, and cheaper procedures. Second, structural infrastructure should be provided in a timely manner, especially for new urban extensions not yet connected to urban services (in particular roads, electricity, and water). Third, land should be serviced to enable investment by particular activities.

Resolved property rights and tenure security increase the fluidity of the land market. An inclusive definition of property rights is needed to resolve conflicts between statutory and customary rights. Restrictive and expensive registration, high transaction costs, and limited knowledge of procedures (on behalf of citizens and local authorities) can create steep disincentives to formal and planned urban development. Tools to gather and communicate information about properties are also essential.

Clearly defined tenure and property rights are the first requirement for building solid and transparent valuation systems. Meeting this need will also provide city planners with the necessary tools and information to plan future urban expansion. Adapting legal frameworks and expanding the formally recognized definitions of property rights are critical tasks for land management and planning. In Côte d'Ivoire, the absence of an inclusive definition of property rights and tenure status restricts land use and is at the root of land insecurity and conflicts, as discussed above. That customary practices (urban and rural) are more widely used than the law is a fact that calls for more inclusive definitions of property rights. Other countries with diversity of tenure types have adopted similar approaches, allowing left-out groups to invest and eventually access finance through their land. Clear and transparent land valuation supports effective functioning of land markets. Thus, solid valuation methods that more sensitively reflect market prices and institutions that systematically collect this information are essential. The Republic of Korea and the Philippines have moved in this direction (box 1.6).

For valuation methods to better reflect market prices, data-gathering and disseminating institutions must be nurtured. Tools for urban expansion and redevelopment are successful usually when robust systems for assessing land values are in place. Without accurate information, city leaders will be unable to plan for the future or take coordinated actions across institutions. And, when cities cannot assess land value accurately and understand existing land markets, they are unable to capture part of the land's value, which may become a major loss of municipal revenue and reduce the municipality's ability to increase funding for urban services and infrastructure to urbanizing areas. In Hong Kong SAR, China, for example, a land-value capture tool of betterment taxes has allowed the city government to generate sustainable funding, exceeding a third of the transit agency's annual budget. Ivorian cities could capture land values through improved tax recovery (see chapter 4).

High transaction costs, uncoordinated institutions, and unclear land use management constrain the supply of land. One way of counteracting inefficiency is

---

Box 1.6 International Experience with Multiple Property Regimes and Land Valuation

In Mexico, social/communal properties are recognized under the land law, and communities that own the land can subdivide and sell, lease, or retain communal management. Many communal plots are located in peri-urban areas and are under high pressure to develop. But, because they are included in the legal framework, national incentives emerged to encourage adherence to legal processes. Peru integrated different tenure types into one national law (no. 29415/2010), which allowed established community groups residing on long-abandoned or contested properties to petition for formalized occupancy rights, along with transfer of land title into community trusts.

As these examples illustrate, a more inclusive legal framework giving the government a clearer understanding of traditional land property dynamics would allow much of the peri-urban land to be registered, potentially leading to more formal development and allowing authorities to plan future expansion and coordinate it with developers.

Developed and emerging economies have explored and successfully applied innovative methods to value land. In many developed countries, land valuation methods rely on several forms of data and types of institutions to assess land prices. Data sources include market data on transactions, information about property attributes, and information on potential income and costs of construction inputs. In addition, independent institutions help maintain transparency and accessibility of data. In the Republic of Korea, the state requires that land and buildings be assessed by certified private appraisers rather than by government officials, and, to make the process transparent, at least two assessments are required. When appraisals differ by more than 10 percent, a third is required. The final value is settled on the average of the private appraisals.

National systems for robust land valuation are rare in emerging economies. But some countries, such as the Philippines, have improved land assessment. Public valuations there used to be conducted infrequently and independent of market values. In 2006, some local governments started using market-based valuations; and, three years later, the national government adopted a modified version of the International Valuation Standards for private sector appraisals. The country is set to approve a Valuation Reform Act that will develop a national transactions database and strengthen centralized oversight of local government valuations, reevaluation, and assessors.

---

to increase property registrations by providing clear, easily accessible information about existing procedures, while also reducing the time and costs of those procedures. The Rural Land Law of 1998 is seldom followed for lack of information. To enforce it, the government should ensure that the correct information reaches people (landowners). And, although the Decree of Definitive Concession has cut the time taken to acquire a document of title, more people need to be informed about the procedure and the Land and Housing Single Window. The government must also plan to train officers who will be able to cope with higher demand for land registration and ownership documents while maintaining efficient service.

Simplifying procedures can reduce barriers to formally developing land. Improving the registration rate of rural and peri-urban lands and clarifying their ownership can also increase the rate of formal conversion from rural to urban land, as well as the registration of new urban subdivisions that reduce informal developments. Likewise, improved coordination between local and national officers in the approval of building permits is vital to encouraging formal urbanization. Better engagement of local actors in urban expansion decisions—in close coordination with the MCLAU—can prevent invalid authorization and subsequent demolition and relocation costs incurred by the national government. Actions and decisions at the local and national levels must be synchronized and only one message sent to people and developers.

Reducing transaction costs of formal development can also encourage the construction and supply of affordable housing. And high costs and stringent conversion regulations can increase informality and exacerbate affordability gaps for housing units. Much of the housing for middle-income households has been built informally on unregistered and unplanned land. And high prices for land and its development, even when informal, have left low-income populations with few housing alternatives to informal settlements.

Reforms in land-management law and reduced barriers to registration and formal development require accurate information on land types and availability. There are several efforts to gather information on land ownership and transactions in the BNETD, MCLAU, and AGEF, which could be unified or exchanged through shared platforms. In Tunisia, the Topography and Cadastral Service, and the Land Registry, have identified a shared platform between public entities as a key initiative. Resources and capacity building would expand the operations of cadastral and registry offices in urban (and rural) areas.

The Rural Land Law—if modified and enforced to include customary law—could help regulate the conversion of rural into urban land. This would increase formal developments and facilitate the coordination of urban expansion with infrastructure and services. But as insecurity of tenure for urban land also exists within cities, an urban code is essential—urgently—to govern land transactions, management, and use, as well as to strengthen the regulatory environment for future development.

The roles of the public and private sectors in the land market should be better distributed to maximize their contribution and boost land production. The roles of public institutions are too broad, including clearing land tenure, creating land reserves, and reallocating land to developers. But they lack the instruments—regulatory or, more important, financial—to perform those tasks. Thus the private sector is seen as a competitor to the public authorities in accessing land when it should instead work in partnership with it. The public institutions could be mostly involved in regulating and facilitating the land market whereas the private sector is more efficient in providing investments. The government can enhance the fluidity of land markets to encourage better land use by relaxing current land transaction regulations and nurturing institutions to systematically and accurately value land. Municipalities and public land development authorities can provide the primary and secondary infrastructure necessary to the housing developers. Land subdivisions (for self-construction) and housing and real estate development can be left primarily to private developers, while public developers can still operate in the "social" niche.

Expanding Service Delivery

Efforts to promote serviced land need to be sustained. The law on development concessions, adopted in 1997, authorizes the state to grant concessions to land management companies to develop serviced land and housing. The government has committed to clear the land titling backlog in order to develop a market for such development (World Bank 2001). This is the most effective way to support development of the housing market for lower-income groups, for which affordability is better with incremental self-construction. This is by far more cost-effective in providing urban services than urban upgrading. Hence a proper balance should be found between prevention and upgrading policies.

As Ivorian cities continue to grow, and new cities emerge as Domestic Connectors, the rate of unserviced developments will continue to grow, as will the cost to the government of extending services after urbanization. Thus, informal markets will form, leading to more expensive services, overexploitation of current infrastructure, and conflict among communities. Better coordination of land use and infrastructure will require a better definition of the role of local governments in service provision, sustainable tariff models based on the needs of different populations, and better ways to invest in maintenance and extensions. Regulating density, properly balanced with available infrastructure, can also prevent overspending by the state on network extensions. Identifying the spatial limitations of cities will also prevent excessive spending to connect peri-urban areas.

The government should increase the supply of formal and affordable housing in areas with infrastructure and services, address informal settlements, and cut the costs of relocation. The huge housing gap calls for several actions that can promote private—not just public—housing interventions. The state is the only actor allowed to access and bundle land for large housing projects, making it harder for private developers to access land and develop formally, discouraging them from following legal and formal processes and creating developments that are disconnected from infrastructure and services. By reducing land use barriers and promoting fluid land markets, the government could increase the supply of formal and affordable housing in areas with infrastructure and services and reduce the cost of upgrading, infrastructure extension (postdevelopment), and relocation (in case of occupation of nondevelopable state land). To meet the needs of the lower-income groups, adapted levels of services can be determined and provided at a lower cost. Those special norms may allow for reduced levels of services at installation while paving the stage for incremental servicing.

Urban construction codes should be upgraded and enforced. More flexible codes that meet the needs of current cities, particularly in Regional and Global Connectors facing higher densities, are essential. Upgrading low-income and informal neighborhoods in areas with service infrastructure and connections is expensive, but can target high densities and reach out to large populations. In Recife, Brazil, some upgrading programs operate in areas that permit higher-density development, with some streamlined regulations encouraging formalization and development of affordable housing. These areas averaged 225 people per hectare, compared with 65 in the rest of the city, and housed nearly 40 percent of the urban population.

Most basic infrastructure services need to be provided for all city residents. Besides creating functioning land markets, city planners must also ensure that most basic infrastructure services reach all city residents—urban and peri-urban—because existing Global and Regional Connectors will continue to grow and new domestic connectors will demand basic services. Investing in infrastructure will require that local and national authorities work together to prioritize needs and design sustainable financing models.

Besides expanding and improving infrastructure, Côte d'Ivoire needs to implement financially sustainable service models and regulate prices to increase investment and coverage. In some infrastructure service sectors, such as for drinking water, decisions have been made on regulatory frameworks to improve financial sustainability, adjust tariffs, and engage local governments. The country needs to create financially sustainable service models through tariff adjustment and cost recovery. Almost all sectors must coordinate planning with efficient providers that leverage private sector participation (and decentralize to match the real cost of provision and capital improvements). Adopting and enforcing these reforms is a first step to expanding basic services to urban citizens. Countries like Algeria and Colombia have set tariffs to cover operating and nonoperating costs, while keeping prices affordable. In Algeria, new legislation allows consumers to choose between an elevated fixed fee and a progressive metered fee—most consumers opted for the latter.

Cities at all levels—Domestic, Regional, and Global Connectors—have growing populations demanding increased physical structures, infrastructure, housing, and amenities. To meet these needs, city authorities and planners need to coordinate provision of basic services with land use and urban growth plans. But the reduced responsibilities of local and district governments affect intergovernment coordination and the development of urban strategies and plans. Global Connectors like Abidjan are dominated by a strong central government, to the point that local authorities are seldom consulted in planning, leading to tensions and miscommunication between actors at different government levels. Basic service delivery, for example, is contracted by the central government to private suppliers, who deliver through a countrywide strategy, rather than with an urban and locality-specific approach.

Up-to-date information is required to ensure an efficient urbanization of, particularly, Domestic Connectors. Recent data on land use, land values, basic infrastructure, service provision, connectivity to social and economic centers (jobs), and informal settlements are needed. Local authorities could be key actors in gathering these data, helping serve their constituents and enforce plans and regulations.

This approach could complement the government's urbanization efforts. The early intervention of land use planning by Domestic Connectors will help them to urbanize efficiently. Comparisons with other cities suggest that the cost of upgrading infrastructure can be much higher than building it in advance. Global and Regional Connectors that have developed informally face a more complex challenge. They will require a combination of infrastructure upgrading, land use planning, and enforcement, and a coordination of infrastructure and land use for future urbanization.

Simpler and More Efficient Planning

Land use plans help city authorities ensure compliance with planning guidelines and building codes, guide development by allocating budgets to different zones, and develop zoning regulations. These plans can ensure that public and private developments in various zones are developed harmoniously, and that developments provide mixed economic and residential activities as well as green and protected areas. Mixed land use can also lead to short commuting times, particularly in a "horizontal" city like Abidjan, where growth is limited by the sea to the south and the protected green areas to the north.

Improved allocation of responsibilities across governing authorities at different levels is essential. Nurturing an environment of good governance is a prerequisite for planning, connecting, and financing cities, requiring that decision makers at all levels have well-defined roles and work in a coordinated manner. The structural decisions of city planning in Abidjan (and other cities) are in the hands of the MCLAU rather than mayors and the chairpersons of regional councils. This framework provides an opportunity to improve the capacity of local governments and their participation in regulating land use and providing basic services—provided that their responsibilities are accompanied by funding opportunities. As revealed by the urban audits, local governments in Côte d'Ivoire had significant knowledge of their commune's needs, as well as experience in the provision of facilities and amenities, and delivery of services. However, in all 10 communes that were audited (see box 1.1), local governments faced more difficult challenges of poverty and deterioration of infrastructure in the last two decades because of the sociopolitical crises—while at the same time having very limited funding and losing their abilities to govern and plan effectively. Based on their experience, local governments may have more accurate information on the service deficits in their communities and so should become involved again in managing service provision. They should thus be granted increased responsibilities in enforcing building and planning regulations and in helping reduce informal settlements.

Updated land use policies and planning standards should be aligned with infrastructure availability and plans. One way to do this is to coordinate density with planned use and current infrastructure, as in Singapore, where areas with a metro station have higher densities. The Urban Master Plan of Greater Abidjan (2015–30) seeks to concentrate higher densities in the core (and older) municipalities, where infrastructure for basic services already exists. Other planning regulations include minimum distances to the front, rear, and sides of a plot and maximum building heights. In Abidjan, buildings cannot be higher than the width of their adjacent streets, posing a strict limitation on the construction of dense and vertical housing. These limitations—along with poor coordination of basic services, transport, and housing developments—incentivize low-density developments on nonserviced areas, expand the urban perimeter, and add long-term costs for cities and national governments to deliver services and for residents to access jobs.

Another advantage of coordinating land use and infrastructure is the ability to manage informal settlements. This applies particularly when settlements evolve in inner city areas where infrastructure already exists but does not meet the needs of the population. In Tunisia, for instance, an upgrading program implemented between 1975 and 1995 reduced slum housing. National utilities made massive investments in water and sewage infrastructure and upgraded informal settlements. Postdevelopment provision of infrastructure and services is more expensive than planning land use and infrastructure in advance, and less efficient than taking advantage of existing urban infrastructure in low-density areas and improving it.

Housing affordability can also be improved with relaxed construction and land use regulations. In Abidjan, where housing production is insufficient, higher densities can be important in increasing the provision of housing in strategic locations that are well connected to the job market. The increase in production would relax pressure on the rental market and eventually have a positive impact on prices. Likewise, higher densities achieved in self-construction will increase housing affordability for lower-income groups, reducing the unit cost of housing with, for example, lower land plot surface allowed and increasing the potential revenues from renting for commercial or residential purposes. Higher density in incremental construction can be achieved by a combination of factors: first, more flexible urban regulation; second, improved access to finance; and third, a more professional construction sector (better-trained and informed construction workers). Other prerequisites mentioned above—those essential to encourage private investments—are improved security of tenure and better access to serviced land.

Notes

1. A technical seminar using the team alignment process was held on June 28–29, 2014, to identify constraints and solutions to harmonious urban development. Participants were director-level staff from all ministries involved in the urbanization, representatives of the chairpersons of the association of municipalities and regions, representatives of the major private sector associations, and representatives of the Parliament and Economic and Social Council.

2. World Bank calculations based on satellite imagery classification. See Global Human Settlement Layer, European Commission Joint Research Centre. http://ghslsys.jrc.ec .europa.eu/. Years covered in this analysis: 1975, 1990, 2000, and 2014.

3. *L'Urbanistique* No. 002, October 2014.

4. According to the urban audit developed by the World Bank and the Commune of San-Pédro in 2013, organized and provisioned housing has access to water and electricity networks, a paved road, and pipeline networks. Many homes in this area were built by real estate companies, such as SOGEFIHA and SICOGI. Most of these houses are inhabited by middle-income residents, and 5 percent correspond to "high-standing" houses (300–400 sq m and even 1,000 sq m) where public officials and company managers reside.

5. Interview with Cadaster Office, BNETD.

6. See CAHF 2014. The access rate is calculated based on the national daily revenues per person and taking a household of three persons for a studio. With a lower rent of $189 and a maximum outlay of 40 percent, only a small proportion at the top of the pyramid earning more than $4 per day can afford this rent.

7. Government authorities are aware of the importance of having these plans and are discussing carrying them out in 25 cities. Since 2013, JICA and MCLAU have been developing a new Schéma Directeur d'Urbanisme for Greater Abidjan (2015–2030). This plan oversees the 13 municipalities of the district and six peri-urban areas (Alépé, Azaguié, Bonoua, Dabou, Grand-Bassam, and Jacqueville). Yamoussoukro also seems to be discussing updating its Schéma Directeur d'Urbanisme. Other cities (excluding the two districts) are meant to have a current Schéma Directeur de Planification Urbaine, but most do not (or still have to update them).

8. Aide-mémoire mission, World Bank 2014.

9. Aide-mémoire mission, World Bank 2014.

10. Decree No. 77–906 of November 6, 1977, on village land subdivisions, for instance, approves in its first article "subdivision for construction on non-registered land, for the benefit of one or more villages, in the framework of development and a restructuring of the rural area." This decree has often been used to convert rural peri-urban land into urban developable land.

11. The minimum land plot surface area for an individual house developed by AGEF is 100 sq m. Taking a conservative value of the net land production of two-thirds, the gross land requirement for 25,000 new houses would be 375 ha. This is a density of 67 households per hectare, which is relatively conservative considering some international standards (in Tunisia, a technical commission recommended in 1988 a density of 40 to 50 individual houses per hectare).

Bibliography

AGEF (Agence de Gestion Foncière, Côte d'Ivoire). n.d. "Présentation Général de l'Agence de Gestion Foncière." AGEF.

Atta, K. 2011. "Urbanisation et Développement, défis et perspectives pour la Côte d'Ivoire, Abidjan." Ministère du Plan et du Développement, Projet d'Appui à la Mise en Œuvre de la Politique Nationale du Développement (REPCI 2009–2010), 295.

Baharoglu, Deniz. 2002. "World Bank Experience in Land Management and the Debate on Tenure Security." Background Series 16, Urban and Local Government (draft), TUDUR, World Bank, Washington, DC.

BERGEC (Bureau d'Études et de Réalisation en Génie Civil) and GERAD (Groupe d'Études, de Recherche et d'Appui au Développement). 2013a. Audits Urbain Financier et Organisationnel de la Commune de Bouaké. Rapport Provisoire, République de Côte d'Ivoire, Département de Bouaké, Commune de Bouaké.

———. 2013b. *Audits Urbain Financier et Organisationnel de la Commune de San-Pédro.* Rapport Provisoire, République de Côte d'Ivoire, Département de San-Pédro, Commune de San-Pédro.

Blanc, Aymeric, and Lise Breuil, Lise. 2009. "Les partenariats public privé peuvent-ils bénéficier aux exclus des services d'eau?" *Secteur Privé et Développement* 2 (July).

Buckley, Robert M., and Jerry Kalarickal. 2006. *Thirty Years of World Bank Shelter Lending.* Washington, DC: World Bank.

CAHF (Centre for Affordable Housing Finance in Africa). 2014. *Housing Finance in Africa Yearbook 2014.* Parkview, South Africa: CAHF.

Centre for Liveable Cities and Urban Land Institute. 2013. *10 Principles for Liveable High-Density Cities.* Singapore and Hong Kong: Centre for Liveable Cities Urban Land Institute.

Chauveau, Jean-Pierre. 2007. "La loi de 1998 sur les droits fonciers coutumiers dans l'histoire des politiques foncières en Côte d'Ivoire: Une économie politique des transferts de droits entre autochtones et étrangers en zone forestière." In *Enjeux fonciers et environnementaux*, Dialogues afroindiens, 155–190. Pondichéry: Institut Français de Pondichéry (accessed December 4, 2014), http://www.dhdi.free.fr /recherches/environnement/articles/chauveaufoncier.pdf.

Coulibaly, Gofaga, et al. 2014. "Guide de Restructuration des Quartiers Précaires," Revised document, Ministère d'État, Ministère de l'Intérieur et de la Sécurité, République de Côte d'Ivoire.

Crook, Richard, Simplice Affou, Daniel Hammond, Adja F. Vanga, and Mark Owusu-Yeboah. 2007. "The Law, Legal Institutions and the Protection of Land Rights in Ghana and Côte d'Ivoire: Developing a More Effective and Equitable System." IDS Research Report 58, Institute of Commonwealth Studies, University of London; Institut pour le recherche en développement (Abidjan), Université de Bouaké; and Kwame Nkrumah University of Science and Technology (KNUST).

GoCI (Government of Côte d'Ivoire). 1998. "Loi relative au domaine foncier rural." Loi n°98–750 du 23 décembre 1998 modifiée par la loi du 28 juillet 2004 (accessed July 7, 2014), http://www.droit-afrique.com/images/textes/Cote_Ivoire/RCI%20-%20 Domaine%20foncier%20rural.pdf.

———. 2009. "Stratégie de relance du développement et de réduction de la pauvreté." Abidjan.

———. 2010. Rapport pays de suivi des Objectifs du Millénaire pour le Développement. Document de travail, Abidjan.

———. 2013. Ordonnance No. 2013-481 du 2 juillet 2013 fixant les règles d'acquisition de la propriété des terrains urbains.

———. 2014. Analyse Environnementale Pays 2014. Abidjan.

Groupe Huit, Terrabo, and BEPU (Bureau d'Études et de Planification Urbaine). 2013. *Audit Urbain, Organisationnel et Financier de la Commune de Korhogo.* Rapport à mi-parcours, Republique de Côte d'ivoire, Ministère des Infrastructures Économiques, Cellule de Coordination de PUIUR, Projet d'Urgence d'Infrastructures Urbaines.

Gulyani, Sumila, and Genevieve Connors. 2002. "Urban Upgrading in Africa: A Summary of Rapid Assessments in Ten Countries." Regional Urban Upgrading Initiative, Africa Infrastructure Department, World Bank, Washington, DC.

Hauhouot, Asseypo A. 2002. *Développement, aménagement, régionalisation en Côte d'Ivoire, Abidjan*. Édition Universitaire de Côte d'Ivoire, 372.

ICF International. 2015. "Demographic and Health Surveys." http://www.dhsprogram .com/.

INS (Institut National de la Statistique). 2002. *Enquête sur le Niveau de Vie des Ménages de Côte d'Ivoire*. Abidjan: Institut National de la Statistique.

———. 2008. *Enquête sur le Niveau de Vie des Ménages*. Abidjan: Institut National de la Statistique.

———. 2014. Recensement Général de la Population et de l'Habitat 2014 : Principaux Résultats Préliminaires. Abidjan: Institut National de le Statistique.

INS (Institut National de la Statistique) and ICF International. 2012. *Enquête Démographic et de Santé et à Indicateurs Multiples de Côte d'Ivoire, 2011–2012*. Calverton, MD: INS and ICF International.

Kouassi, Selay Marius. 2011 "Hand Pumps: A Losing Battle for Ivory Coast?" Pulitzer Center on Crisis Reporting, December 1. http://pulitzercenter.org/reporting/ivory-co ast-ouattara-election-violence-water-hand-pumpstanks.

———. 2012. "Côte d'Ivoire: In Search of Water in Urban Ivory Coast." Radio Netherlands Worldwide, April 5. http://allafrica.com/stories/201204050982.html?viewall=1.

Legendre, R. 2014. Recommandations pour l'optimisation des modes opératoires de délimitation de territoires villageois et de certification foncière. Rapport final phase 1. Washington, DC: World Bank.

LIEPSC–CEFILD (Ligue internationale pour l'Étude et la Promotion de la Santé Communautaire–Cabinet d'Études et de Formation aux Initiatives Locales de Développement). 2013a. *Audit Urbain, Organisationnel et Financier de la Commune de Koumassi*. Rapport Provisoire, République de Côte d'Ivoire, Ministère des Infrastructures Économiques, Projet d'Urgence d'Infrastructures Urbaines, Programme d'Assistance à la Cellule de Coordination à la Mise en Œuvre des Contrats de Ville.

———. 2013b. *Audit Urbain, Organisationnel et Financier de la Commune de Port Bouet*. Rapport Provisoire, République de Côte d'Ivoire, Ministère des Infrastructures Économiques, Projet d'Urgence d'Infrastructures Urbaines, Programme d'Assistance à la Cellule de Coordination à la Mise en Œuvre des Contrats de Ville.

Lozano-Gracia, Nancy, and Cheryl Young. 2014. "Housing Consumption and Urbanization." Policy Research Working Paper 7112, World Bank, Washington, DC.

Marin, Philippe. 2012. Public-Private Partnerships for Urban Water Utilities: A Review of Experiences in Developing Countries. Washington DC: World Bank.

Matar, F., P. Marin, A. Locussol, and R. Verspyck. 2009. Reforming Urban Water Utilities in Western and Central Africa: Experiences with Public-Private Partnerships. Volume 1: Impact and Lessons Learned. PPIAF, Water Sector Board. Washington, DC: World Bank.

MCLAU (Ministère de la Construction, du Logement, de l'Assainissement et de l'Urbanisme), SDUGA, and JICA (Japan International Cooperation Agency). 2014. *Le Projet de Développement du Schema Directeur d'Urbanisme du Grand Abidjan (SDUGA)*. Rapport Interimaire, Volume I, Resume. Oriental Consultants Co. Ltd., Japan Development Institute, JICA, and Asia Air Survey Co. Ltd.

MEMPD (Ministère d'État, Ministère du Plan et du Développement). 2006. *Pre-Bilan de l'Aménagement du Territoire*. République de Côte d'Ivoire.

———. 2012. *Plan National de Developpement 2012–2015*. Republique de Côte d'Ivoire.

Ministere de l'Environnement et du Développement Durable. 2012. *Plan National du développement durable en Côte d'Ivoire dans la perspective de rio+20*. Republique de Côte d'Ivoire.

Ministere des Infrastructure Economiques. 2014. "Communication en Conseil des Ministres." Republique de Côte d'Ivoire.

Ministère du Logement et de l'Urbanisme. n.d. *Création de l'Agence de Gestion Foncière*. Rapport Final Definitif, Projet d'Appui Institutionnel à la Politique de l'Habitat Banque Mondiale, Agence Française de Développement, Gouvernement du Japon.

Pesaresi, M. X. Blaes, E. Daniele, S. Ferri, L. Gueguen, F. Haag, S. Halkia, H. Johannes, M. Kaufmann, T. Kemper, G.K. Ouzounis, M. Scavazzon, P. Soille, S. Vasileios, and L. Zanchetta. 2012. *A Global Human Settlement Layer from Optical High Resolution Imagery—Concepts and First Results*. Publications Office of the European Union.

Rakodi, C. 1997. *The Urban Challenge in Africa: Growth and Management of Its Large Cities*. United Nations University Press, Tokyo (accessed September 10, 2014), http://archive.unu.edu/unupress/unupbooks/uu26ue/uu26ue00.htm.

Sabaliauskas, K., L. D. Zalo, and S. Deveikis. 2010. *L'acquis du cadastre et du registre foncier et immobilier de Lituanie pour les pays africains*. Un bref rapport sur la mission du cadastre foncier rural de Côte d'Ivoire en Lituanie 2010, presented at FIG Working Week 2011, "Bridging the Gap between Cultures," Marrakech, Morocco, May 18–22, 2011.

Siyali, W. I. 2012. "Le marché foncier et immobilier à Abidjan." Thèse de doctorat unique en géographie urbaine, Abidjan, Université Félix Houphouët-Boigny.

Stamm, Volker. 2007. *The Rural Land Plan: An Innovative Approach from Côte d'Ivoire*. Darmstadt, Germany: Ministry of Agriculture in Abidjan.

Terrabo, BEPU (Bureau d'Études et de Planification Urbaine), and PWC (PriceWater houseCoopers). 2013. *Audit Urbain, Organisationnel et Financier de Ia Commune d'Abobo*. Rapport Provisoire, Association International de Développement (IDA).

Thiriez, A., Ibo Jonas, and V. Butin. 2011. *Étude Strategique pour la Gestion des Dechets Solides dans le District d'Abidjan*. Rapport Final Définitif, BURGEAP and STE, Ministère des Infrastructures Economiques, Abidjan.

UN-Habitat (United Nations Human Settlements Programme). 2012. *Côte d'Ivoire: Urban Profile of Abidjan*. UN-Habitat.

———. 2013a. *The Relevance of Street Patterns and Public Space in Urban Areas*. Working Paper. UN-Habitat.

———. 2013b. *Streets as Public Spaces and Drivers of Urban Prosperity*. UN-Habitat.

USAID (United States Agency for International Development). 2013. "Land Tenure Côte d'Ivoire Profile." USAID Land Tenure and Property Rights Portal (accessed September 3, 2014), http://usaidlandtenure.net/cote-divoire.

World Bank. 2001. "Côte d'Ivoire - Urban Land Management and Housing Finance Reform Technical Assistance Project." Implementation Completion Report. http://documents.worldbank.org/curated/en/2001/12/1677819/cote-divoire-urban-land-management-housing-finance-reform-technical-assistance-project

———. 2014. Doing Business Indicators (database), World Bank, Washington, DC (accessed July 15, 2014), http://www.doingbusiness.org/data/exploreeconomies/c%C3%B4te-divoire.

———. 2015a. *World Urbanization Prospects*. Washington, DC: World Bank.

————. 2015b. *Cote d'Ivoire—Analyse Environnementale Pays: Rapport Définitif*. Washington, DC: World Bank.

————. Forthcoming. *Spatial Development of African Cities, Regional Study*. Washington, DC: World Bank.

World Bank and BURGEAP. 2011. "Etude Stratégique pour la Gestion des Déchets Solides dans le District d'Abidjan."

Yapi-Diahou, Alphonse, Marthe Adjoba Koffi-Didia, Emile Brou Koffi, Gilbert Assi Yassi, and Martin Kouakou Diby. 2011. "Les périphéries abidjanaises: Territoires de redistribution et de relégation." In *Les métropoles du sud vues de leurs périphéries*, edited by J. L. Chaléard, 107–122. Grafigéo.

Yapi -Diahou, A., G. A. Yassi, and T. A. Doho Bi. 2014. "Les classes moyennes dans les périphéries d'Abidjan: La clientèle des promoteurs dans des espaces en recomposition." In (dir), *Métropoles aux Suds: Le défi des périphéries?* edited by J. L. Chaléard, 115–132. Paris: Karthala.

Yassi, G. A., 2013. "Akouédo une décharge hors normes à Abidjan." In Vol. 1 of *Variations ivoiriennes, Revue des Hautes Terres*, edited by Yapi-Diahou et Kamdem, 11–22. Yaoundé, Cameroon: IRESMA Editions.

CHAPTER 2

Connecting Cities

Tuo Shi and Ibou Diouf

Introduction

A city's connections—external and internal, physical and economic—bear heavily on its future. Where cities and city neighborhoods are disconnected, labor and product markets are not integrated. The results are forgone productivity and higher product prices, costs felt by producers and consumers alike. And as weak connections limit the growth of cities, so feeble cities will stunt growth of the country.

The benefits of strong connections are well understood.[1] Between cities, connections enable firms to access local, regional, and global markets, both for buying inputs and for selling outputs. They also give consumers options and, in many cases, better prices. Within cities, connections enable people to access employment; and they enable firms to attract workers, access other inputs, and sell their products in local markets. Enhanced connections can expose cities to new economic opportunities, allowing them to flourish. Policy makers who make markets and jobs more accessible open the door to unforeseen possibilities, facilitating economic transformation.

Cities need to be spatially connected in a way that supports their particular agglomeration economies. Global Connectors must have world-class infrastructure facilitating international connectivity (ports, airports, and information and communications technology [ICT]), good interurban infrastructure to link industrial zones with domestic raw material sources, and efficient intraurban transport systems integrating labor markets and making cities livable. The most needed inputs for Regional Connectors are trade and transport that seamlessly connect the domestic economy to regional markets, with lower transport costs. Because most Domestic Connectors are in predominantly agricultural or resource-based regions of emerging urbanization with low economic density, agglomeration forces need to be reinforced via market institutions to regulate land use and transactions and delivery of basic services.

But city leaders who envision stronger connections for their cities and city neighborhoods face difficult choices. With limited resources, they cannot invest in everything. It is hard to know which new or improved connections will yield the highest returns over time. As facts change, cities will need to adapt. Setting priorities for investment means picking winners and losers in the short run—but in the long run it can make a vast difference for entire cities, even countries. Some decisions lock cities and countries into patterns that last a century or more; others have outcomes that are simply irreversible.

Leaders need to tighten intraurban, interurban, and international connections. Given the constraints of Côte d'Ivoire, Ivorian policy makers—to support the diversified urbanization it needs to fully reap the benefits of agglomeration economies—should focus on improving intraurban mobility in Abidjan; reducing interurban transport costs between its Global, Regional, and Domestic Connectors; and improving international transport and ICT for strategic Global and Regional Connectors.

Intraurban Mobility

In planning to increase access and to ensure affordability, policy makers need to consider options that enable cities to strengthen agglomeration economies and spatially integrate labor markets. International experience suggests that agglomeration economies and integrated labor markers foster productivity and stimulate economic growth by triggering two interrelated processes. First, integrated labor markets allow for matching between firms and workers, and at lower cost. Making jobs more accessible facilitates economic transformation toward industrialization, specialization, and diversification. Second, learning spillovers increase with urban mobility. Knowledge is embedded in people and passed on by "those who know" (Duranton 2009). Spreading knowledge between large numbers of people increases knowledge generation, accumulation, and diffusion. Getting these connections right can enable cities like Abidjan to become "nurseries" for smaller ones, and thus knowledge spreads across cities (Duranton and Puga 2001).

Therefore, improving connections within a city is critical for integrating labor markets, particularly in large cities such as Abidjan where there are spatially large footprints and long distances. Weak connections between workers and firms in large cities can lead to a fragmented labor market. In such conditions, workers and firms face higher search costs. Workers can find a job, but they do not benefit from the "thickness" of the labor market, which usually allows them to find a better job for the same search cost. Cities therefore lose the potential agglomeration benefits that a unified labor market would offer. Constrained labor mobility within cities further dampens the diffusion of knowledge. If higher-skilled workers cluster in a location, they have no incentive to move, and their accumulated knowledge remains there.

Limited Internal Connections in Abidjan

The central municipalities of Abidjan appear to be disconnected from the periphery. A survey in the District of Abidjan conducted in 2013 by the Japan International Cooperation Agency (JICA) and Ministry of Construction, Housing,

Sanitation, and Urbanism (Ministère de la Construction, du Logement, de l'Assainissement et de l'Urbanisme [MCLAU]) found that most people walk or bike to work, which constrains their employment opportunities (JICA and MCLAU 2014). Work and business activities are concentrated in the center of Abidjan, with far fewer jobs in the periphery. People travel to work in Yopougon, Abobo, Cocody, Adjame, and Koumassi. Whereas Yopougon, Abobo, and Koumassi show more people traveling to other places to work, Cocody and Adjame (more central) attract more workers than those leaving. In the periphery (Songon, Anyama, Grand-Bassam, Bingerville), there is much less mobility. Adjame, which is located in the center of Abidjan, is clearly an attractive place for people traveling for business. However, a large share of people is disconnected from where the jobs are. Traffic routes are different for motorized workers and nonmotorized workers, with workers walking or cycling to work much less connected than the motorized ones. Only two axes seem to be linked for nonmotorized workers: Adjame–Attecoube and, to a lesser extent, Koumassi–Marcory.

Public transport is not used by most people in Abidjan: most travel on foot or by bike, especially the poor (figure 2.1). The survey reports estimates of spending on public transport of only 1 percent of the population, suggesting that a marginal number of the population living in Abidjan actually use public transport to go to work, school, or shop. Among the trips recorded by the survey, 53.2 percent are undertaken by nonmotorized transport such as by bike or on foot. Only 4.8 percent of trips are done by car or motorcycle. A few people use water transport or meter taxis. Collective taxis (*wôrô-wôrô*), vans (*gbaka*), and buses

Figure 2.1 Most People in Abidjan Walk or Bike, Limiting Job Opportunities

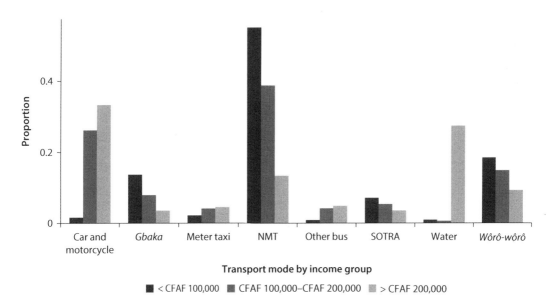

Transport mode by income group

■ < CFAF 100,000　■ CFAF 100,000–CFAF 200,000　▨ > CFAF 200,000

Source: JICA and MCLAU 2014.
Note: NMT = nonmotorized transport; SOTRA = Société des Transports Abidjanais.

(SOTRA [Société des Transports Abidjanais] and other buses) were used for the remaining trips in the survey.

The poorest have access only to a small share of the labor market. Distance traveled increases slightly with income, through better access to faster modes of transport (figure 2.2). Most people work and live in nearby places. The average trip is less than 5 km. Since most people walk or bike, they can only travel that far. For those using motorized transport, one of the more frequently used routes from home to work is Adjame–Abobo, about 8 km on the highway. Surprisingly, very few walking or biking trips are undertaken on that axis.

Abidjan is losing out on potential agglomeration benefits that come from a unified labor market. International evidence shows that, as income rises, people travel farther and faster and transport modes change. There is an increase in usage of buses, cars, trains, and planes relative to walking and cycling, which are the transport modes of the poor—see, for example, Schäfer (1998), Gakenheimer (1999), and WBCSD (2001). Figure 2.3 shows the correlation between the under-five mortality rate (U5MR), as a proxy for income or poverty, and the proportion of people traveling to work by foot or bike in cities of Africa (UN-Habitat 2002). This shows that U5MR is positively correlated with the proportion of people traveling to work by nonmotorized means and is inversely correlated with the proportion of people taking motorized means (excluding bus and trains).

Coordinating Land Use for Intraurban Connectivity
To enhance mobility within cities, land use planning and urban transport need to be better integrated. Transport and mobility are best addressed as part of an integrated urban strategy that can cater to various user groups and can anticipate

Figure 2.2 Distance Traveled Increases with Income

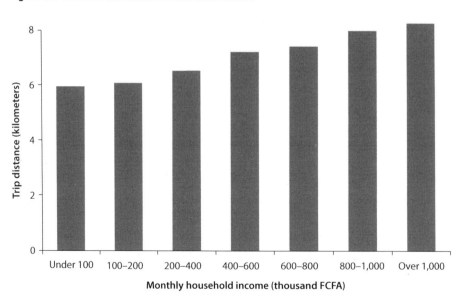

Source: JICA and MCLAU 2014.

Figure 2.3 Development Level and Mode of Urban Transport

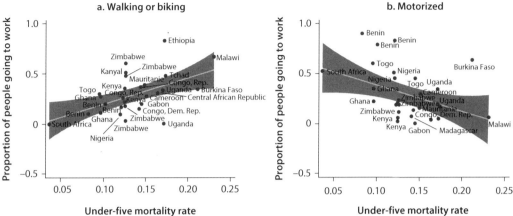

Source: UN-Habitat 2002.

long-term needs. Policy measures could be developed on managing land use through transit-oriented development or smart growth that gives preference to new developments along established public transport routes.

Ivorian cities need an urban transport master plan that promotes a reliable, safe, modern, and sustainable multimodal transport system accessible to all urban dwellers. There is no national transport master plan,[2] and the national road master plan needs to be updated to reflect the government's spatial development strategy. The sector is poorly coordinated: many informal, unqualified actors operate with obsolete vehicles that pose safety and pollution problems. In the Greater Abidjan area, public transportation is not diversified despite a navigable lagoon and is not commensurate with a metropolis of more than 6 million.

The dominance of informality presents a constraint to urban transport services. Public transport in Abidjan principally operates on only two rights-of-way, namely that of the road and that of the lagoon, attracting about 9 million boardings each day. In Abidjan, both the formal and the informal sectors operate on both rights-of-way. A key issue is that the public transport service is provided largely by the informal sector. Bus services are concentrated in routes originating from suburban areas and ending in several city terminals such as Adjame or the Plateau. The informal sector, consisting of *gbaka*, meter taxis, *wôrô-wôrô*, and intercommunal taxis, accounts for 85 percent of public transport trips, and has grown at the expense of formal transport.

Public transport should be given priority through traffic regulation and pricing. Measures to enhance the attractiveness of public transport are important for improving overall efficiency, such as upgrading traffic signal control, implementing traffic information systems and traffic management on highways, controlling overloaded vehicles, and enforcing traffic regulations. Parking management and priority treatment for traffic safety are also important. Policies must be guided to provide a comprehensive and integrated public transport network that is convenient, user-friendly, and accessible to all income groups in all urban centers, district and neighborhood, while providing access to local community facilities, employment centers, leisure sites, and tourism sites.

Pricing mechanisms can be effective in encouraging use of public transport and reducing reliance on private vehicles. International experience shows that urban areas shrink in size as transit subsidies increase, but they increase in size with auto subsidies. Instruments that take advantage of market mechanisms include congestion charges or tolls, emission or pollution tax, fuel tax, vehicle tax, and subsidies. Singapore, London, Amsterdam, and Stockholm have congestion taxes to reduce peak-time car traffic (World Bank 2009). These policies are implemented to promote the use of public transport, which reduces congestion costs and increases livability, eventually leading to higher productivity in cities.

Interurban Connectivity

Among cities, transport costs are like an implicit trade barrier. Global evidence shows that falling transport costs caused by large infrastructure investments and breakthroughs brought closer economic integration and specialization within countries. Transport links between cities reinforce agglomeration economies and generate complementary and specialized functions. Declines in transport costs should encourage trade among cities and enable specialization across cities and the growth of secondary cities. Falling transport costs can enable standardized manufacturing industries to thrive in secondary cities where land and labor costs are much lower. As cities specialize, intercity infrastructure becomes a priority in the most dynamic areas.

Connections among Global, Regional, and Domestic Connectors are limited, reflected in the slow growth of secondary cities and their weak economic specialization. Most firms are in a few southern cities, encouraging migration to these cities and their hinterlands. Between 1999 and 2011, 89–96 percent of registered firms were in the south (mostly in Greater Abidjan). This area also has 80 percent of the country's formal jobs and is the main employment zone for sectors such as services to households and industry, transport, telecommunications, wholesale and retail, and food and agriculture (Coulibaly et al. 2014). The concentration of companies in the south and lack of secondary-city growth is due to Abidjan's position as the country's main economic hub; it has one of the largest ports in Sub-Saharan Africa—the Autonomous Port of Abidjan—as well as a deep-sea port at San-Pédro. It is also related to the limited intercity and regional connectivity, which make it difficult to move standardized manufacturing industries out of the primary city into secondary cities. The rest of the country subsists mainly by growing cash or food crops.

Road Infrastructure

The Ivorian road sector has been growing fast. Expanding from 10,570 km before independence to 85,000 km in the early 2000s, the road network has made it the first choice of transit for the landlocked countries of WAEMU (the West African Economic and Monetary Union, comprising Burkina Faso,

Mali, and Niger). The density of the road network is relatively low (82 km/1,000 km² compared with an average of 133 km for low-income countries). However, the primary and secondary networks provide sufficient coverage of primary and secondary cities and international borders (World Bank 2010).

The 2011–15 National Development Plan allocated about 25 percent of the nearly US$6 billion capital investment plan to infrastructure development and transport. The renovation and extension of the northern highway to Yamoussoukro have been completed and a third bridge in Abidjan inaugurated. The government is also considering extending the northern highway to Bouaké and building a highway to the Ghanaian border through Grand-Bassam.

The main Ivorian cities are linked by an extensive road network, with four main axes starting from Abidjan. The east axis goes to Bondoukou and Bouna in the northeast, passing by Abengourou and Agnibilékro (map 2.1). The second goes to Korhogo (Regional Connector), Ferkessédougou, and Ouangolodougou through the cities of Bouaké (Regional Connector) and Yamoussoukro

Map 2.1 Main Routes and Cities in Côte d'Ivoire

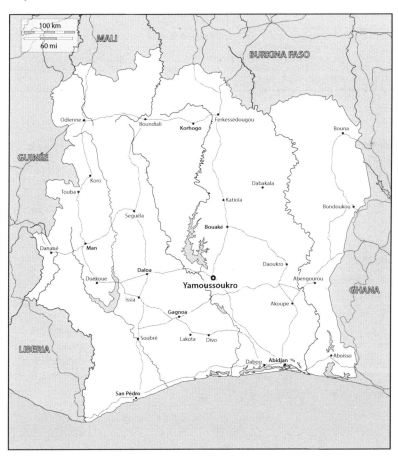

Source: d-maps.com.

(Global Connector). The west axis goes to Daloa (Regional Connector) through Man (Regional Connector), connecting the neighboring countries of Liberia and Guinea. The south axis follows the coast to San-Pédro (Global Connector). The north axis is an international road in the direction of Burkina Faso and Mali. Trade in goods is very frequent between Côte d'Ivoire, Ghana, Togo, and Nigeria using the Abidjan–Lagos axis, passing through Aboisso and Noe. The majority of road freight (83 percent) in Côte d'Ivoire is over long distances (over 180 km), from Global to Regional to Domestic Connectors (figure 2.4). The road network linking these connectors has to be rehabilitated.

Côte d'Ivoire's transport infrastructure requires rehabilitation. The country's ambition to become an emerging nation and to be a hub for transport in West Africa requires rehabilitation of roads, especially to the 31 regional capitals and Domestic Connectors, and modernization of the vehicle fleet. Informal payments and roadblocks should also be tackled. In particular, the following policy measures and respective time frame can be considered:

- Zero tolerance enforced on harassment and bribe extortion by traffic police of road users, especially on international corridors (short term)
- The rehabilitation of roads connecting the region, including capitals and domestic-oriented communities and the construction of new transport infrastructure (medium term)
- Incentives or financial services to facilitate the renewal of the car fleet in order to lower operating costs (medium)
- Implementation of the reforms in the transport sector (medium and long term)

Figure 2.4 The Majority of Trade Flows among Global Connectors and from Domestic to Global Connectors

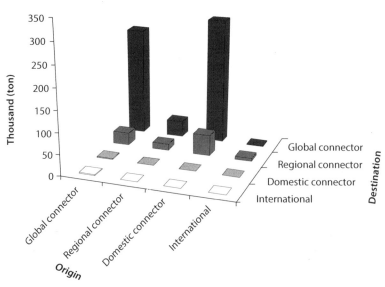

Source: ENSEA 2014.

These institutional actions should be matched by initiatives improving the efficiency of the regional corridors. For the Abidjan–Ouagadougou corridor, an extension of the highway beyond Yamoussoukro to connect Bouaké, Korhogo, and Ferkessédougou is an essential medium- to long-term priority. To support diversified urbanization, it is also important to diversify the corridors connecting the domestic economy to attractive regional markets. The Abidjan–Lagos corridor offers denser market potential, and extending the highway to Grand-Bassam and Aboisso on to the border with Ghana is a sound investment. A third corridor westward could be considered to link Abidjan to Nzérékoré in Guinea. The road connecting Abidjan, Yamoussoukro, Daloa, and Man to the border with Guinea could then be set as a regional corridor and provide enticing regional trade opportunities to Daloa and Man. As these three regional corridors develop, a focus should be on providing efficient logistics, distribution infrastructure, and institutions in the Regional Connector cities.

Transport Costs

Economic connectivity—measured by transport costs—can be useful for measuring a city's external connections. These typically include direct vehicle operating costs (maintenance, tires, fuel, labor, and capital), as well as indirect costs (licensing, insurance, road tolls, and roadblock payments). A survey of 448 truckers (ENSEA 2014) was carried out to estimate transport costs, following the methodology developed and used in India, Tunisia, Vietnam, and other countries (box 2.1).

Domestic transport costs in Côte d'Ivoire are among the highest in the world. The ENSEA (2014) trucking survey reports that the average freight transport cost is $0.35 per ton-kilometer (figure 2.5 ; important to note is that the median trucking cost is $0.17 per ton-kilometer). The average transport cost is much higher than in other developing countries such as India and Vietnam and also considerably higher than in the United States, where labor costs and overheads are much higher.

Box 2.1 Identifying Road Connection Constraints in Vietnam: The World Bank's Trucking Industry Survey

To understand Vietnam's transport infrastructure bottlenecks and reveal the main drivers of its transport costs, the World Bank urbanization review team commissioned a route-specific trucking survey. It comprised structured, face-to-face interviews with key managers and owners of trucking companies as well as with individual operators who owned or leased their trucks as independent businesses. The final sample included 246 respondents answering questions on 852 data points (origin–destination combinations).

The survey suggested that corruption and poor road conditions were the main causes of bottlenecks in Vietnamese truck transport. On average, truck operators rated the severity of corruption at 3.7 out of 5 and the severity of poor road conditions at 3.1 out of 5.

---

box continues next page

Box 2.1 Identifying Road Connection Constraints in Vietnam: The World Bank's Trucking Industry Survey *(continued)*

Map B2.1.1 Origin Cities in the Vietnam Trucking Industry Survey

Source: World Bank 2011.
Note: "City class" refers to the Vietnam urban classification system, established in 2001 and updated in 2009. It is a hierarchical system constituted of six classes of urban centers that are defined by different levels of economic activities, physical development, population, population density, and infrastructure provision. "Special" cities = Hanoi and Ho Chi Minh City; 1 = population over 500,000 in provincial towns (1 million in government-run cities); 2 = population over 300,000 in provincial cities (800,000 in government-run cities); 3 = population over 150,000.

box continues next page

Box 2.1 **Identifying Road Connection Constraints in Vietnam: The World Bank's Trucking Industry Survey** *(continued)*

Trips in the vicinity of Hanoi and Ho Chi Minh City appeared to have higher transport costs. About 13 percent of transport costs around Ho Chi Minh City, and 6 percent around Hanoi, consisted of informal facilitation payments (such as bribes). On average, such payments account for about 8 percent of all trucking operation costs.

Source: World Bank 2011.

Figure 2.5 Transport Costs within Côte d'Ivoire

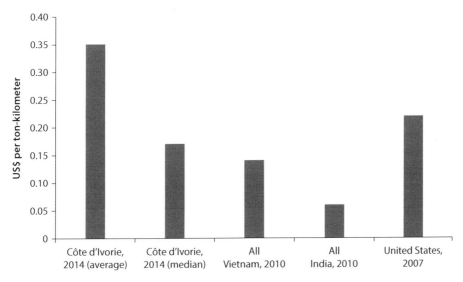

Source: ENSEA 2014.

Transporters that serve Domestic Connectors face the highest costs. The transport costs (per ton-kilometer) are the highest along routes connecting Regional and Domestic Connectors ($0.47 per ton-kilometer) and those connecting Domestic and Global connectors ($0.39 per ton-kilometer). In comparison, transport costs within Global Connectors are more in line with the national average ($0.32 per ton-kilometer), and routes connecting Global and Regional Connectors have lower transport costs ($0.17 per ton-kilometer; table 2.1).

High transport costs are detrimental to the growth of secondary cities and reduce connectivity for economically lagging areas with higher poverty incidence. The routes connecting Domestic and Global Connectors carry considerable freight and serve as integrators between the domestic and global economy. Further, the routes connecting Domestic and Regional Connectors link the country's lagging areas with markets. Disproportionately high costs of connections are likely to hurt national economic competitiveness as well as the development potential of cities in lagging areas.

Table 2.1 Transport Costs in Côte d'Ivoire, by Type of City

	GC–GC	GC–RC	RC–DC	GC–DC
Cost ton-km (US$)	0.32	0.17	0.47	0.39
Fuel (%)	53.75	59.44	39.47	50.77
Salary (%)	13.88	11.47	17.30	15.89
Bonus (%)	1.72	2.67	6.98	3.79
Maintenance (%)	12.32	12.81	14.40	12.08
Overhead (%)	15.19	5.25	3.58	5.18
Other fees (%)	3.15	8.37	18.27	12.29
Distance (km)	143,146.22	90,813.08	44,825.14	67,464.77

Source: ENSEA 2014.
Note: GC–GC = within Global Connector; GC–RC = connecting Global and Regional Connectors;
RC–DC = connecting Regional and Domestic Connectors; GC–DC = connecting Global and Domestic
Connectors; km = kilometer.

Fuel costs appear to be the major constraint faced by truckers on all routes. While truck drivers across most routes report fuel costs, empty backhauls, corruption, and road safety to be constraints, drivers between Domestic and Global Connectors report fuel costs to be a major constraint (over 90 percent report this), likely driven by the quality of infrastructure. Empty backhauls are also reported as major constraints along Regional Connector–Domestic Connector and Domestic Connector–Global Connector routes. For Global Connectors, licensing and authorization regulations tend to be much more of a constraint than along other routes: over 72 percent of drivers along Global Connector routes report licensing to be a constraint, compared with only 34 percent for Global Connectors to Regional Connectors, and 29 percent for Regional Connectors to Domestic Connectors (table 2.2). This might be explained by truckers being harassed in the greater Abidjan area and being asked for bribes for any missing vehicle document.

The physical constraints on connections among Ivorian cities are exacerbated by market structure and policy. In addition to examining physical connectivity and transport costs, this study looks at transport prices—what is paid by producers and consumers. Transport prices reflect various factors: transport costs, operator overhead, operator profit, regulatory constraints, and market structure. The last of these—market structure—is a key determinant of prices in the transport industry. As seen in table 2.3, along Global Connector routes—with high demand and large freight volumes—prices are lower than costs, presumably driven down by competition. However, in areas with lower traffic volumes, such as Regional and Domestic Connectors, transport prices are much higher than costs. Transport-scale economies lead to a vicious circle between higher costs and lower trade and traffic—and areas with lower demand will attract only a few providers who are likely to seek excessive profits.

The freight transport sector needs to be better organized and be more competitive. Until the new legislative framework goes into effect, entry into the transport sector is quite easy, leading to a fragmented market dominated by

Table 2.2 Major Constraints Reported by Truckers

	GC–GC	GC–RC	RC–DC	DC–GC	All
Fuel cost (% reporting)	63.64	87.69	87.37	91.82	88.69
Empty backhaul (% reporting)	72.73	68.21	80.00	82.16	77.16
Road accident (% reporting)	72.73	62.56	54.74	59.48	58.97
Corruption and roadblocks (% reporting)	90.91	82.56	89.47	84.39	86.32
Licensing and authorization (% reporting)	72.73	34.02	28.87	25.47	30.26

Source: ENSEA 2014.

Table 2.3 Transport Prices between Global, Regional, and Domestic Connectors

Route	Transport price (US$ per ton-kilometer)	Transport cost	Margin
CG–CG	0.27	0.32	−0.05
CG–CR	0.40	0.17	0.23
CR–CD	0.55	0.47	0.08
CD–CG	0.53	0.39	0.14

Sources: ENSEA 2014.

informal and small players relying on obsolete trucks and overage vehicles. As a result, they are vulnerable to informal payments because many of them do not comply with regulations. Multiple local trade unions translate into "vested interests poles" that fragment the market and distort prices. Indeed, practices such as freight repartition and *tour de rôle* (a queuing system) have a negative impact on the quantity, quality, and prices of transport services. Therefore, greater efficiency of transport services will imply new measures and mechanisms to improve transparency of transport prices. In this regard, the establishment of a robust and transparent market information system (MkIS) will be instrumental.

Establishment of an MkIS can better connect transporters with customers. For both freight and passenger transports, *tour de rôle* and oligopolistic behavior of unions and professional associations are long-standing practices that are jeopardizing the market efficiency. Promoting an MkIS can help coordinate better the supply and demand side of transport services. The system would provide a platform where information could formally be centralized, analyzed, treated, and made accessible to all market players. The MkIS could build upon the ICTs with two-legs: a virtual freight exchange and customer management applications for passengers.

International Connectivity

Infrastructure for transport and ICT is vital for boosting the economic efficiency of the Global, Regional, and Domestic Connectors. Policy makers need to treat their cities as an interlinked portfolio of assets, each differentiated by size, location, density of settlement, and function that connect their economy to local, regional, and global markets. Worldwide evidence highlights that businesses and people can exploit economies of scale and agglomeration if their settlements perform their intended functions. This is very much dependent on a city's connections, whether external or internal. External connectivity of a country passes through node cities at or along international transport and communication infrastructure: ports, airports, railways, and the ICT backbone.

Maritime Connectivity

Abidjan and San-Pédro are world-class ports. The Autonomous Port of Abidjan (with one container terminal and another under construction), and the deep-sea port of San-Pédro (built under the country's first development plan) provide maritime transport for Côte d'Ivoire and landlocked countries such as Burkina Faso, Mali, and Niger. Abidjan's port is the country's main port, accommodating 80 percent of maritime traffic in the country. Abidjan handles larger freight volumes than do most ports in West Africa and has a capacity of about 650,000 twenty-foot equivalent units (TEUs) per year. It was, however, one of the most expensive ports in 2009. Limited competition among port operators is also keeping prices high. San-Pédro port is dedicated mainly to timber traffic and part of the export of agricultural products (primarily coffee and cocoa).

Abidjan port's operation was seriously interrupted by the sociopolitical crises in Côte d'Ivoire. After the end of the postelection crisis of 2011, it has been slowly regaining its place among the busiest ports in Africa although its container traffic is still low (about 700,000 TEUs in 2013) compared with South Africa (over 4 million TEUs in 2013). Traffic in transit toward hinterland countries (such as Burkina Faso and Mali) saw a resurgence of activity after the end of the crises. In 2013, the volume of traffic in transit toward the hinterland was double that in 2011 (1.76 million tons versus 0.76 million tons).

Activities at the Port of San-Pédro have also witnessed a strong recovery over the past three years. The volume of exports increased by 16 percent, from 980,000 tons in 2011 to 1.139 million tons in 2013. The volume of transshipment traffic increased more than four times over the same period. The number of ships accommodated in the port rose from 369 in 2010 to 533 in 2013.

One of the major challenges of the port sector is the specialization of quays at the Autonomous Port of Abidjan. Expansion of the port to Boulay Island will allow it to increase its capacity. The port will also need to increase its capacity in deep water to promote its role as a major transshipment center for West Africa. Alternatively, cabotage between the port of Abidjan and San-Pédro can make them complementary to better serve domestic and regional clients. The construction of a bridge between the port of Abidjan and the northern highway will enable the delivery of cargo to the hinterland countries, bypassing the city of Abidjan and helping to reduce congestion. These projects fit into the vision of the current port authorities, which is to make Côte d'Ivoire a major regional maritime hub.

Air Connectivity

Côte d'Ivoire has three international airports—Félix Houphouët-Boigny in Abidjan, Yamoussoukro, and Bouaké. Commissioned in 1939, Félix Houphouët-Boigny Airport (which dominates air traffic) has been expanded several times, notably in 1996. The work consisted of lengthening by 300 meters the airstrip that was originally 2,700 meters long. The terminal was also expanded.

Félix Houphouët-Boigny Airport has yet to regain its precrisis level of cargo exports. The highest level (111,215 tons) was in 2002, a figure not seen since, because the crises led many airlines to relocate their operations (Dabité and Nassa 2011). Normalization after the postelection crisis of 2011 led to an increase of passenger and air traffic freight. In 2013, 22 companies served the airport with 1,178,362 passengers, but air cargo traffic in 2013 was still low (17,869 tons in 2013 against 16,754 tons in 2012).

After 1990, domestic traffic was nonexistent until 2012. With the new national company Air Côte d'Ivoire, domestic air traffic has resumed with flights to and from Regional and Global Connectors such as Bouaké, Korhogo, and San-Pédro. The company plans to serve the following other Regional Connectors: Man, Odienne, Bouna, and Bondoukou. To increase domestic demand for passengers, the government has begun subsidizing airline tickets from Abidjan to San-Pédro and Korhogo.[3]

The country recently obtained international certification of airport security in Abidjan. This will allow Félix Houphouët-Boigny Airport to make direct flights to the United States. Extension and improvement of the runway allowed the airport in 2014 to accommodate the Airbus A380, which now makes a weekly flight to Abidjan.

Rail Connectivity

The Abidjan–Ouagadougou railroad allows Burkina Faso to have a seamless connection to the sea while connecting Ivorian manufactured goods to domestic and regional markets. The railroad is 1,260 km long. Originally planned to reach Niamey in Niger, the project stopped short in Ouagadougou. The rail line is now operated by a private company, SITARAIL, after the operator was privatized in 1995. The railroad handles 40 freight trains and 12 passenger trains per week. The line carries 910,000 tons of goods per kilometer per year and 300,000 passengers per kilometer per year.[4]

SITARAIL transports bulk cargo to Burkina Faso. The main goods are clinker, cement, grain, containers, oil, and fertilizer. Traffic in the other direction includes cattle, cotton, shea nuts, sesame, vegetables, fruits, and manganese. SITARAIL is one of the largest railway companies in West Africa. The statistics for 2000–05 indicate that SITARAIL and Transrail (linking Mali and Senegal) had the best performance, with the density of SITARAIL traffic reaching nearly 500,000 ton-kilometer compared with 15,000 ton-kilometer for Nigeria's Railway Company. Côte d'Ivoire's major cities along the line are Abidjan, Bouaké, and Ferkessédougou; in Burkina Faso, they are Bobo-Dioulasso, Ouagadougou, Banfora, and Koudougou. Of the 66 stations and stops along the railroad, only eight were used frequently (Tape Bidi and Fodouop 2010), leading the operator to close many domestic stations between Dimbokro and Agboville.

Railroad repair is one of the country's main challenges, in addition to the need to diversify markets. The current state of the railway sector allows the connection of economies of Côte d'Ivoire and Burkina Faso. The country should pursue railway expansion by offering more service for internal traffic. It is in this context that construction of the Abidjan Tramway is planned to ease congestion in the capital. Building such a transit transport system should greatly modernize this sector. A domestic integration initiative tapping the agricultural potential of some Regional Connectors might make these stops profitable again, promoting rail–road intermodal logistic facilities to be profitable activities.

ICT Connectivity

Connectivity through ICT is relatively developed compared with regional peers. Mobile phone coverage is above the average for the Economic Community of West African States (ECOWAS)—95 percent against 78 percent (see table 2.4, below). In Abidjan, as with other cities, most citizens live within reach of a 3G-enabled mobile telephone network, and access to the Internet is relatively good through Wi-Fi and 3G. Furthermore, three major fiber optic cables land in Abidjan: the West African Cable System (WACS), the African Coast to Europe (ACE), and the SAT3/WASC (South Atlantic 3/West Africa Submarine Cable) (See Map 2.2, below). This fosters competition among three major Internet service providers (MTN, Orange, and Côte d'Ivoire Telecom), which has driven Internet connection costs down a little; however, connectivity charges remain high compared with countries like Ghana and South Africa, and access outside urban centers is relatively low. Advanced 4G technology is also being introduced. However, much more investment is needed because many Domestic Connectors are not on the Internet (map 2.3). High-speed Internet is generally lacking. According to the United Nations E-Government Survey 2014, Côte d'Ivoire is currently 171st (out of 193 countries) in the world, near·the average of ECOWAS

Table 2.4 Population and Mobile Phone Coverage

Country	Population (2013)	Coverage (%)
Benin	10,323,474	93
Burkina Faso	16,934,839	66
Cabo Verde	498,897	100
Côte d'Ivoire	20,316,086	95
Gambia, The	1,849,285	100
Ghana	25,904,598	108
Guinea	11,745,189	63
Guinea-Bissau	1,704,255	74
Liberia	4,294,077	60
Mali	15,301,650	129
Niger	17,831,270	39
Nigeria	173,615,345	73
Senegal	14,133,280	93
Sierra Leone	6,092,075	44
Togo	6,816,982	63
ECOWAS	327,361,302	78

Source: World Bank 2014.

Map 2.2 Submarine Cables Landing in Abidjan

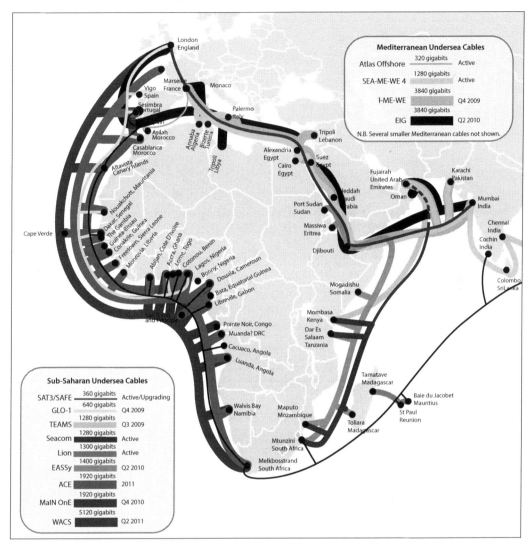

Source: Shuttleworth Foundation.

countries but significantly behind Ghana (123rd) and Senegal (151st). Mobile broadband is also relatively low with only about 6.8 percent penetration (end 2013), which is on par with Senegal and Nigeria, but significantly lower than Ghana (28.2 per 100 inhabitants).

There is an opportunity to make Yamoussoukro a technology hub in West Africa. Because the government's growth pole initiative for Abidjan, Bouaké, and San-Pédro is integral to its growth and employment strategy, it is important to back it up by establishing a technology hub in Yamoussoukro based in the Polytechnic Engineering School. Domestic technology firms (wherever they are) and external private partners could form a cluster around the polytechnic school to tap the numerous and low-wage skilled workers graduating every year.

Diversified Urbanization • http://dx.doi.org/10.1596/978-1-4648-0808-1

Map 2.3 ICT Connectivity in Côte d'Ivoire

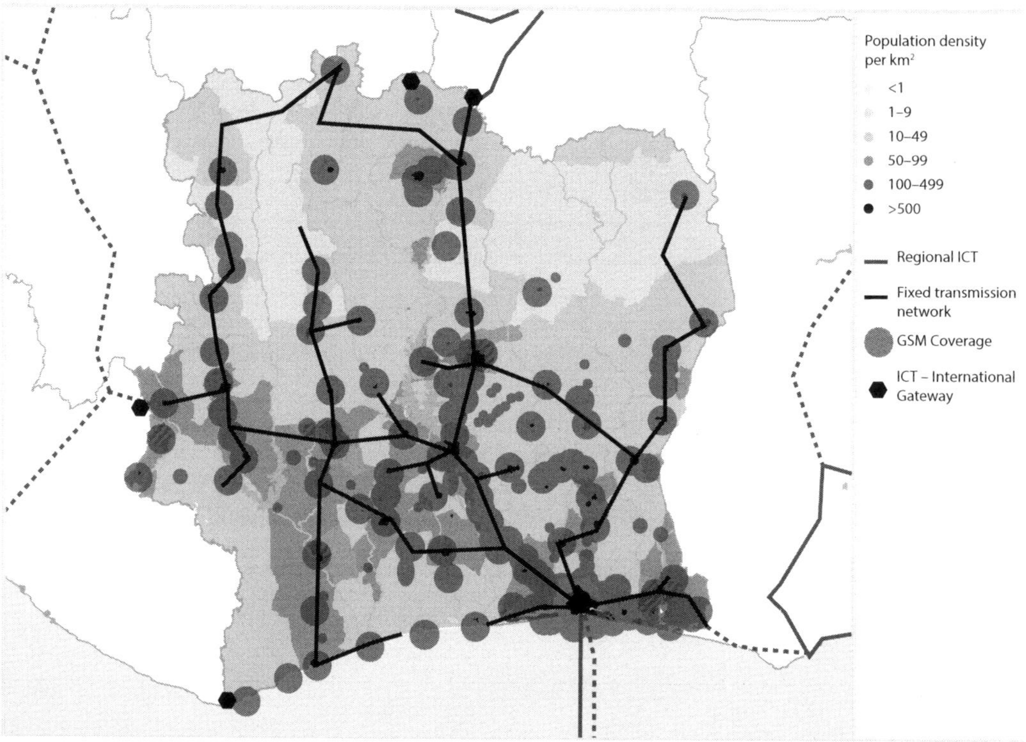

Source: Foster and Pushak 2010.
Note: GSM = global system for mobile communication; ICT = Information and communications technology.

This would mean securing world-class ICT connectivity to at least the three Global Connectors (Abidjan, San-Pédro, and Yamoussoukro) to take advantage of recent ICT innovations—such as massive open online courses (MOOCs) that could be developed in partnership with the Polytechnic Engineering School—and technology-oriented city redevelopment as New York is currently experimenting with in partnership with Cornell University to catalyze spinoff companies and increase the probability that the next high growth company—a Google, Amazon, or Facebook—will emerge in New York City (http://www.nycedc.com/project/applied-sciences-nyc).

Notes

1. A vast literature shows positive links between market access and the growth of cities (see, among others, Beeson, DeJong, and Troesken 2001; Henderson and Thisse 2004; and Tao, Hewings, and Donaghy 2010. For example, research on Brazil shows that a 1 percent increase in market potential leads to an increase in city size of 2.7 percent, while a reduction in transport costs of 10 percent leads to a 1 percent increase in city growth over a decade (da Mata et al. 2007).

2. However, JICA is assisting the government with the Greater Abidjan Transport Master Plan.

3. *Fraternité Matin* No. 14980 of November 10, 2014.

4. bollore-africa-logistics.com

Bibliography

Baum, Herbert, and Judith Kurte. 2001. "Transport et développement économique." Discussion Paper for Round Table 119, Conférence Européenne des Ministres des Transports, Centre des Recherche Économiques.

Beeson, Patricia E., David N. DeJong, and Werner Troesken. 2001. "Population and Growth in U.S. Cities, 1840–1990." *Regional Science and Urban Economics* 31: 669–99.

Brunel, J. 2005. "Le transport de marchandises et la croissance économique." Paper presented at the conference, ASRDLF, Villes et territoires face aux défis de la mondialisation—XIe colloque de l'ASRDLF, Dijon, France, September 5–7.

Bullock, Richard. 2009. "Off Track: Sub-Saharan African Railways." AICD Background Paper 17, Africa Region, World Bank, Washington, DC.

Cotton, Anne Marie. 1974. *Les cahiers d'outre mers, revue de géographie*. Bordeaux, France: ORSTOM (Office de la Recherche Scientifique et Technique d'Outre-Mer).

Coulibaly, Souleymane, Jacques Esso, Charles Fe Doukoure, and Desire Kanga. 2014. "Revue l'Urbanisation: Analyse Économique." Background paper prepared for this report.

Dabité, Désiré, and Axel Nassa. 2011. "Zone franche en Côte d'Ivoire, entre mondialisation, objet et effets géographiques." HAL (Archive ouvert en Sciences de l'Homme et de la Société) 00580353.

da Mata, Daniel, Uwe Deichmann, J. Vernon Henderson, Somik Lall, and H. G. Wang. 2007. "Determinants of City Growth in Brazil." *Journal of Urban Economics* 62: 252–72.

Didier, Michel, and Remy Prud'homme. 2007. "Infrastructures de transport, mobilité et croissance." *La documentation française*. Paris: La documentation français.

Duranton, Gilles. 2009. "Are Cities Engines of Growth and Prosperity for Developing Countries?" In *Urbanization and Growth*, edited by Michael Spence, Patricia Clarke Annez, and Robert M. Buckley. Washington, DC: World Bank.

Duranton, Gilles, and Diego Puga. 2001. "Nursery Cities: Urban Diversity, Process Innovation, and the Life Cycle of Products." *American Economic Review* 91 (5): 1454–77.

Ecole Nationale Supérieure de Statistique et d'Economie Appliquée (ENSEA), World Bank. 2014. Côte d'Ivoire Urbanization Review: Urban Connectivity: Repositioning cities based on their respective comparative advantage. Background paper for the Côte d'Ivoire Urbanization Review.

Foster, Viven, and Nataliya Pushak. 2010. *Côte d'Ivoire's Infrastructure: A Continental Perspective*. Washington, DC: World Bank.

Gabella-Latreille, C. 1997. "Le modèle Quin-Quin Fret, un modèle de simulation à l'horizon 2015 des flux de transport de marchandise." Doctoral Thesis, Université Lyon 2.

Gakenheimer, Ralph. 1999. "Urban Mobility in the Developing World." *Transportation Research Part A* 33 (1999): 671–89.

Gwilliam, Ken, Vivien Foster, Rodrigo Archondo-Callao, Cecilia Briceño-Garmendia, Alberto Nogales, and Kavita Sethi. 2008. "The Burden of Maintenance: Roads in

Sub-Saharan Africa." AICD Background Paper 14, Africa Region, World Bank, Washington, DC.

Henderson, J. Vernon, and Jacques François Thisse, eds. 2004. *Handbook of Regional and Urban Economics*, vol. 4. Amsterdam: Elsevier.

JICA (Japan International Cooperation Agency) and MCLAU (Ministère de la Construction, du Logement, de l'Assianissement et de l'Urbanisme). 2014. The Project for the Development of the Urban Master Plan in Greater Abidjan. Interim Report, Annex, Working Paper 1: Household Interview Survey.

Lee, H. L., and C. Billington. 1993. "Material Management in Decentralized Supply Chains." *Operations Research* 41: 835–47.

Lenormand, A. 2002. "Prévisions dans les modèles cointégrés avec rupture: Application à la demande de transports terrestres de marchandises et de voyageurs." Doctoral Thesis, Université Paris 1, Panthéon-Sorbonne.

MEMPD (Ministère d'État Ministère du Plan et du Développement). 2012. *Plan National de Développement, 2012–2015*. République de Côte d'Ivoire.

Meyer, F. 1998. "La concurrence rail-route: Analyse économétrique des trafics de marchandises et des perspectives du transport combiné." Doctoral Thesis, Université Paris 1, Panthéon-Sorbonne.

Mundy, Michael, and Andrew Penfold. 2008. "Beyond the Bottlenecks: Ports in Sub-Saharan Africa." Background Paper 8, Africa Infrastructure Country Diagnostic, World Bank, Washington, DC.

Polèse, Mario. 2010. "Le rôle des villes dans le développement économique: Un autre regard." Working Paper, Institut National de la Recherche Scientifique, Quebec.

Schäfer, A. 1998. "The Global Demand for Motorized Mobility." *Transportation Research A* 32 (6): 455–77.

Tao, Zhining, Geoffrey J. D. Hewings, and Kieran P. Donaghy. 2010. "An Economic Analysis of Trends in Mid-Western U.S. Pollutant Emissions from 1970 to 2000." *Ecological Economics* 69 (8): 1666–74.

Tape Bidi, Jean, and Kengne Fodouop. 2010. *L'armature du développement en Afrique. Industries, transports et communication*. Vol. 6. Paris: Éditions Karthala.

Teravaninthorn, Supee, and Gael Raballand. 2009. *Le prix et le coût du transport en Afrique: Étude des principaux corridors*. Directions in Development Series. Washington, DC: World Bank.

UN-Habitat. 2002. *Global Urban Indicators Database 2*. Nairobi: UN-Habitat.

WBCSD (World Business Council for Sustainable Development). 2001. *Mobility 2001: World Mobility at the End of the 20th Century and Its Sustainability*. Geneva: WBCSD.

World Bank. 2009. *World Development Report: Reshaping Economic Geography*. Washington, DC: World Bank.

———. 2010. *Infrastructure de la Côte d'Ivoire: Une perspective continentale*. Country Report. Washington, DC: World Bank.

———. 2011. *Vietnam Urbanization Review*. Washington, DC: World Bank.

———. 2014. World Development Indicators. 2013 data. Washington, DC: World Bank. http://data.worldbank.org.

CHAPTER 3

Greening Cities

Nancy Lozano-Gracia and Alexandra Panman

Introduction

Failures in infrastructure and coordination deepen Côte d'Ivoire's urban pollution and its vulnerability to natural disasters. The cities face a severe lack of basic sanitation, solid waste management, and storm water infrastructure, so untreated water from industry and households is disposed directly into urban and coastal water bodies. Inadequate storm water drainage and poor solid waste management mean that cities flood easily—exacerbating problems from extreme weather events and washing additional pollutants into lakes, lagoons, and the ocean. As transport motorizes, inefficiencies are leading to rising per capita emissions, whereas green spaces in and around cities—which help filter pollutants and absorb flood water—are disappearing through lack of green management.

These impacts can be mitigated with coordinated, forward-looking, and context-specific decisions. Thinking about "green cities" does not require any new paradigm. Greening should not impose large new costs on urban development at the expense of other social and economic goals. It is about building understanding of existing costs into decision making, and taking coordinated and contextual actions to promote sustainable development. In Côte d'Ivoire, priority greening initiatives are those that help address key development challenges throughout the system of cities. They are initiatives that will help cities, individually, anticipate future costs of today's decisions, leading to efficiency gains and building resilience to environmental risks.

For Global Connectors, greening can improve competitiveness and productivity. The economy of Abidjan and other Global Connectors is based on international trade, innovation, and productivity. High rates of urban pollution threaten their quality of life, making them unattractive to high-skilled labor and undermining productivity. Coastal cities are also particularly vulnerable to natural disasters, such as flooding associated with sea-level rise. Greening initiatives potentially offer myriad solutions to these challenges. As this chapter highlights, integrated planning to upgrade basic infrastructure in Abidjan's 144 precarious settlements can result in a triple win of social, economic, and environmental benefits. Protection of green and open spaces along the waterfront can make the city more attractive and livable while providing a vital buffer against climate change–related risks. Further, coordinated efforts to provide a system of public, nonmotorized transport can help stem rising congestion and air pollution, while providing a wide range of social and economic advantages.

For Regional Connectors, green policies can be aligned with the bigger priority to support growth through regional trade and transport. The economy of the Regional Connectors is grounded in regional trade related to extractive industries and small manufacturing. As highlighted in this chapter, a fuller understanding of the environmental costs and trade-offs associated with these activities is important to ensure more efficient use of resources, which will help cities plan ahead. It will also help cities save in the long run by building, into infrastructure investment, resilience to environmental risks: for example, roads should be designed to withstand landslides, coastal erosion, and heavy rains to prevent waste of public investment.

International experience indicates that there are opportunities to reduce the environmental footprint and improve the economic efficiency of light manufacturing, often at industrial zones where economies of scale can be attained in pollution-treatment infrastructure. The government has already identified the economic and social gains of better-regulated and modernized freight transport, which could help minimize the environmental costs of trucking. The natural beauty and ecological uniqueness of regions such as Man present underexploited economic opportunities, in a context where ecotourism is the fastest-growing area of the tourism industry (TEEB 2010) and is an important area for growth in green jobs (OECD 2012).

For Domestic Connector cities, establishing greener growth patterns will stimulate localization economies. Domestic Connector cities are important in the system of cities and national economy because they connect agricultural inputs and outputs to markets. These cities need to get basic services right from the outset to support more sustainable growth patterns. Planning can greatly reduce the long-term costs of urban development by laying the foundation for basic service infrastructure such as sewage systems and roads (chapter 1). This can help insulate small cities from unnecessary future costs, such as those now faced by larger cities like Abidjan, where, for example, solid-waste collection trucks cannot reach 40 percent of houses because of the physical layout of the city. Domestic Connector cities can also explore alternative technologies to potentially reduce costs for basic services, as smaller cities in Kenya are doing, by exploring off-grid photovoltaic street lighting.

The national government also has a vital role to play in enabling greener urban development across cities because this is too great a burden for city governments alone. The central authorities can provide information and create incentives to change behavior and support more efficient, sustainable development. Policy makers and consumers require better information on the environmental costs of their decisions. The government can ensure that this information is collected and disseminated, for example by establishing reporting standards for firms, monitoring national data on water and air quality, and supporting cities in measuring urban indicators that help urban households, businesses, and policy makers better consider future costs and challenges in their decision making today. It can also educate through schools. It can provide incentives by creating regulations and using price instruments to stimulate behavior change among firms and households. Although the effect of such measures is hard to predict, international experience with fuel standards and vehicle-upgrading programs suggests that important transformations can occur through a well-designed and integrated system.

Why Think about Greening Cities?

Policy makers shape their cities and determine the environmental costs of urbanization. As chapters 1 and 2 show, infrastructure and land use decisions determine the form and growth patterns of urban areas, but the environmental dimension is rarely considered when these decisions are made. For example, policy makers regulate urban land uses such as maximum permitted densities and make infrastructure investment decisions such as road construction projects. These decisions frame the mobility needs of urban residents, such as commuting distances to work and to school, and their transport options, all of which are important variables in determining an urban area's per capita air pollution and carbon emissions.

Environmental externalities can impose heavy environmental, social, and economic costs on cities. In economic theory, negative externalities are uncompensated damages imposed by one economic agent on another. A textbook example is air pollution. The consequences of burning fossil fuels are not included in the market price for energy consumption but are paid by everyone who breathes harmful particles and who is affected by climate-related events. These costs can be steep: in China the health costs of air pollution alone have been estimated at 3.8 percent of gross domestic product (GDP) (World Bank 2007). Other costs can include knock-on effects for economic development of a city as a whole, as health problems undermine worker productivity, pollution makes a city unattractive to skilled workers, and climate-related extreme weather events disrupt businesses and destroy infrastructure.

As urbanization intensifies and wealth grows, the production of environmental externalities is likely to be amplified. As urban systems grow, negative externalities of congestion and air pollution generally rise, affecting humans' well-being and the environment (Whitehead et al. 2010). In addition, as cities become wealthier and incomes increase, the consumption and waste associated with each urban resident is also likely to grow, straining solid waste services and, unless managed properly, raising pollution and health risks (Hoornweg and Bhada-Tata 2012). Cities need to plan ahead to make sure that the costs of these externalities do not undermine the benefits of growth.

Greener cities are often more productive, competitive, inclusive, and resilient to risks. There are solutions that connect environmental objectives and other policy priorities. Initiatives to reduce the environmental costs of urban activities can also generate social and economic benefits. For example, improved infrastructure for basic services such as urban waste collection and treatment not only helps maintain water quality and biodiversity in urban lakes but also reduces the burden of diseases such as diarrhea and cholera. Getting basic services right can also help mitigate the costs of extreme weather: damage from flooding is amplified when sewage systems are not prepared for water surges.

Greening is about informed, coordinated, and context-specific decision making. Thinking about green cities does not require a new paradigm. Greener cities are efficient in their use of natural resources, clean because they minimize pollution and consider the environmental impacts of policies and infrastructure decisions, and resilient in that they account for natural hazards and the role of environmental management in disaster preparedness (World Bank 2012a). Making a city greener requires thinking about the externalities that planning and management decisions may bring. As Côte d'Ivoire grows and becomes wealthier, it is likely that negative externalities of urban activities will intensify. If these challenges are ignored, they could undermine hard-won gains in quality of life.

Greening is also about awareness of how projected increases in flooding, extreme weather events, and other climate change–related effects are likely to hit cities (see the discussion later in the chapter of climate change's effects on cities in developing countries). Cities across the world face a growing risk of extreme weather events that can put lives in danger and cause extensive damage to public and private infrastructure. Côte d'Ivoire's coastal cities such as Abidjan, Grand-Bassam, and San-Pédro are highly vulnerable to sea-level rise and damage tied to coastal erosion, placing a large portion of the country's population and economic activity under threat. Greening means bringing the best available information about risks into planning decisions and infrastructure investment today, in order to build resilience and avoid unnecessary losses. For example, improvement to the San-Pédro–Abidjan road link is a clear national development priority. The design of any new investment in roads in this area, however, must consider the long-term viability of the infrastructure: design decisions about the location and materials of the road will directly affect exposure to risks like coastal erosion and—as the destruction of newly resurfaced areas in 2013 highlights—heavy rains.

Data collection to support coordinated action across sectors is essential. Monitoring and evaluation of environmental risks such as water and air quality, as well as coastal erosion, are vital to support informed decision making. Greening initiatives do not come in "one size fits all." Their effects are specific and usually vary from one city to another. Studies show that initiatives to promote increased use of nonmotorized transport could improve the health of urban citizens in cities such as London and New York because improved air quality and increased physical activity reduce respiratory- and obesity-related illnesses.[1] But the same outcome cannot be expected in all cities. In highly polluted cities such as Beijing and Delhi, additional efforts may be needed to reduce emissions before the health benefits of increased walking or cycling come through. Evidence-led initiatives are needed.

In Côte d'Ivoire, greening initiatives can be tailored to the patterns and priorities of individual cities. Cities of all sizes can benefit from greener growth patterns. But support for environmentally sustainable development should be prioritized by need. Global Connector cities such as Abidjan and San-Pédro can prioritize green initiatives that align with the need for innovation and competitiveness because greener, healthier, happier, and more livable cities are likely to attract skilled workers and reap productivity gains. They can also minimize exposure to the growing threat of natural disasters by building approaches against sea-level rise and coastal erosion into urban planning. In Regional Connector cities such as Bouaké and Man, greening initiatives can help promote localization economies needed for efficient regional trade and transport by providing a framework to better manage trade-offs and support more efficient growth. Greening is also important in Domestic Connector cities, but, there, priorities to improve basic services can lay the foundations for greener urban development.

How Green Are Ivorian Cities?

There is an urgent need for better information on the economic costs of environmental degradation in Côte d'Ivoire. Indeed, comprehensive analysis of the economic costs of environmental degradation in the Africa region as a whole is missing, even though such analysis has become increasingly common in Latin America and East Asia. The few studies that exist suggest that the costs are steep: World Bank studies estimated annual losses of about 9 percent and 10 percent of GDP in Nigeria and Ghana respectively (Bromhead 2012). The Water and Sanitation Program on the economic impact of sanitation estimated that poor sanitation costs Ghana, Kenya, Nigeria, and Tanzania US$290 million, $324 million, $3 billion, and $206 million each year, respectively. More information of this kind is needed to guide policy decisions in Côte d'Ivoire. The following section therefore aims to provide an indicative picture of the current state of Ivorian cities, as a starting point for further analysis. It draws together a wide range of information about pollution in Côte d'Ivoire with information about the social, environmental, and economic costs of pollution and environmental degradation from around the world.

Urban Pollution in Côte d'Ivoire Effects Productivity and Livability

The environmental costs of pollution are increasingly evident for all cities. Pollution threatens species loss in protected forest areas and destruction of fragile mangrove habitats.[2] Mangrove habitats are often the source of ecosystem services and resilience to natural disasters such as flooding, and their destruction is likely to hit the poorest hardest because the poor are most reliant on those ecosystem services and vulnerable to risks of disasters (Kumar and Yashiro 2014). Pollution is also an important factor in the decline of renewable internal freshwater sources[3] and the dramatic decrease of dissolved oxygen and hydrogen sulfide enrichment in water bodies near urban areas, such as Bietri Bay (Hayé et al. 2009). Indeed, water quality in the Ébrié Lagoon of Abidjan is considered inappropriate for any use by World Health Organization (WHO) standards

(Ministére des Infrastructure Économiques 2011), and the lagoon has many dead fish (World Bank, forthcoming). Along with the decrease in water quality, air pollution is widespread in Africa (map 3.1).

Urban air and water pollution negatively affect the environment: they cause biodiversity loss[4] and are associated with global warming, acid rain, deoxygenation of water sources, and toxic poisoning of animal, fish, and plant life. These losses are unquantifiable; biodiversity underpins all ecosystem services,[5] and its destruction not only threatens the flow of benefits such as crops, timber, freshwater, and other inputs to economic activity but can also lead to a loss of intangible social, economic, and cultural value that can stress communities and lead to human suffering (TEEB 2010; Brink et al. 2012). Biodiversity loss can also increase exposure to natural disasters—in the Lao People's Democratic Republic, for example, it was estimated that conservation of wetlands could save the country some US$5 million a year in avoided flood damage.[6]

Urban pollution also has heavy health costs. Although there have been no comprehensive studies to monetize the health costs associated with air and water pollution in Côte d'Ivoire, evidence suggests they are not trivial. Air pollution is linked to lower respiratory diseases such as asthma and pneumonia, which make up the third-biggest factor in the country's disease burden.[7] Indeed, lower respiratory diseases account for 6,417 years of life lost per 100,000 due to disability or death.[8] Chemical and inorganic pollution of drinking water is also connected with chronic diseases such as cancer of the digestive system (World Bank 2007). Polluted water is associated with the spread of waterborne diseases such as diarrhea and cholera. The WHO estimates that 842,000 people die every year from diarrhea related to unsafe drinking water and poor sanitation, including 361,000 children under five years of age (WHO 2015). The number of disability-adjusted life years (DALYs) lost due to diarrhea alone are 7,897 per 100,000 (map 3.2).

Map 3.1 Air Pollution Worldwide

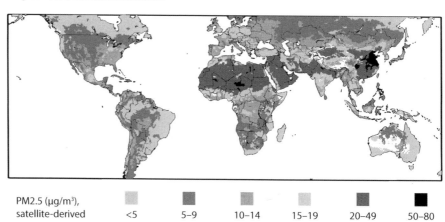

| PM2.5 (µg/m³), satellite-derived | <5 | 5–9 | 10–14 | 15–19 | 20–49 | 50–80 |

Source: Van Donkelaar et al. 2010.
Note: PM2.5 = Particulate Matter, 2.5 micrometers or less.

Map 3.2 Respiratory and Diarrheal Diseases, DALYs per 100,000 People, 2010

    a. Lower respiratory infections   b. Diarrheal diseases

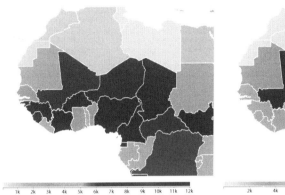
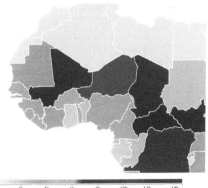

Source: IHME 2013. GBD Compare. Seattle, WA: IHME, University of Washington. Available from http://vizhub.healthdata.org /gbd-compare/.
Note: Data shown are for both genders and all ages. DALY = disability-adjusted life year.

Urban pollution is further associated with economic costs such as reduced labor productivity, which can have a powerful effect on Global and Regional Connectors. There are productivity costs to respiratory and communicable diseases in the form of lost work and other indirect household costs from caring for sick children and relatives. A 2012 analysis of the household costs of childhood diarrheal illnesses found that more than half the total household costs of diseases in The Gambia and Kenya were indirect costs and productivity losses of this kind (Rheingans et al. 2012).

These diseases are also linked to lower educational attainment among children. They can cause absences from school and less concentration in class, which may ultimately lead to lower productivity among adults in the labor force. The economic costs of this productivity loss can be heavy. The effects are likely to be spatially concentrated in areas with high pollution. A study in Nigeria, for instance, found a significant positive statistical relationship between proximity to an open dump and health risks, as well as to reduced labor market performance (Ogunrinola and Adepegba 2012).

The economic costs of urban pollution are also felt through losses in competitiveness and in economic opportunities. Air quality is a key component of a city's environmental attractiveness because pollution and traffic congestion, as well as safety and public space, affect the quality of life. Reducing pollution can make a city attractive to high-skill workers and raise competitiveness.[9] High levels of pollution can also constrain economic activity. Water pollution hurts tourism, property values, fishing, and other sectors that depend on clean water. In the United States, the Environmental Protection Agency estimates that tourism-industry losses related to water pollution reach as much as US$1 billion a year. Clean water bodies are estimated to raise neighboring real estate values by

25 percent relative to those affected by pollution. Although data limitations prohibit estimates for Côte d'Ivoire, anecdotal evidence suggests that the findings are comparable; the highly visible and pungent pollution in the Cocody Lagoon area undoubtedly lowers the real estate, tourism, fishery, and public space potential of the area (Rabbi 2014).

Unreliable basic services and coordination failures amplify the costs of urban pollution in Côte d'Ivoire, imposing challenges on Global, Regional, and Domestic Connector cities. The main sources of air pollution affecting urban residents are emissions from transport, industrial processes, and household fuel consumption.[10] Urban water pollution is mainly associated with discharge of household and industrial waste, storm water runoff, and atmospheric deposition.[11] Although comprehensive estimates of water pollution costs in Sub-Saharan Africa are rare, a study in Uganda in 2002 estimated that contaminated water costs the economy US$22 million–$35 million every year (Moyini et al. 2002). Pollution from these sources is likely to grow with continued urbanization and economic growth. Infrastructure for basic services and improved coordination are vital to minimize all the costs of this pollution.

Unreliable Basic Services Increase the Social, Economic, and Environmental Pressures of Pollution from Urban Activities

The absence of household sanitation systems is a major contributor to urban pollution. Less than 40 percent of urban households in the country are connected to an appropriate sanitary system (World Bank, forthcoming). Wastewater collection infrastructure is also limited. In Abidjan, one-third of households discharge their used water directly into the street or gutter (UN-Habitat 2012), directly affecting the quality of urban water sources. An estimated two-thirds of urban pollutants in the Ébrié Lagoon are from domestic effluents (Scheren et al. 2004). The potential health costs of this pollution are high: diseases such as cholera and diarrhea can spread through water sources contaminated by human waste, and stagnant water can become a source of harmful bacteria and a breeding ground for malarial mosquitos. These problems are likely to be exacerbated by sea-level rise and climate change–related extreme weather because the sanitation infrastructure is ill equipped to cope with an influx of water (Hammer et al. 2011).

Facilities to treat industrial water pollution are scarce. Water sources in the urban areas of Abidjan and San-Pédro are particularly affected by industrial waste because most of the country's industrial activity is in these areas. The 98 enterprises in the port area of Abidjan generate 60 percent of Ivorian industrial production and employ 50,000 workers. Additional water pollution risks are associated with port activities because shipping involves highly toxic waste chemicals and fuels that are not permitted in other forms of transport and can be complex to manage. According to a 2009 United Nations Environment Programme (UNEP) evaluation, the Autonomous Port of Abidjan lacks operational facilities for residues and also lacks staff training in identifying and managing hazardous materials. The health consequences can be serious, as the high number of fatalities in Abidjan associated with illegal dumping in 2006 demonstrated.

Both household and industrial waste collection and disposal mechanisms lag far behind waste production, compromising urban air and water quality. Despite major improvements in the collection and disposal of waste in Abidjan in recent years, most cities do not have the capacity to manage waste. In 1998 it was estimated that coverage levels were less than 30 percent in cities outside Abidjan, and it is likely that this has declined as urban population growth[12] has outstripped coverage gains (World Bank, forthcoming). Nor do the country's landfills meet international standards, and the main Abidjan Akouédo landfill has operated for 30 years.

Inadequate solid waste collection has worrying implications for water and air pollution. Low levels of solid waste collection can result in high levels of waste discharging into water bodies in rainy seasons, and can also increase flooding risks by blocking sewage and storm water drainage systems. This can increase the health costs of flooding because it can bring human waste into direct contact with humans. Even when waste is collected, it can have a highly polluting effect if not disposed of properly. The decomposition of waste produces methane as well as dust and volatile compounds that can escape into the atmosphere if the process is mismanaged (IFC 2014).[13] And metals and chemicals from poorly managed landfills can infiltrate surface and ground water; research conducted in 2010 found lead and zinc in the land near the Akouédo landfill in Abidjan and evidence that iron, cadmium, copper, and chromium migrated downstream to the Ébrié Lagoon (Kouame et al. 2010).

Limited coverage of storm water drainage systems increases vulnerability to floods and undermines urban resilience. Urban flooding is a growing challenge in cities throughout Côte d'Ivoire, particularly in Abidjan where it is estimated that more than 20 people died in flood-related incidents in June 2014 alone. A 2006 United Nations Children's Fund (UNICEF) Multiple Indicator Cluster Survey (MICS) found that 4.4 percent of the population of Abidjan lives in areas prone to flooding and 7 percent on the border of the river. The rainwater drainage system has received little investment since the 1990s, and in some neighborhoods, such as Abobo in the north, only an estimated 11 percent of the land mass is serviced with rainwater drainage (UN-Habitat 2012). This has a knock-on effect on urban mobility because unchecked rainwater increases the speed with which road networks deteriorate.

Unreliable electricity service forces households and firms to rely on energy sources that expose urban residents to harmful pollutants. Air quality in cities is compromised by unreliable electricity for domestic and industrial energy, which increases reliance on diesel generators and biomass for home cooking. Firms across the country rely heavily on diesel generators that produce emissions potentially very harmful for people living close by. Statistics from the United States indicate that diesel generators emit 50 percent more nitrogen oxide (NOx) per megawatt-hour (MWh) than do gas-fired power plants.[14] Further, nearly 60 percent of Ivorian households rely on biomass for cooking and lighting fuel, exposing household members involved in cooking and domestic tasks to concentrated air pollution (figure 3.1). The health effects of this pollution are high: in 2010 household air pollution was responsible for 5 percent of the total disease burden, up from 2002's estimated 3.4 percent (WHO 2012).

Coordination Failures Increase the Costs of Pollution from Urban Mobility and Industrial Activity

Coordination is a key ingredient for the sustainable development and growth of cities. When transport investment decisions are not made in close coordination with land use planning, a city can grow into ways that set back its development and affect its livability for decades if not centuries. The physical structure of a city, once established, can remain in place for over 150 years (Hallegatte 2009). Coordinated land use and infrastructure planning involves bringing together decisions on infrastructure investments with the development of productive and other logistical infrastructure, as well as accompanying investments in connectivity with flood protection investments and efforts to enhance structural drainage to increase resilience. By bringing together the different pieces of the puzzle, coordination between land use management and connectivity has the potential for reducing pollution and enhancing a city's efficiency.

But, in Côte d'Ivoire, poor coordination has led to urban mobility trends that point to increasing reliance on environmentally inefficient forms of transport. Air pollution from transport is determined by factors such as mode of transport, quality of fuel used, and length of trip. Although fuel and vehicle age standards are in keeping with regional trends,[15] there has been a rapid growth in the number of cars on the roads—fivefold between the early 1990s and 2006 and potentially in line with per capita GDP growth of 8.6 percent between 2007 and 2013 (figure 3.2).[16]

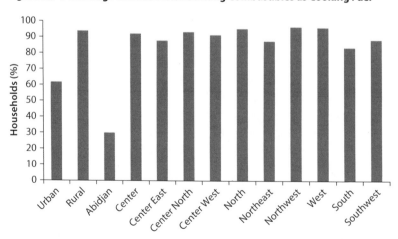

Figure 3.1 Percentage of Households Burning Combustibles as Cooking Fuel

Source: INS 2012.

Figure 3.2 Number of Cars and Emissions by Vehicle Mode

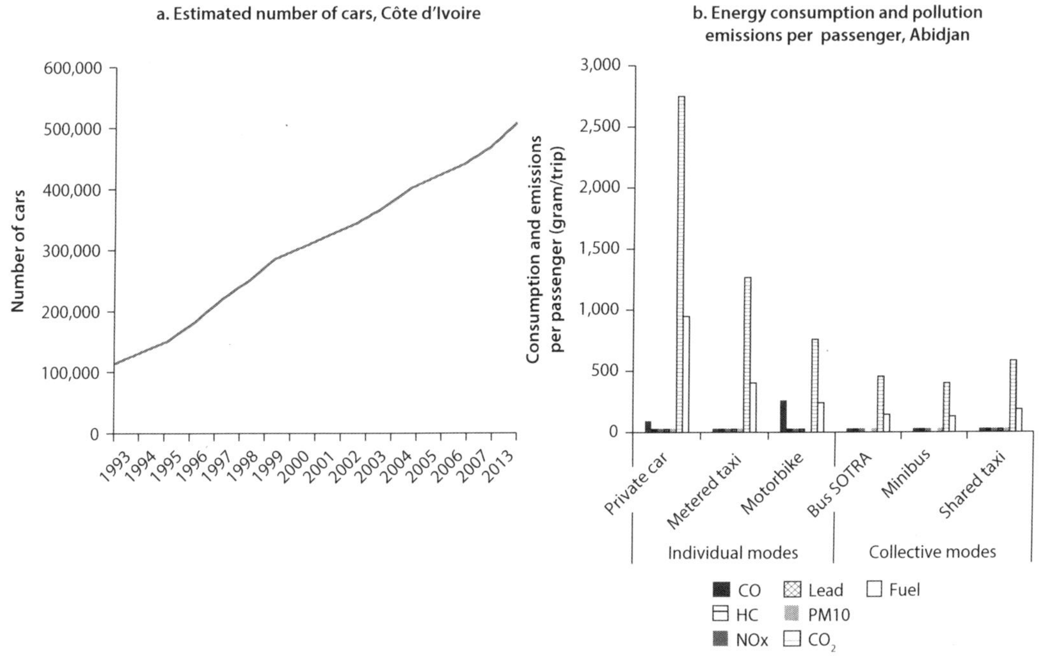

a. Estimated number of cars, Côte d'Ivoire

b. Energy consumption and pollution emissions per passenger, Abidjan

Source: World Bank calculations, based on World Development Indicators. 2006–13 estimates based on broad global estimate that vehicle ownership increases in line with per capita income.

Source: Certu 2002 as quoted in UN-Habitat 2012.
Note: CO = carbon monoxide; CO_2 = carbon dioxide; HC = hydrocarbon; NOx = nitrogen oxide; PM10 = Particulate matter under 10 micrometers in diameter; SOTRA = Société des Transports Abidjanais (Abidjan Transport Company).

The existing public transport system does not provide a safe, efficient, and affordable alternative to private vehicles. The only city in Côte d'Ivoire with dedicated public transport is Abidjan, where SOTRA (Société des Transports Abidjanais) is mandated to provide regulated bus services. However, given declining numbers of buses and quality of services, the share of motorized transport served by SOTRA has been overtaken by informal collective alternatives such as minibuses (*Gbakas*) and shared taxis (*wôrô wôrôs*) (figure 3.3). User criticisms, however, suggest that none of these options is adequate: they are either unreliable (SOTRA) or unsafe (minibuses and shared taxis—figure 3.4).

Inefficiency in truck freight transport is associated with high emissions that threaten Regional Connectors. As seen in chapter 2, large port cities and medium cities such as Bouaké are receiving growing levels of truck freight transport, which is likely to bring economic benefits to them and to the country; but the environmental impacts must be appreciated (figure 3.5). Freight transport in low- and middle-income countries uses mainly two- and three-axle rigid trucks that are often 15–20 years old (World Bank 2009a). These trucks consume more fuel than newer, more efficient trucks, and can be highly disruptive to traffic because they may break down often (OSAC 2014). It could be that the

Figure 3.3 Collective Transport Market Share, 1988–2002

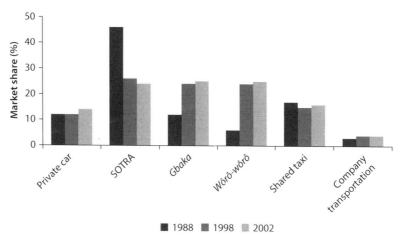

Source: World Bank estimates based on UN-Habitat 2012.
Note: SOTRA = Société des Transports Abidjanais (Abidjan Transport Company).

Figure 3.4 User Criticisms of Abidjan Public Transport, 2007

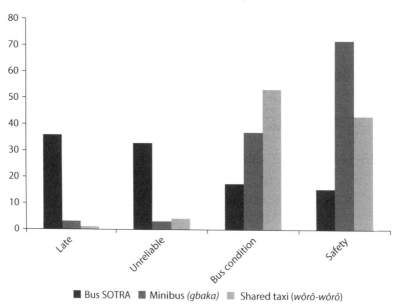

Source: Zoro-Fofana 2007, quoted in UN-Habitat 2012.
Note: "Bus condition" refers to quality of the environment in the bus. SOTRA = Société des Transports Abidjanais (Abidjan Transport Company).

environmental costs of this trade are greater than they would be if newer trucks or alternative modes of transport were used.

Transport infrastructure is vulnerable to damage from extreme weather events. Transport networks in cities across the world are facing disruption related to climate change impacts such as heat extremes and flooding, and one

Figure 3.5 Freight Emissions by Transport Mode

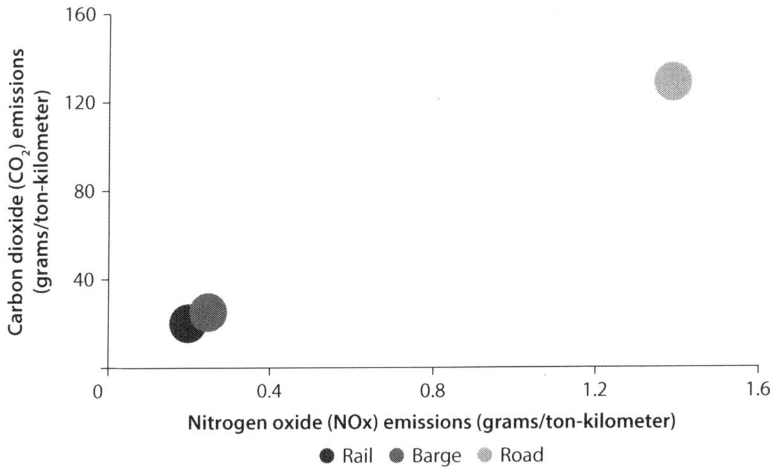

Source: Adapted from Kruk and Donner 2010.

of the areas where transit system agencies have started to react has been in developing plans for protecting infrastructure from coastal flooding (Hammer et al. 2011). In Côte d'Ivoire, coastal road infrastructure is particularly vulnerable. Planning of new roads should take into account the impact of location: placing the roads at a larger distance from the coast could safeguard the infrastructure and support a shift from axial development of settlements along the coast, thereby promoting more resilient urban development (UEMOA 2010). Indeed, the International Union for the Conservation of Nature's analysis of risks of coastal erosion notes that most risk situations in West Africa "are largely due to the fact that in the past, coastal risks have not been taken into account for the location and configuration of human developments and settlements" (UEMOA 2010).

Without improved oversight of industrial pollution, it is likely that urban air quality will continue to decline. Although there is no current information on the spatial distribution of industrial air pollution throughout the country, data from before the crises show that industrial air pollution was highly concentrated around major urban centers.[17] This trend will likely have intensified as industrial output picks up. But it is not only large industry that affects air quality. Small industries can be very polluting, too: light industry is associated globally with respiratory complications from air pollution. Thus medium cities such as Bouaké, which are home to light industry and manufacturing such as tobacco, cashew nuts, alcohol, and textiles, may face the high health costs linked to local air pollution.

The deterioration of green spaces in and around cities contributes to increased exposure to flooding and landslide risks. Current planning regulations specify a minimum of 5 percent green or public space in each of the country's 197 municipalities. But anecdotal evidence suggests a lack of coordination in maintaining and preserving green spaces, leading to a decline in their quantity and quality in urban areas. Although Abidjan has two national parks, two botanical gardens, and several well-known squares and public gardens such as Briand and Bressoles in Plateau, these spaces are increasingly encroached on by urban development or are becoming rundown. The amount of green spaces (public or private) varies widely across municipalities (Djibril et al. 2012).

Urban green spaces are important for urban resilience because they can help reduce pollution, storm water runoff, and heat-island effects. They filter pollutants and dust from the air and phosphorus from the water. By some estimates, one tree can absorb as much as 48 pounds of carbon dioxide per year and supply oxygen for two people.[18] Green areas can also help contain flooding—a 5 percent increase in tree cover leads to a 2 percent decrease in storm water runoff (Wolf 2006). They also have a positive impact on urban heat-island effects. According to the Forest Service of the U.S. Department of Agriculture, well-placed trees can reduce air-conditioning needs in buildings by 30 percent. The urgency of the need to preserve these green spaces is likely to be particularly pronounced for coastal cities such as Abidjan and San-Pédro, which are highly vulnerable to climate change–related flooding (box 3.2).

Green areas offer social and health benefits. Well-lit public spaces are thought to improve social interaction in a city, creating inclusive spaces vital to cultural life. Whereas dilapidated public areas can become the focus of crime and antisocial activity, when well kept and safe they are linked to the inclusion of women and minority groups in city life and to the general perception of well-being. A robust literature also links green areas to improved physical and mental health; Roger Ulrich's 1984 study found that hospital patients with a view of green spaces took fewer painkillers and had a shorter recovery time than those who did not (Ulrich 1984). (And, as discussed earlier, factors affecting human health also have knock-on effects for productivity and economic competitiveness.)

Unregulated urban expansion on forestland can weaken urban resilience. Côte d'Ivoire is home to rainforests, wetlands, and other fragile natural habitats, including eight national parks and five reserves. Although the main causes of deforestation are the conversion of forestland to agriculture and the reliance on wood for energy, some of the country's key urban centers are in environmentally diverse and fragile ecosystems. Urban expansion and cultivation of cash crops threaten the Western Guinean lowland forest and the vegetation near the Sassandra River in the southwest. Both areas are home to distinctive flora and fauna, including many endemic species and unique plant associations (IFPRI). Of the country's 6.4 million hectares of forest, 4.2 million are considered "highly degraded."[19] The costs of this deforestation likely outweigh the benefits gained by the industries that conducted the logging. Estimates from Kenya indicate that economic losses there totaled as much as US$64 million in 2010, considerably more than the benefits to the industries from this deforestation (UNEP 2013). More generally, Côte d'Ivoire is likely to pay a very heavy economic, social, and environmental price for climate change (box 3.1).

Box 3.1 Climate Change and Cities in Developing Countries

Climate change is a growing threat to cities all over the world, and cities in developing countries are particularly vulnerable. As the World Bank's *Turn Down the Heat* report argues, the world is on a path to warming of 4°C by the end of the century, and this increase will have devastating impacts on agriculture, water resources, ecosystems, and human health (World Bank 2013b). Cities across the world are likely to be increasingly affected by extreme weather events, water scarcity, air pollution, and other climate change–related effects. Developing-country cities are particularly vulnerable to the effects of climate change because their resilience and adaptive capacity are low (Hammer et al. 2011; OECD 2012). In 2011 the African Development Bank estimated that adaptation costs will be in the region of US$20 billion–$30 billion above the existing infrastructure and service spending deficit in the region.

Climate change is associated with serious economic, social, and environmental costs in Côte d'Ivoire (GoCI 2010). Over the last three decades rainfall has declined by about 20 percent, and the climate is marked by greater rainfall variability and longer dry seasons. These changes are likely to hurt agricultural production, which accounts for 27 percent of GDP, two-thirds of jobs, and 20 percent of exports (World Bank, forthcoming). Overall temperatures are thought to have risen by 1°C over the last 25 years, and biodiversity loss is apparent in forest and water ecosystems, particularly in protected areas such as the Comoe, Marahoue, and Tai National Parks, as well as the Abokouamekro Game Reserve (World Bank, forthcoming).

There is a pressing need to build resilience to sea-level rise and coastal erosion. Two-thirds of the country's coast is exposed to erosion, with records showing loss of land of 1 to 2 meters a year but sometimes up to 20 meters. The coastal area is home to the major cities of Abidjan and San-Pédro, where a large portion of the country's population and economic activity are located. Sweeping erosion has been recorded off Abidjan harbor, which is likely to increase exposure. Economic vulnerability on this metric is measured by the anticipated losses as a share of a city's wealth, taking into account the exposure of assets and population as well as infrastructure-based adaptation. It could make Abidjan one of the world's five most vulnerable cities to sea-level rise (Hallegatte et al. 2013; OECD 2013).

Adaptation is needed to reduce these risks. Measures should combine upgrading protection, managing subsidence, planning land use to direct new development from floodplains, setting up flood-warning and evacuation systems, and selectively relocating away from highly vulnerable areas (Hammer et al. 2010). It is also possible to develop waterfront reinforcement to protect key infrastructure. In Venice (Italy), for example, massive infrastructure protects buildings but is costly (€4.3 billion) and must generally be very carefully designed to ensure it does not itself lead to ecological resource destruction and so increase risks over the longer run (Hammer et al. 2011; Nicholls et al. 2008).

Sources: Hammer et al. 2011; Nicholls et al., 2008; OECD 2010; World Bank, forthcoming.

A Green Toolbox: Instruments for Decision Makers

Policy tools can help decision makers minimize environmental costs and amplify social and economic gains of urbanization. This section draws on real-world examples in cities around the world of institutional frameworks or infrastructure investments that have helped reduce the costs of urban pollution and increased urban resilience. It highlights how these initiatives can align with policy priorities for Global, Regional, and Domestic Connector cities in Côte d'Ivoire.

Building a Data Collection and Dissemination Platform

Improved monitoring of environmental costs of decisions made by government, firms, and households is the first step. As highlighted throughout this chapter, the environmental costs of urban activities are poorly appreciated by those who generate externalities and those affected by them. Improved environmental monitoring is needed to inform better decision making, in order to provide greater information about current costs and potential future challenges, and to gather evidence about the effectiveness of policies designed to improve the urban environment. Policy priorities include improving the reliability of collection and dissemination of existing data initiatives, such as monitoring water quality by the Centre Ivoirien Antipollution (CIAPOL), whose activities were partly revived in 2014 after more than 15 years of inactivity due to financing constraints related to the conflict. Priorities also cover establishing new data collection for unmeasured factors.

The national government could support cities' participation in emerging data-collection efforts led by other cities around the world. As the World Council on City Data (WCCD) highlights, there may be advantages to aligning data collection with international indicators, including that participation creates opportunities for cross-city learning and knowledge exchanges with other cities on cost-effective policy. There may also be other benefits: WCCD argues that participating in a transparent and independently verified international data-collection initiative can improve a city's investment attractiveness and can become a means for cities to leverage funding.[20] One example is WCCD's ISO 37120 "Sustainable Development of Communities: Indicators for City Services and Quality of Life."[21] This set of 100 standardized indicators and data collection methodologies was developed by cities, for cities, and offers flexibility, so that it is up to each participating city to set targets according to its own priorities.

Improved data can create new, formal approaches to decision making in natural resource management and public investment. International experience suggests that the introduction of procedures for reviewing environmental costs into the evaluation of public procurement processes can yield solid, green dividends (box 3.2). Public procurement accounts for about 25–30 percent of GDP in developing countries (OECD 2012), a large enough amount that,

Box 3.2 Green Accounting

The management of national economies requires improved understanding of the value of natural resources and associated ecosystem services. As Nobel Laureate Joseph Stiglitz has emphasized, although a private company is judged by its income statement and balance sheet, most countries know very little about their national balance sheet because they focus on measuring GDP, which is only the income statement. Natural resource accounting and ecosystem service accounting seek to address this imbalance by building understanding of a country's natural assets into public policy decision making.

Under the *Strategic Plan for Biodiversity 2011–2020*, the United Nations has supported initiatives to improve and standardize measurement and accounting of ecosystem services, such as Satellite Economic and Environmental Accounts (SEEA). The World Bank's WAVE project also seeks to support developing countries in formulating and implementing work plans to compile accounts for natural resources such as forests, water, and minerals (in keeping with the SEEA central framework).

However, no single approach is used for valuing natural resources and ecosystem services. There are a variety of approaches, each of which has its strengths and weaknesses. Policy makers therefore use a mix of qualitative, quantitative, and monetary assessments to identify the benefits of environmental interventions. These assessments are by their nature highly context specific: the costs and benefits of measures to protect or conserve natural assets, and the distribution of these costs and benefits across different groups, are likely to vary considerably from one place to another.

For instance, although the benefits of protecting tropical forests' ecosystems often out-weigh the costs, there are questions about how best to do so and about how to ensure that the costs and benefits of the intervention are evenly distributed. There are important challenges in ensuring that people who live in areas placed under conservation or protection also share in the benefits of these measures. One example is Payment for Environmental Services, in Mexico, where a portion of water charges is legally allocated to public payments to landowners in exchange for forgoing certain activities on their land (TEEB 2010).

Sources: Brink et al. 2012; Bromhead, 2012; TEEB 2010; U.S. EPA; WAVE website.

if directed toward greener products and projects, it could help build a market for green goods.

Dissemination of environmental information can help support behavior shifts among households and firms. Studies from around the world suggest that consumers are often willing to incorporate environmental considerations into their consumption decisions. Similarly, publicizing firms' environmental practices can sometimes be enough to change their production practices because consumers exert pressure on firms to reduce their environmental footprint. Through an initiative known as PROPER, Indonesian companies were publicly assigned a color ranking based on their environmental performance. This straightforward system provided new information to the consumer on how companies were adhering to national and international standards, and is credited with having improved sustainability practices among companies through social pressure (Zinnes 2009). But firms are unlikely to release this kind of information voluntarily. For this system to work, governments must capitalize on their unique capacity to oblige firms to report their practices (Kahn 2013).

Improved dissemination of risk information can help "future-proof" development. Urban flooding increasingly places lives and livelihoods at risk in Côte d'Ivoire. The design of appropriate flood risk reduction measures such as development planning, forecasting, and early warning systems requires reliable data: information on the type, source, and probability of current urban flooding risks to identify patterns and priorities (Jha, Bloch, and Lamond 2012). Some of these data are already collected in Côte d'Ivoire: the National Office of Civil Protection (l'Office National de la Protection Civile [ONPC]), municipalities, and even some universities are engaged in recording natural risks in cities. Participation in regional watch keeping and vigilance direction initiatives under the West African Coastal Observatory (WACO) shoreline monitoring program will also lead to improved ability to identify and anticipate risks related to coastal flooding (UEMOA 2010).

Clarifying responsibility and improving the quality of comprehensive collection, use, and dissemination of flood-risk information could help cities deal with existing risks and prepare for future challenges. For example, improved dissemination of risk information in the form of comprehensive risk maps can help raise awareness among the public and facilitate prompt evacuation from at-risk areas (World Bank Institute 2012). Dissemination of risk maps can also help inform decisions about future development planning and help avoid unnecessary costs associated with information failures in the construction of new houses or commercial activity in risk areas.

Information can be used to create economy-enhancing regulations and standards. A government has the authority to impose environmental standards in sectors that directly affect the environmental costs of urban activities. When well designed, environmental standards can provide incentives to change behavior. By increasing the costs of pollution, such change can reduce environmental degradation and depletion (World Bank 2012a). The government can influence the "price" of pollution through tools such as regulation, minimum standards enforcement, and positive or negative financial incentives such as new taxes or tax breaks. The introduction of fuel and vehicle standards, for example, has been credited with significantly reducing black carbon emissions in many countries worldwide (World Bank 2014).

Effective environmental standards weigh up trade-offs and are supported by credible enforcement capacity. Accurately predicting the economic costs associated with introducing environmental standards can be difficult. Firms may respond to increased production costs from pollution regulations by reducing production and cutting jobs, or by relying more on labor-intensive jobs and increasing employment. Analysis of four different industry sectors in the United States found that the impact of regulation was specific to each industry (World Bank 2012a). Nor should the costs of enforcing compliance be underestimated.

Improving the Quality and Coverage of Basic Services

There is a need to ensure that urban areas receive basic service coverage. As outlined above, lack of sewage and wastewater infrastructure has strong negative impacts on the urban environment and increases urban vulnerability to natural disasters such as flooding. Cities of all sizes in the urban system need to prioritize investment in basic services. For Domestic Connector cities, which are at early stages of development in which foundational infrastructure decisions will determine future growth, this means avoiding the mistakes of larger cities by laying the foundations for greener growth.

It is efficient to establish rights-of-way for future infrastructure investment. International experience suggests that simply establishing rights-of-way for *future* infrastructure investment can yield long-term economic and environmental savings, because acquiring rights-of-way is costly and time consuming once development has already taken place (World Bank 2013a). The famous New York street grid plan, for example, was conceived in the early nineteenth century. Many of the roads were not built until much later, but the land was reserved in advance, minimizing the costs of putting in the roads later. This approach has been used in cities as far apart as Buenos Aires and Barcelona (World Bank and AusAID 2015).

New technological solutions are emerging that can bring environmental benefits and cost savings in delivering basic services. Cities in Côte d'Ivoire may be able to take advantage of these innovations to avoid costly traditional approaches used by most advanced industrial countries. This could be an opportunity to "leap frog" the old-fashioned approaches straight to new solutions (OECD 2012). For example, by extending the grid, new technology provides cleaner and cheaper ways of delivering power to hard-to-reach areas, as shown by the use of photovoltaic sources in the One Million Solar Streetlight Project, conducted by the German Development Agency (Deutsche Gesellschaft für Internationale Zusammenarbeit [GIZ]) and Laptrust, the Kenyan government workers' pension scheme.[22]

In Côte d'Ivoire's Regional and Global Connector cities—where settlements have already taken root without basic services—upgrading will be a priority. Abidjan has an estimated 144 precarious settlements characterized by insecurity of tenure, irregular settlement patterns, poor building materials, and lack of basic services. Improving basic services there could benefit the city as a whole, despite multiple challenges. For example, an evaluation of recent efforts to expand access to sanitation in Abidjan, Bouaké, and other selected cities estimated that the interventions might have resulted in annual health expenditure

Box 3.3 Urban Upgrading in São Bernardo do Campo, Brazil: Integrated, Coordinated, and Evidence Based, with Comprehensive Resettlement Policies

The Metropolitan Region of São Paulo is home to close to 20 million inhabitants and accounts for almost 20 percent of the country's GDP. But its water resources are strained: soaring population growth, unplanned and unserviced land use, and rapid industrial development have all polluted drinking-water reservoirs and contributed to water scarcity and flood vulnerability.

The city of São Bernardo do Campo is one of 39 municipalities in the region. On the edge of the Billings reservoir, it protects the water resources for the entire urban area. Billings is one of the three main watersheds in the Mananciais water system, which provides 70 percent of the region's drinking water.

One-third of São Bernardo's 1 million inhabitants live in one of the 261 precarious and informal settlements. At least 65 settlements are in zones of high exposure to natural risks such as landslides and flooding. And, given that 151 of these settlements are in environmentally fragile areas of the Mananciais, these areas also contribute heavily to water pollution through storm water runoff and untreated sewage.

In response to these challenges, the Municipality of São Bernardo—with support from the São Paulo Water Utility SABESP, the national government, and the World Bank—developed a comprehensive approach to upgrade the settlements. The objective was to formalize and improve living conditions, remove households from at-risk environments, and reduce water pollution in the Billings reservoir.

The approach is interesting for several reasons. First, it is highly integrated—the municipality opted to address multiple dimensions of deprivation and environmental degradation together. Interventions were designed to integrate housing policies, transport interventions, and basic services provision. Green public spaces along the water's edge were included in the design in order to grant some flood protection, to filter water runoff, and to offer space for community and recreational activities. This effort required coordination among municipal departments, the state utility company, and state entities responsible for environmental protection.

Second, it is highly coordinated. Infrastructure investments were combined with information campaigns on environmental practices and on behavior change in areas such as waste disposal, water use, and sanitation to ensure long-term impact.

Third, its design is evidence based. The project is well aligned with a wider initiative of SABESP to improve data collection and monitoring on water quality in Billings, and the municipality conducted extensive mapping and assessment of infrastructure and housing material to be able to prioritize interventions. (See http://sihisb.saobernardo.sp.gov.br.)

Fourth, Brazilian law since 2013 requires comprehensive resettlement policies to be integrated with the concept and planning stages of projects receiving federal government funds. An assessment must evaluate alternatives to displacement before the project begins and must provide guiding principles to identify under which circumstances the decision to involuntarily relocate households or economic activities from a target area can be considered. If relocation is inevitable, a resettlement plan must be drafted and measures to compensate the affected people must be approved by Brazil's Ministry of Cities.

Sources: Cities Alliance 2013; World Bank 2012c, 2013c.

savings per project beneficiary of US$16 (with a total saving of US$3.2 million for the 200,000 beneficiaries).[23] Examples from across the world indicate that these benefits can be further leveraged when projects are designed around an integrated approach (box 3.3).

All cities need to extend solid waste collection. A city cannot function properly without good, solid waste management (IFC 2014). Collection in Côte d'Ivoire is the responsibility of a national agency—Agence Nationale de Salubrité Urbaine (ANASUR)—rather than of the municipal governments. Collection rates in cities outside Abidjan are very low. Establishing well-financed systems in all cities is a priority, and they should be integrated with urban planning (see next section, "Integrated Planning"). As noted earlier, 40 percent of houses in Abidjan are inaccessible to collection trucks and must therefore be serviced by "precollectors."

Solid waste collection in Abidjan has picked up over the past few years, but with room for further gains. Collection rates are estimated at about 70 percent, markedly better than in 2009 when the city had many informal dump sites (PPIAF 2012). This improvement is partly attributed to reforms that adjusted payment for services from remuneration for removing waste *from* a municipality to payment for delivering waste *to* the Akouédo landfill. But there is considerable room for improvement. In addition to challenges in waste disposal in the absence of sanitary landfills (above), waste quantities could be made more manageable with improved source separation, and efficiency in the collection system could be improved with the introduction of transfer stations. Industrial waste management in particular needs to be upgraded.

Needs assessments could support better-informed solid waste management investment and help ensure that decision making today anticipates the needs of tomorrow. Government officials frequently find it hard to reach informed decisions on how to improve their local solid waste management system. As cities grow, challenges will grow, placing new strains on already struggling systems. Such challenges are typically associated with lack of information and technical expertise, which can lead to inappropriate solutions. Many cities in developing countries adopt expensive, hard-to-maintain waste management practices from industrialized countries (Coffey and Coad 2010; Zurbrügg 2003). A city's solutions should take account of local infrastructure and resources, considering factors such as inaccessible roads (Henry, Yongsheng, and Jun 2006) and local technical skills (Hazra and Goel 2009), as well as the flexibility to scale up operations as needs grow. Thus, in Côte d'Ivoire solid waste priorities differ between Global, Regional, and Domestic Connector cities.

Integrated Planning

In large cities, integrated transport planning could reduce traffic congestion, improve air quality, and promote economic efficiency. It can improve the economic and environmental efficiency of daily commuting because individual mobility decisions can have strong negative externalities. Integrated mobility planning can help create a framework of incentives that promotes more sustainable behavior. Integrated planning involves looking toward the future: by integrating information about environmental cost and benefits into short-term decision making, it can yield important benefits to ensure more sustainable development over the longer term.

Affordable, efficient, and safe urban mobility should be planned around mobility needs. Data are lacking on commuting times, modes, and patterns in Ivorian cities. Improved understanding of these movements will be vital to minimize the environmental and social costs of daily commutes and will improve economic efficiency in urban areas by better connecting workers to firms. This is a high priority for Global Connector cities, where long commutes, traffic congestion, and air pollution are a strain on livability. Improved planning for urban mobility should integrate multiple considerations to help support more efficient, affordable, and environmentally sustainable commuting. With support from the Japan International Cooperation Agency (JICA), the government is taking steps to integrate understanding of mobility needs into its transport planning. International case studies highlight the importance of ensuring that this information is also integrated into land use planning and public transport management.

Initiatives are under discussion to combine information dissemination, standards, and financial incentives to change behavior in the trucking sector. The government expressed commitment to reforming the freight transport sector and, with the support of the World Bank, is exploring a series of activities that would reform the trucking industry with the objective of improving its competitiveness. Many of the initiatives under discussion may also be expected to reduce the environmental footprint of the industry. Modernizations such as containerization, storage reforms, improved management methods, and more stringent driving requirements and incentives to upgrade the truck fleet could all improve efficiency and so reduce associated environmental harm.

Integrated planning is needed to ensure that long-term environmental costs are better incorporated with current development decisions to help "future-proof" development. This will help manage tensions between competing uses of natural resources and increase resilience to natural disasters. The economies of Côte d'Ivoire's Regional Connector cities are based in the exploitation of natural resources (including agriculture) and their transport. Man and San-Pédro are hubs for agricultural markets in the west and south of the country and important centers for the exploitation of iron, nickel, and fossil fuels[24] and are also hubs for international trade (from Man toward Guinea and Liberia, as well as through the port of San-Pédro). These activities yield important economic and social benefits, but they also result in high costs in the form of biodiversity degradation and deforestation because these cities are in areas of very rare and fragile ecosystems. In the case of Abidjan and San-Pédro, the destruction of mangrove ecosystems increases vulnerability to sea-level rise (box 3.4). Indeed, conservation of these areas is one of the leading environmental priorities for the country (World Bank, forthcoming).

Box 3.4 Shoring Up Coastal Cities

Improving management of coastal risks is a central recommendation of the International Union for the Conservation of Nature's report of coastal erosion in West Africa. The key principles advocated include the following:

- Reducing exposure to contingencies. This is a principle that needs to be incorporated into planning of new areas, which should be developed away from coastal areas, and into understanding the risks faced by existing settlements. Natural defenses should be protected and can even be introduced as "buffers" between the shore and human settlements. These must be designed in light of local needs: the necessary width of the buffer will vary from one place to another, reflecting location of people and goods and the dynamics of the coastal ecosystem in that area.
- Protecting natural morphological and plant formation in coastal areas because they play an important role in coastal sediment dynamics. The report stresses that any new development of heavy infrastructure along the coast of Côte d'Ivoire will create new needs in terms of coastal management because the infrastructure can place new pressure on the coastal ecosystem and may require coordinated protection. These considerations should be given a prominent and central consideration, for example, in plans to extend the port of San-Pédro.
- Protecting segments of coast where defenses are most needed, bearing in mind the local, national, and subregional impacts that defenses can have given the interdependence of water systems.
- Ensuring that land use planning incorporates understanding of coastal dynamics, such as the important role that mangroves play in safeguarding coastal areas from flooding. Wetlands provide ecological services and are important resources for local livelihoods such as fishing.

The regional report identifies seven high- and very-high-risk areas in Côte d'Ivoire: Grand Lahou, Port-Bouet, Port-Bouet East, Grand-Bassam, Grand-Bassam West Coast, Bassam Estuary right bank, and the Abidjan East peri-urban area. These are areas with considerable risks to human lives, industrial output, and tourism infrastructure from coastal erosion and sea-level rise. The report highlights the need to ensure that risks are better incorporated into new urban development on the beachfronts of these areas (particularly Port Bouet, Port Bouet East, and Abidjan East), provision of resilient basic service and transport infrastructure (Abidjan East), development of risk plans and dissemination of evacuation and disaster preparedness among at risk populations (Port-Bouet and Abidjan East), and the development of a detailed flood-submersion risk prevention plan (Grand-Bassam and Bassam Estuary right bank).

Source: UEMOA 2010.

Box 3.5 Integrating Port and Regional Development Planning with Coastal Management: The Case of Colombia's Caribbean Coast

The cities of Cartagena, Barranquilla, and Santa Marta are on the northern Caribbean coast of Colombia. These three ports all play an important role in the national economy: they receive 69 percent of the country's imports and exports (tons) and are each important centers of tourism. The three cities share strong growth potential; however, they also face serious shared environmental threats. The coastal area is highly exposed to coastal flooding, and unbridled economic growth and urban expansion threaten the fragile and unique ecosystems in the area that include coastal and freshwater ecosystems, mountains, and tropical rainforest.

The government acknowledges the benefits of regional planning and has undertaken reforms in recent years to help address obstacles to increased coordination in infrastructure projects. The government has also set up a dedicated fund to finance regional infrastructure, through the Systema General de Regalias. These Regalias are royalties and taxes that the government applies to the extraction of natural resources, such as mining activities. The creation of this Regalias fund represents an effort to ensure that the benefits of extracting natural resources in Colombia will contribute to sustainable long-term development of the country and that these benefits will be shared equitably across the nation. The founding principles of the fund include emphasis on the objective of promoting cooperation between local government bodies and stimulating regional competitiveness and development.

Since 2012, more than 200 project proposals have been received, approved, and in some cases initiated in the coastal Caribbean region. These projects include environmental recuperation initiatives focused on water quality improvements, the introduction of sustainable forestry practices, and recuperation of beaches. Infrastructure projects to date have ranged from basic sanitation systems and new public parks to larger transport infrastructure projects such as support for preparing a project to introduce railroad access to the port of Barranquilla. In Cartagena, linear parks and boardwalks along the urban seafront are a visual manifestation of the power of green infrastructure to combine social, economic, and environmental gains: they are public spaces that support the city's tourism potential while providing some protection from sea-level rise as part of an integrated coastal management plan.

This integrated and participatory regional planning framework has several potential advantages. The first is efficiency: planning in light of regional economic and resilience needs is likely to yield economies of scale and avoid wasteful duplication in infrastructure investment. The second is more effective inclusion of social and environmental costs and benefits, achieved by bringing together national and local stakeholders from different sectors and interests in the planning process. The third is oversight and accountability, through clear and transparent allocation of roles, responsibilities, and flow of funds for projects once they are approved.

Source: Samad, Lozano-Gracia, and Panman 2012.

Examples from around the world highlight the importance of better-integrated infrastructure planning. They show that more integrated approaches to infrastructure planning can help balance the short-term benefits of resource extraction with long-term costs of biodiversity loss, as well as help build resistance to natural disasters. An interesting example is the case of Colombia, where regional infrastructure to protect fragile ecosystems has been financed through royalties from natural resource extraction (box 3.5).

Environmental conservation can also promote economic growth and create jobs. In addition to long-run advantages to protecting biodiversity, environmental conservation can also secure benefits in the short term. In 2000, 7 of the 13 protected areas in Côte d'Ivoire received an average of 5,540 foreign visitors yearly, the majority of which were European, and generated revenues of around CFAF 10 billion (World Bank, forthcoming). The country has considerable tourism potential, which when realized can be a tool for peace building and poverty alleviation, as The Gambia illustrates (Christie et al. 2013). Ecotourism is the fastest-growing area of the tourism industry (TEEB 2010) and important for growth in green jobs (OECD 2012). In South Africa, for example, about 486,000 jobs have been created through environmental rehabilitation programs since 1995 (UNEP 2013).

Integrated planning can also improve the efficiency of industrial production, reducing the environmental costs and supporting productivity gains through industrial zones. There are many potential competitiveness and productivity gains from industrial zones or estates. But there can be significant efficiency gains in environmental infrastructure, such as building wastewater treatment facilities that can be shared by all industry within an estate, removing industry from downtown locations where a large number of residents are directly exposed to pollutants, and making it easier for environmental regulators to oversee industrial activity and ensure compliance with standards.

Where the selection of firms included within the estate allows, there is potential for environmental and economic gains through synergies in waste management. Perhaps the most famous example is that of the Kalundborg estate in Denmark: it includes a coal-fired power plant that exchanges waste products with other industrial facilities in the industrial estate, which are able to use them as inputs into their productive activity. Thus, fly ash from the plant is used in the neighboring cement factory, the steam produced is used by a pharmaceutical plant, recovered heat from coal production is used by fish-farming facilities, and sludge is recycled as an input in the fertilizer factory (World Bank 2012b). Although the Kalundborg waste-sharing approach appears to have developed organically, there have been successful attempts to encourage this kind of exchange in ecoindustrial estates in China (Dalian Industrial Estate) and India (Naroda Industrial Estate).

Annex 3A: Carbon Dioxide Emissions in Côte d'Ivoire

Figure 3A.1: Carbon Dioxide Emissions, by Sector and Total

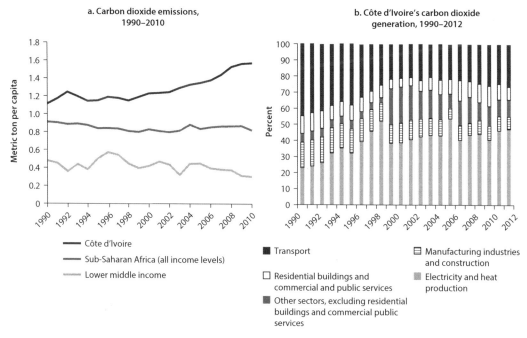

a. Carbon dioxide emissions, 1990–2010

b. Côte d'Ivoire's carbon dioxide generation, 1990–2012

— Côte d'Ivoire
— Sub-Saharan Africa (all income levels)
— Lower middle income

■ Transport

☐ Residential buildings and commercial and public services

■ Other sectors, excluding residential buildings and commercial public services

☐ Manufacturing industries and construction

▨ Electricity and heat production

Source: World Development Indicators 2014.

Notes

1. A Monash University study on the "Effects of Enhancing Land Use" found that a 30 percent increase in land use density and associated decrease in distances to public transport would result in about a 25 percent increase in physical activity and a 1–5 percent reduction in exposure to particulate matter in London and New York. In contrast, in highly polluted cities such as Delhi and Beijing, greater physical activity could actually *increase* health challenges; the associated reductions in air pollution would not compensate for increased exposure to particulate matter. Targeted air-quality improvements, in this case, may prove more effective for greening.

2. These fragile mangrove ecosystems are extremely important fish breeding areas and are home to more than 430 rare plant species, forest elephants, pigmy hippos, chimpanzees, turtles, and other wildlife (World Bank CEA forthcoming).

3. Internal renewable freshwater has declined from 5100 cubic meters per capita in 1990 to 3963 in 2004 (WDI). There are many sources of water pollution, including natural sources and agricultural practices such as the use of pesticides and fertilizers in cash crops (Pare and Bonzi-Coulibaly 2013).

4. Biodiversity is defined by the 1992 Convention on Biological Diversity as "the variability among living organisms from all sources including, terrestrial, marine and other aquatic ecosystems and the ecological complexes of which they are part; this includes

diversity within species, between species and of ecosystems." Full text of the accord is available at https://www.cbd.int/doc/legal/cbd-en.pdf.

5. Ecosystem services can be defined as flows of value to human societies resulting from the state and quantity of natural capital. The Millennium Ecosystem Assessment identifies four categories of ecosystem services that are each underpinned by biodiversity: provisioning services, such as wild foods, crops, freshwater, and plant-derived medicines; regulating services, which include disaster protection, carbon storage, water cycling, and filtering of pollutants; cultural services, such as recreation, spiritual and aesthetic values, and education; and supporting services in the form of soil formation and nutrient cycling (TEEB 2010).

6. TEEB case: Wetlands reduce infrastructure damage, Lao PDR.

7. As measured by the Global Burden of Disease Study, which is a collaborative project of nearly 500 researchers in 50 countries led by the Institute for Health Metrics and Evaluation at the University of Washington.

8. Disability-adjusted life years (DALYs) combine the years of life lost due to disability with the years of life lost due to death attributed to specific causes.

9. Research by the OECD using a projection model (IMACLIM) suggests that long-run improvements in environmental quality can strengthen the economic attractiveness and thus the competitiveness of cities (Hammer et al. 2011).

10. At the national level the two largest contributors to air pollution are electricity generation and transport. In contrast to other low- and middle-income countries, Côte d'Ivoire has not experienced a sharp increase in carbon dioxide emissions over the last 15 years (annex 3A). This may reflect effects of disruptions in industrial and manufacturing output related to the recession of the late 1990s and military and political crises of the early 2000s. Emissions may climb steeply as the economy rebounds.

11. For example, analysis of pollution loads in 2000 estimated that, of the 33 kilotons of annual nitrogen loads in the Ebrié Lagoon, 45 percent came from urban sources, 42 percent from water runoff, and 13 percent from atmospheric deposits. Measures were similar for the 2.5 kilotons of phosphorous loads: 39 percent urban, 48 percent runoff, and 13 percent atmospheric (Scheren et al. 2004).

12. Solid waste generation can be expected to grow as urban areas expand and as Côte d'Ivoire's income rises, because higher-income and urban residents generate more waste. Urban waste generation in Africa averages 0.65 kg per capita per day, or 169,119 tons. By 2050 this will have increased to 0.85 kg per capita per day, or 441,840 tons (Hoornweg and Bhada-Tata 2012).

13. See also "Nutrient Pollution: The Effects," from the U.S. Environmental Protection Agency website (accessed September 9, 2014), http://www2.epa.gov/nutrientpollution /effect-economy.

14. A typical standby diesel generator produces 25–30 pounds of nitrogen oxide (NOx) per megawatt-hour of power generated, 50–60 times the NOx pollution produced per megawatt-hour by the typical mix of California gas-fired power plants. The California Air Resources Board estimates that operation of an uncontrolled 1 megawatt diesel engine for only 250 hours per year would result in a 50 percent increase in cancer risk to residents within one city block. http://www.sbcapcd.org/generators .htm.

15. Although diesel sulfur specifications allow for higher than average emissions, gasoline (petrol) sulfur specifications are comparatively strong (maximum of 150 parts

per million). The country does, however, lag behind regional leaders Nigeria and South Africa in adopting Euro 2 Vehicles emission standards (UNEP 2014).

16. GDP per capita (constant 2005 $) increased from 933.63 in 2007 to 1,014.40 in 2013, or 8.6 percent (WDI). Internationally, a 10 percent increase in per capita GDP is associated with a 10 percent increase in vehicle ownership (Kahn 2013).

17. Data are from the Emissions Database for Global Atmospheric Research 3.2 (EDGAR), http://themasites.pbl.nl/tridion/en/themasites/edgar/documentation /citation/index-2.html.

18. Data from North Carolina State University's "Tree Facts," http://www.ncsu.edu/project /treesofstrength/treefact.htm.

19. Data are from the REEGLE page "Ivory Coast Country Profile (2012)," (accessed March 15, 2016), http://www.reegle.info/policy-and-regulatory-overviews/CI.

20. WCCD, online, http://www.dataforcities.org/wccd/.

21. The indicators are established around 20 themes that integrate dimensions of sustainable development, grouped under (i) city services indicators: education, energy, finance, recreation, fire and emergency response, governance, health, safety, solid waste, transportation, urban planning, wastewater, water; and (ii) quality of life: civic engagement, culture, economy, environment, shelter, social equity, and technology and innovation (WCCD, online), http://www.dataforcities.org/wccd/.

22. http://www.gicafrica.diplo.de/Vertretung/suedafrika-dz/en/__pr/2014/04/04-Kenya -street-lights.html.

23. World Bank 2015. The calculation of this benefit is based on WHO's estimated burden of environmental diseases and, more specifically, the estimated share of diarrheal diseases that can be attributed to water, sanitation, and hygiene (WASH) risks. The estimated savings are based on the estimate from the project team that the interventions result in a decrease of about 20 percent in the total incidence of WASH-related disease.

24. There are potentially important offshore oil finds, as with recent discoveries by Total. http://www.offshoreenergytoday.com/total-makes-oil-discovery-offshore-cote -divoire/.

Bibliography

African Development Bank. 2011. *The Cost of Adaptation to Climate Change in Africa.* http://www.afdb.org/fileadmin/uploads/afdb/Documents/Project-and-Operations /Cost%20of%20Adaptation%20in%20Africa.pdf.

BBC (British Broadcasting Corporation). 2010. "Trafigura Found Guilty of Exporting Toxic Waste." July 23. http://www.bbc.com/news/world-africa-10735255.

Bouo Bella, F. X. D., Y. Tchétché, P. Assamoi, J. K. Kouamé, and S. Cautenet, 2011. "Estimation of Domestic and Industrial Emissions in Côte d'Ivoire (West Africa)." *International Journal of the Physical Sciences* 6 (25): 6133–39.

Brink, P., L. Mazza, T. Badura, M. Kettunen, and S. Withana. 2012. *Nature and Its Role in the Transition to a Green Economy.* http://www.unep.org/newscentre/Default.aspx ?DocumentId=2756&ArticleId=9718.

Bromhead, Marjory-Anne. 2012. *Enhancing Competitiveness and Resilience in Africa: An Action Plan for Improved Natural Resource and Environment Management.* Washington, DC: World Bank.

Castán Broto, V. 2014. "Viewpoint: Planning for Climate Change in the African City." *International Development Planning Review* 36 (3): 257–64.

Christie, I., E. Fernandes, H. Messerli, and L. Twining-Ward. 2013. *Tourism in Africa: Harnessing Tourism for Growth and Improved Livelihoods.* Washington, DC: World Bank.

Cities Alliance. 2013. "Brazil Passes Landmark Involuntary Resettlement Policy." http://www.citiesalliance.org/brazil-involuntarydisplacementpolicy.

Coffey, Manus, and Adrian Coad. 2010. *Collection of Municipal Solid Waste in Developing Countries.* UN-Habitat.

Djibril, K., A. Coulibaly, X. Wang, and D. Ousmane. 2012. "Evaluating Green Space Use and Management in Abidjan City, Côte d'Ivoire." *International Journal of Economics and Management Engineering* 2 (3): 108–16.

Dowall, D., and N. Lozano-Gracia. 2012. "Planning for the Future: Accommodating Growth through Effective Planning in Urban India." Background paper prepared for *Urbanization beyond Municipal Boundaries: Nurturing Metropolitan Economies and Connecting Peri-Urban Areas in India,* by Tara Vishwanath and others. Washington, DC: World Bank.

EMBARQ. 2013. "Social, Environmental and Economic Impacts of BRT Systems: Bus Rapid Transit Case Studies from around the World." http://www.embarq.org/sites/default/files/Social-Environmental-Economic-Impacts-BRT-Bus-Rapid-Transit-EMBARQ.pdf.

Hallegatte, S. 2009. "Strategies to Adapt to an Uncertain Climate Change." *Global Environmental Change* 19 (2009): 240–47.

Hallegatte, S., C. Green, R. J. Nicholls, and J. Corfee-Morlot. 2013. "Future Flood Losses in Major Coastal Cities." *Nature Climate Change* 3: 802–06.

Hammer, S., L. Kamal-Chaoui, A. Robert, and M. Plouin. 2011. "Cities and Green Growth: A Conceptual Framework." OECD Regional Development Working Papers 2011/08, OECD Publishing, Paris.

Hayé, C. V., B. K. Dongui, J. Pellerin, and A. Trokourey. 2009. "Pollution Evaluation in the Estuary Bay of Bietri (Abidjan, Côte d'Ivoire)." *Journal of Oceanography, Research and Data* 2: 1–11.

Hazra, Tumpa, and Sudha Goel. 2009. "Solid Waste Management in Kolkata, India: Practices and Challenges." *Waste Management* 29 (1): 470–78.

Henry, Rotich K., Zhao Yongsheng, and Dong Jun. 2006. "Municipal Solid Waste Management Challenges in Developing Countries—Kenyan Case Study." *Waste Management* 26 (1): 92–100.

Hoornweg, D., and P. Bhada-Tata. 2012. *What a Waste: A Global Review of Solid Waste Management.* World Bank Urban Development Series 15. Washington, DC: World Bank.

Hoornweg, D., L. Sugar, and C. L. Trejos Gomez. 2011. "Cities and Greenhouse Gas Emissions: Moving Forward." *Environment and Urbanization,* April 13, http://eau.sagepub.com/content/early/2011/01/08/0956247810392270.

IFC (International Finance Corporation). 2014. "Solid Waste Management." *Handshake,* January 12. http://www.ifc.org/wps/wcm/connect/81efc00042bd63e5b01ebc0dc33b630b/Handshake12_WastePPPs.pdf?MOD=AJPERES.

IHME (Institute for Health Metrics and Evaluation). 2013. *GBD Compare.* Seattle, WA: IHME, University of Washington (accessed September 5, 2014), http://www.healthdata.org/data-visualization/gbd-compare.

INS (Institut National de la Statistique). 2012. *Enquête Démographique et de Santé.* Abidjan: Institut National de la Statistique.

IPCC (Intergovernmental Panel on Climate Change). *The Regional Impacts of Climate Change*. Online report: http://www.ipcc.ch/ipccreports/sres/regional/index.php?idp=30.

Jha, Abhas K., Robin Bloch, and Jessica Lamond. 2012. *Cities and Flooding: A Guide to Integrated Urban Flood Risk Management for the 21st Century*. Washington, DC: World Bank.

Kahn, Matthew E. 2013. "Sustainable and Smart Cities." Policy Research Working Paper 6878, World Bank, Washington, DC.

Kouame, Innocent Kouassi, Brou Dibi, Kouadio Koffi, Issiaka Savane, and Ion Sandu. 2010. "Statistical Approach of Assessing Horizontal Mobility of Heavy Metals in the Soil of Akouedo Landfill Nearby Ebrie Lagoon." *International Journal of Conservation Science* 1 (3): 149–60.

Kruk, C. Bert, and Michel Donner. 2010. *Freight Transport for Development Toolkit: Ports and Waterborne Transport*. Washington, DC: World Bank.

Kumar, P., and M. Yashiro. 2014. "The Marginal Poor and Their Dependence on Ecosystem Services: Evidence from South Asia and Sub-Saharan Africa." In *Marginality*, edited by J. Von Braun, and F. W. Gatzweiler, 169–180. Dordrecht, The Netherlands: Springer.

Liousse, C., E. Assamoi, P. Criqui, C. Granier, and R. Rosset, 2014. "Explosive Growth in African Combustion Emissions from 2005 to 2030." *Environmental Research Letters* 9: 1–10.

Ministère des Infrastructures Économiques. 2011. *Étude Stratégique pour la Gestion des Dechets Solides dans le District d'Abidjan*. PUIUR (Programme d'Urgence d'Infrastructures Urbaines).

Ministry of Environment, Water, and Forests of Côte d'Ivoire; African Refiners Association (ARA); and the United Nations Environment Programme (UNEP). 2009. "West and Central Africa Regional Framework Agreement on Air Pollution (Abidjan Agreement-2009)." Recommendations from the West and Central Africa Subregional Workshop on Better Air Quality (BAQ), Abidjan, Côte d'Ivoire, July 20–22. http://www.unep.org/urban_environment/PDFs/BAQ09_AgreementEn.Pdf.

Moyini, Y., E. Muramira, L. Emerton, and F. Shechambo. 2002. "The Costs of Environmental Degradation and Loss to Uganda's Economy with Particular Reference to Poverty Eradication." Policy Brief 3, International Union for Conservation of Nature.

New York City Mayoral Website. http://www.mikebloomberg.com/index.cfm?objectid=4FF5F4D5-C29C-7CA2-FD895D2C4AFF5B3D.

Nicholls, R. J., S. Hanson, C. Herweijer, N. Patmore, S. Hallegatte, J. Corfee-Morlot, J. Château, and R. Muir-Wood. 2008. "Ranking Port Cities with High Exposure and Vulnerability to Climate Extremes: Exposure Estimates." OECD Environment Working Papers 1, OECD Publishing, Paris. http://dx.doi.org/10.1787/011766488208.

OECD (Organisation for Economic Co-operation and Development). 2012. *Green Growth and Developing Countries: A Summary for Policy Makers*. Paris: OECD.

———. 2013. "Future Flood Losses in Major Coastal Cities." *Nature Climate Change Magazine*.

Ogunrinola, I.O., and E.O. Adepegba. 2012. "Health and Economic Implications of Waste Dumpsites in Cities: The Case of Lagos, Nigeria." *International Journal of Economics and Finance* 4 (4): 239–251.

OSAC (Overseas Security Advisory Council). 2014. *Côte d'Ivoire 2014 Crime and Safety Report*. Washington, DC: United States Department of State, Bureau of Diplomatic Security.

Pare, S., and L. Y. Bonzi-Coulibaly. 2013. "Water Quality Issues in West and Central Africa: Present Status and Future Challenges." Proceedings of H04, IAHS-IAPSO-IASPEI Assembly, IAHS Publications 361, Gothenburg, Sweden, July.

PPIAF (Public-Private Infrastructure Advisory Facility). 2012. "PPIAF Assistance in the Republic of Côte d'Ivoire Information Document." http://www.ppiaf.org/sites/ppiaf .org/files/documents/PPIAF_Assistance_in_C%C3%B4te_d'Ivoire.pdf.

Rabbi, J. 2014. "Dépollution de la Lagune Ebrié: Où en sont les travaux d'assainissement?" lebanco.net, http://www.lebanco.net/banconet/bco21688.htm.

Rheingans, Richard, Matt Kukla, Richard A. Adegbola, Debasish Saha, Richard Omore, Robert F. Breiman, Samba O. Sow, Uma Onwuchekwa, Dilruba Nasrin, Tamer H. Farag, Karen L. Kotloff, and Myron M. Levine. 2012. "Exploring Household Economic Impacts of Childhood Diarrheal Illnesses in 3 African Settings." Clinical Infectious Diseases 55: S317–26.

Sadik-Kahn, J. 2013. "New York's Streets? Not So Mean Any More." TEDCity2.0, https:// www.ted.com/talks/janette_sadik_khan_new_york_s_streets_not_so_mean_any_more.

Samad, T, N. Lozano-Gracia, and A. Panman. 2012. Colombia Urbanization Review: Amplifying the Gains from the Urban Transition. Washington, DC: World Bank.

Scheren, P. A. G. M., C. Kroeze, F. J. J. Janssen, L. Hordijk, and K. J. Ptasinski. 2004. "Integrated Water Pollution Assessment of the Ebrié Lagoon, Ivory Coast, West Africa." Journal of Marine Systems 44: 1–17.

Sukuzi, H., R. Cervero, and K. Iuchi, 2013. Transforming Cities with Transit: Transit and Land Use Integration for Sustainable Urban Development. Washington, DC: World Bank.

Syeda, Maria Ali, Aroma Pervaiz, Beenish Afzal, Naima Hamid, and Azra Yasmin. 2014. "Open Dumping of Municipal Solid Waste and Its Hazardous Impacts on Soil and Vegetation Diversity at Waste Dumping Sites of Islamabad City." Journal of King Saud University—Science 26 (1): 59–65.

TEEB (The Economics of Ecosystems & Biodiversity). 2010. Mainstreaming the Economics of Nature: A Synthesis of the Approach, Conclusions, and Recommendations of TEEB. Geneva: TEEB.

UEMOA (Union Économique et Monétaire ouest-africaine). 2010. "Management Scheme of the Regional Study for Shoreline Monitoring and Drawing Up a Development Scheme for the West African Coastal Area." http://cmsdata.iucn.org/downloads /sdlao_1__general_management_scheme.pdf.

Ulrich, Roger S. 1984. "View through a Window May Influence Recovery from Surgery." Science 224 (4647): 420–21.

UNEP (United Nations Environment Programme). 2009. "Côte d'Ivoire Country Needs Assessment." http://www.unep.org/gpwm/InformationPlatform/CountryNeeds AssessmentAnalysis/CotedIvoire/tabid/106545/Default.aspx.

———. 2010. Share the Road: Investment in Walking and Cycling Infrastructure. Nairobi: UNEP.

———. 2013. "Placing Economic Value on Africa's Natural Resources." UNEP News Centre, December 4. http://www.unep.org/newscentre/Default.aspx?DocumentId =2756&ArticleId=9718.

———. 2014. "Africa Region." Presentation by Wanjiku Manyara (PIEA) and Lidia Ikapi-Neyer (ARA), Africa Region Updates. http://www.unep.org/transport/new/pcfv /pdf/10gpm/10GPM_AfricaRegionalUpdates.pdf.

UN-Habitat (United Nations Human Settlements Programme). 2012. *Côte d'Ivoire: Profil Urbain d'Abidjan*. UN-Habitat.

UN-Habitat (United Nations Human Settlements Programme). 2013. *Planning and Design for Sustainable Urban Mobility: Global Report on Human Settlements*. New York: Routledge.

van Donkelaar, A., R. V. Martin, M. Brauer, R. Kahn, R. Levy, C. Verduzco, and P. J. Velleneuve. 2010. "Global Estimates of Ambient Fine Particulate Matter Concentrations from Satellite-Based Aerosol Optical Depth: Development and Application." *Environmental Health Perspectives* 118 (6): 847–55.

WCCD (World Council on City Data). 2014. "ISO 37120: The First International Standard on City Indicators." Briefing Paper, http://www.cityindicators.org /Deliverables/WCCD%20Brochure_9-16-2014-178620.pdf.

Whitehead, Christine, Rebecca L. H. Chiu, Sasha Tsenkova, and Bengt Turner. 2010. "Land Use Regulation: Transferring Lessons from Developed Economies." In *Urban Land Markets: Improving Land Management for Successful Urbanization*, edited by S. Lall, M. Freire, B. Yuen, R. Rajack, and J. Helluin, 51–70. Dordrecht, The Netherlands: Springer, World Bank.

WHO (World Health Organization). 2012. "Health Indicators of Sustainable Cities." Initial Findings from a WHO Expert Consultation, May 17–18. http://www.who.int /hia/green_economy/indicators_cities.pdf.

———. 2015. "Drinking Water." Fact Sheet No. 391. http://www.who.int/mediacentre /factsheets/fs391/en/.

Wolf, K. 2006. "Amenities: Trees Are Worth Downtown's Investment: Downtown Idea Exchange: Essential Information for Downtown Revitalization." Alexander Communications Group, Inc., April 1. http://www.cfr.washington.edu/research.envmind /CityBiz/DowntownExchange.pdf.

World Bank. 2002. *Urban Land Management and Housing Finance Reform Technical Assistance Project*. Implementation Completion Report. Washington, DC: World Bank.

———. 2007. *Cost of Pollution in China: Economic Estimates of Physical Damages*. Washington, DC: World Bank. http://siteresources.worldbank.org/INTEAPRE GTOPENVIRONMENT/Resources/China_Cost_of_Pollution.pdf.

———. 2009a. *Freight Transport for Development*. Washington, DC: World Bank. http:// www.ppiaf.org/freighttoolkit/sites/default/files/pdfs/road.pdf.

———. 2009b. "Côte d'Ivoire Protected Area Project." Project Appraisal Document, World Bank, Washington, DC.

———. 2012a. *Inclusive Green Growth: The Path to Sustainable Development*. Washington, DC: World Bank.

———. 2012b. *Getting to Green: A Sourcebook of Pollution Management, Policy Tools for Growth and Competitiveness*. Washington, DC: World Bank. http://siteresources .worldbank.org/ENVIRONMENT/Resources/Getting_to_Green_web.pdf.

———. 2012c. *Integrated Urban Water Management Case Study: São Paulo*. Washington, DC: World Bank. http://siteresources.worldbank.org/INTLAC/Resources/257803 -1351801841279/SaoPauloCaseStudyENG.pdf.

———. 2013a. *Planning, Connecting, and Financing Cities—Now: Priorities for City Leaders*. Washington, DC: World Bank. doi:10.1596/978-0-8213-9839-5.

————. 2013b. *Turn Down the Heat: Climate Extremes, Regional Impacts, and the Case for Resilience*. Washington, DC: World Bank.

————. 2013c. Presentations by Amauri Pollachi and Tassia Regina at the Blue Water Green Cities International Workshop, December 4–6, São Paulo. http://web.worldbank .org/WBSITE/EXTERNAL/COUNTRIES/LACEXT/0,,contentMDK:23328153 ~pagePK:146736~piPK:146830~theSitePK:258554,00.html.

————. 2014. *Reducing Black Carbon Emissions from Diesel Vehicles: Impacts, Control Strategies, and Cost-Benefit Analysis*. Washington, DC: World Bank. http://www-wds .worldbank.org/external/default/WDSContentServer/WDSP/IB/2014/04/04 /000442464_20140404122541/Rendered/PDF/864850WP00PUBL0l0report 002April2014.pdf.

————. 2015. *Emergency Urban Infrastructure Project*. Implementation Completion Report. Washington, DC: World Bank.

————. Forthcoming. *Côte d'Ivoire Environmental Assessment (CEA)*. Washington, DC: World Bank.

————. *Wealth Accounting and the Valuation of Ecosystem Services (WAVE)* website.

World Bank and AusAID. 2015. *East Asia's Changing Urban Landscape: Measuring a Decade of Spatial Growth, 2000–2010*. Washington, DC: World Bank.

World Bank Institute. 2012. "Knowledge Note 5-1 Risk Assessment and Hazard Mapping" (accessed February 17, 2015), http://wbi.worldbank.org/wbi/Data/wbi/wbicms/files /drupal-acquia/wbi/drm_kn5-1.pdf.

Zinnes, Clifford F. 2009. *Tournament Approaches to Policy Reform: Making Development Assistance More Effective*. Washington, DC: Brookings Institution Press.

Zurbrügg, Chris. 2013. "Solid Waste Management in Developing Countries." SANDEC/ EAWAG.

CHAPTER 4

Financing Cities

Jonas Ingemann Parby, Jean-Noel Amantchi Gogoua,
and Gyongshim An

Introduction

Better planning, connecting, and greening of Ivorian cities means scaling up their financing.[1] The country's territorial/spatial development policies need to be translated into regional development plans. The urban master plans—integrating among other issues land use, transport, and sanitation—for each of the 31 regional capitals and the two autonomous districts need to be completed or updated, and all city-level stakeholders mobilized for their implementation. Intraurban transport in Greater Abidjan requires heavy investments to upgrade, diversify, and scale up public transport systems. Missing road links need to be built for all connector cities (Global, Regional, and Domestic) and existing infrastructure upgraded and maintained to stimulate domestic economic integration. And, although the government has recently significantly scaled up infrastructure financing, much still needs to be done to address a two-decade backlog in public investment.

Different levels of government have different responsibilities in infrastructure provision and maintenance. But, given that Côte d'Ivoire has embarked on ambitious decentralization reform, municipalities will play a key role in providing services and managing urban space. Infrastructure requires expansion and upgrading as urbanization accelerates, as well as improved financing and stable mechanisms for revenue generation. Concerted efforts to implement and adjust existing reforms are needed to improve local and national government management and resource oversight. Finally, additional options for infrastructure financing and follow-through on decentralization are needed to reap the benefits of devolution, bring services closer to citizens, and address inequity.

Service delivery in Global, Regional, and Domestic Connector cities is undermined by inconsistencies in their revenue regimes and by lack of finances. This applies to the mandates for decentralization that began in 1980, and were reinforced several times, and to their implementation. But the resources available to municipalities from the central government are negligible and diminishing. Cities are also constrained by limited human resource and institutional capacity, curtailing their ability to attract and retain investment and generate jobs.

The systemic financing gaps across Global, Regional, and Domestic Connectors require immediate attention to address the regulatory framework, volume, and predictability. Given that regions and districts are fairly recent subnational entities, this chapter focuses more on current trends in municipal finance.

Moves to Devolve Responsibility and Finance

Two obstacles still impede public services under a decentralized model in Côte d'Ivoire. The first is systemic, affecting municipal budgets, and includes unpredictable financing, late transfers, and the lack of transparency on shared revenues from the center, combined with low own-source revenue mobilization, even in large urban areas. The provision of services is also affected by the diminishing resources provided to local authorities. The second is related to devolution of responsibilities. While some progress has been made, the framework still features contradictions and overlaps in existing legislation and in the application of existing mandates, leading to confusion between national ministries and local governments about financing and service delivery. This means that devolution is not complete in some cases, or that the related financing for a specific function has not been transferred to local government.

Aims of Decentralization of Municipal Services

The principle of self-administration of local authorities is enshrined in the Constitution.[2] The objectives are to bring decision-making centers and power closer to the populace, to ensure that the latter participates in managing its own affairs and to provide sustainable local development. Decentralization also has an economic component aimed at transforming subnational entities into real centers of development through the responsibilities transferred to them by the national government, on the basis of subsidiarity and cost efficiency. Decentralization is also expected to serve as a catalyst for reducing local and regional disparities.

By their mandates and functions, local authorities are a pillar of development policy. Under Law No. 2003–208 of July 7, 2003, a wide range of responsibilities was in theory devolved to local authorities.[3] The decentralization process is the result of a gradual restructuring of the former municipal system governed by French colonial-era laws, starting with the creation of the first Ivorian commune (box 4.1). However, faced with obvious shortcomings[4] and the need to rationalize the system, the institutional framework governing decentralization and the law was changed in 2012, and the former five levels of decentralized entities were cut to just two, namely regions (31) and municipalities, or *communes* (197).

The establishment of local governments has been implemented in three major phases, in line with the laws governing decentralization. The experimental phase covers the period from 1960 to 1980. Establishment of communes effectively started between 1980 and 1985, with the organization of the first municipal elections in 1980 and the creation of new communes; and the process was consolidated starting from 1985 with the expansion of communes. Five elections have been held since independence (1985, 1991, 1996, 2001, and 2013).

Diversified Urbanization • http://dx.doi.org/10.1596/978-1-4648-0808-1

Box 4.1 Key Laws and Dates for the Establishment of Decentralization in Côte d'Ivoire

In 1978, Law No. 78–07 of January 9, 1978, established 28 fully fledged communes and set up a uniform system of communes in the country.

In 1980, Law No. 80–1180 of October 17, 1980, on municipal organization; Law No. 80–1181 of October 17, 1980, on the system governing municipal elections; Law No. 80–1182 of October 17, 1980, establishing the status of the City of Abidjan; and the subsequent texts of these laws marked the real beginning of a decentralization policy in Côte d'Ivoire, in particular with the increase in the number of communes.

In 2001, a new policy direction in decentralization was instituted through orientation Law No. 2001–476 of August 9, 2001, on the general organization of the territorial administration, which set up five levels of decentralized local authorities. These are—from the lowest to the highest level—communes, towns, departments, districts, and regions. In 2012, however, in a move to rationalize the system, the government decided to postpone the plan to establish communes throughout the national territory and confirmed the number of 197 communes.

Source: Ministry of the Interior and Security 2006.

Given this background, which has been affected by the crises since 1999, decentralization is obviously still only emerging as a tool for service delivery and improved accountability.

Devolution is based on two key principles: subsidiarity and cost efficiency. Local authorities[5] are in a better position to identify and manage basic services because they are closer to, and have a more in-depth knowledge of, their populations. With less bureaucracy, the cost of basic services is expected to decline, and the involvement of the local population in managing municipalities should lead to greater transparency and efficiency in service delivery.[6] Water and electricity have their own arrangements, although the actual transfer of responsibilities to local authorities could improve service delivery (box 4.2).

The objective of transferring responsibilities was to increase accountability of the representative bodies, executive organs, and working committees involved in decentralization. The council is a representative body that assumes the function of supreme organ of the local authority. Members of the representative bodies and the executive organs are elected by the population. The government— through the Minister of the Interior and Security's administrative control of decisions, bodies, and advisory services—is in charge of monitoring the implementation of local responsibilities by local authorities. Decisions made by local authorities can enter into force only after approval by the regulatory authority. The latter has power to authorize, inspect, or override local authorities and their decisions and activities. Advisory services to local authorities take the form of assisting and advising municipalities, supporting their activities, and ensuring that their activities are consistent with those of the governments.

Box 4.2 A Different Path for Provision of Water and Electricity

In Côte d'Ivoire, as in most francophone countries, water and electricity are produced, supplied, overseen, and distributed by national companies belonging to an international group. Operations therefore need to be profitable for these companies, although the assets remain the property of the state.

In principle, as responsibilities are devolved to local authorities, these bodies have to be involved in managing these services. It appears, however, that the national companies distribute water and electricity without coordinating with local authorities. For example, the concession contract between the government and the national water company, SODECI (Société de Distribution d'Eau de Côte d'Ivoire), did not take into account the local authorities' responsibilities for sanitation.

The transfer of responsibilities to local authorities could improve service delivery. Such decentralized arrangements are used in many countries, such as South Africa and Mozambique. Although there are also risks in decentralizing water services, there are advantages. For example, water services can be adapted to local needs because locally elected officials would have control of managing them, stimulating competition and potentially reducing costs and consumer prices.

Source: Kouadio and Assande 2014.

The supervisory role is played by the General Directorate for Decentralization and Local Development (Direction Générale de la Décentralisation et du Développement Local [DGDDL]) within the Ministry of the Interior and Security, and by the regional prefects. Article 52 of the orientation Law No. 2001–476 of August 9, 2001, on the general organization of territorial administration states that "Government control of local authorities shall be carried out by the ministry with responsibility for local authorities." As such, any delay at the DGDDL to approve municipal budgets causes delays in the delivery of services in the municipalities. Some mayors interviewed for this review indicated that it takes sometimes up to six months after the start of the financial year for the budget to be approved.

Local authorities have institutional and hierarchical links with other ministries, such as the Ministry of Finance and line ministries. The institutional link with the Ministry of Finance goes through the local Directorate of Operations for Decentralized Collectivities (Direction des Opérations des Collectivités Décentralisées [DOCD]), the General Directorate of Tax (Direction Générale des Impôts [DGI]), and the General Directorate of Treasury and Public Accounting (Direction Générale du Trésor et de la Comptabilité Publique [DGTCP]). The DOCD is responsible for assisting local authorities in drafting their budgets, ensuring consistency, and monitoring the implementation of their operations. The DGI is in charge of operations related to the tax base as well as the assessment and collection of a large portion of the revenue of local authorities.

The DGTCP is responsible for the accounting management of local authorities through the Parastatal Accounting Directorate (Direction de la Comptabilité Parapublique [DCPP]) and its various departments, namely the district, regional, and departmental payment offices, as well as "cash offices."

Incomplete and Inconsistent Decentralization

Responsibilities and functions for core aspects of service delivery critical to urban development have not been fully devolved, and coordination of services between ministries and local governments and in various sectors remains a challenge. Some enabling decrees and orders relating to the law on the devolution of responsibilities have not yet been adopted, leading to a slow progress in devolving powers in many sectors (box 4.3). With the new local government structure, this law is no longer adequate. The devolution and decentralization reforms are affected by unilateral decisions of the central ministries that go against provisions in the legal and institutional framework and often undermine the budget, planning, and decision-making process of the municipalities.[7] The provision of more resources to regions at the expense of municipalities is also seen as unfair by some mayors. Although regions do not produce resources, they are allocated more taxes and subsidies, and their staff are also paid better than those of municipalities. Further, most municipalities[8] and regions do not have a strategic development plan, which precludes their triennial plans and budgets from being aligned with any development objectives and hinders the effective implementation of development programs.

Systemic issues continue to affect the timely and effective formulation and implementation of the budgets of municipalities and regions, leading to inefficiencies in service delivery and project implementation. Local budgets are adopted and implemented with delays. At each level of government, the budget is prepared by the executive—the mayor and the municipal council at the local level, and the president and cabinet office at the regional level. Each of these bodies relies on its own and central government services, which are poorly coordinated. The deadlines set by the programming schedule and budget preparations are hardly ever met, and local budgets are completed late because of delays by local authorities and by the regulatory authority. Also, the budgetary and accounting rules are inconsistent with international standards, although revisions are underway to adapt them to WAEMU Directive No. 01/2011/CM/UEMOA of June 24, 2011, on the financial rules applicable to local authorities.[9] Further, the three-year programs that make up the multiyear budget-programming tool cover only expenditures, not revenues. The credibility of local budgets is hurt by the lack of control and lack of predictability in shared revenues.

Weak financing affects human resources. Each municipality has fewer than two civil servants, far below comparator countries in the region. Local government performance is strongly affected by this scarcity. Local government staff falls into three categories: civil servants, municipal agents, and contract staff (table 4.1). Only a few civil servants are assigned to local entities on the basis of their technical skills. They are usually assigned by the regulatory authority

---

Box 4.3 Slow Sector Progress in Devolving Powers

Apart from education, most sectors are still under the control of the line ministries. Most local authorities disagree with ministries about their role in implementing development activities and hardly ever coordinate among themselves in planning, programming, or implementing them.

Education. Negotiations between the Association of Cities and Communes of Côte d'Ivoire (Union des Villes et Communes de Côte d'Ivoire [UVICOCI]) and the government in March 1998 led to a memorandum of understanding to facilitate the gradual transfer of some responsibilities to municipalities.

Urbanization and housing. The law devolving responsibilities in this area has contradictory elements in that it grant districts powers of land management, whereas this power had, until then, been under municipal authority (in the departments). The attribution commission also appears to be superseded by regional administrative authorities. A new decree issued by the Ministry of Construction, Housing, Sanitation, and Urbanism (Ministère de la Construction, du Logement, de l'Assainissement et de l'Urbanisme [MCLAU]) has centralized decision-making power on land issues (including land tenure management, zoning, and titling) to the central government, going against the decentralization law, and has tended to exclude municipalities (as confirmed by discussions with the mayors of the 14 sampled municipalities) in key decision-making procedures, even though they are meant to be represented in the commission.

Transport. In Abidjan, the main conflict is that the Agency for Urban Transport (Agence du Transport Urbain [AGETU]) issues transport permits and collects transport taxes rather than the municipalities, despite the transfer of responsibilities set in laws and decrees.

Sanitation, environmental protection, and natural resource management. Waste management has been entrusted to the ministry in charge of sanitation, instead of to municipalities. The concession contract between the government and the water agency, SODECI (Société de Distribution d'Eau de Côte d'Ivoire), did not consider local authorities' responsibilities for sanitation, leading to confusion about their role. Although new regulations have now entrusted the ministry in charge of hygiene and sanitation with waste removal, Regional and Domestic Connector cities are still obliged to carry out this activity despite no longer being able to collect taxes for that purpose, thus undermining the sustainability of services.

Fish and animal resources. The consultations conducted under this study (Kouadio and Assande 2014), revealed that the technical departments of the ministry in charge of fish and animal resources do not allow the relevant municipal departments to inspect slaughterhouses or fish warehouses with a capacity below 50,000 metric tons, although existing regulations require them to do so. This creates potential inefficiencies in quality assurance and oversight.

Source: Kouadio and Assande 2014.

(such as the Ministry of the Interior and Security) and occupy senior administrative and technical positions such as secretary general, head of the administrative service, head of finance, and director of technical services. The second and largest category is made up of municipal agents recruited locally, who have at best a secondary school education (*brevet d'études du premier cycle*, or BEPC diploma).

Table 4.1 Number of Municipal Staff, 2007–13

	Civil servants	Municipal agents	Others	Total
2007	184	3,374	408	3,966
2008	250	4,547	776	5,608
2009	1	26	8	35
2010	—	—	—	—
2011	—	—	—	—
2012	403	3,578	543	4,572
2013	348	4,658	886	6,063

Source: World Bank calculations based on data from Direction de la Comptabilité Parapublique and data collected for this report in May–June 2014.
Note: — = not available.

The third category is made up of contract workers recruited for a specific task. Thus there is a large number of basic or implementation agents and a few under-qualified supervisory staff.

The reasons for the lack of qualified staff also include regulatory limitations and few incentives to recruit senior officials. This is particularly true for Domestic Connector cities that struggle to provide better working conditions. There is also the question of appropriate training—municipal agents rarely have the required training. The low investment in human development and abilities hinders local development and hampers implementation of the tasks assigned to local authorities. Local stakeholders (elected officials, workers, and other local actors) do not appear to have the training to undertake the new, devolved responsibilities.

The national government must ensure that municipalities have enough resources to hire qualified staff. It must give municipalities the means to carry out their own recruitment of skilled senior officials if they are to remain autonomous. Above all, municipalities must implement, expand, and revitalize their training plans for public management and local governance.

Municipal Finance and Expenditures

Regulatory Framework Governing Municipal Finance

The legal framework governing local government financing does not grant communes fiscal autonomy. They do not have the power to create taxes or to define the tax base, rate, or method of collection. According to the tax law, the system of local taxation has to be set by the legislative authority. In the absence of an enabling decree relating to the law on financing, local finance agents tend to refer to previous laws. The regulatory framework currently governing commune financing comprises Law No. 2003–489 of December 26, 2003, establishing the local government financial, fiscal, and public property regime, and a number of decrees, orders, and instructions. The fact that these regulations are not aligned with the revised 2012 decentralization law leads to divergent interpretations and applications of law. The legal framework governing commune financing also requires local governments to set aside part of their budget for investment.[10]

There are also limitations to the institutional framework governing local government finance. While the basic institutional framework is in place and is functioning across all dimensions of local government finance (for example, budgeting, planning, budgetary controls, and accounting), the framework is characterized by limitations with related effects on the efficiency in public spending. In addition to not being aligned with the 2012 decentralization law, the regulations for Law No. 2003–489 of December 26, 2003, have not yet been developed; and regulatory laws that govern the management of local finances are old. Some of these texts date back to the colonial era and have not been updated with the new organization of territorial administration. However, work is underway to adapt the financial system of local authorities in Côte d'Ivoire to the Directive No. 01/2011/CM/UEMOA, financial system of local governments within UEMOA (Union économique et monétaire ouest-africaine, or West African Economic and Monetary Union) (World Bank 2014).

Five major financial resources are defined for local authorities under Law No. 2003–489 of December 26, 2003, establishing the local government financial, fiscal, and public property regime: (i) shared revenue resources, comprising taxes and duties collected by the central government and shared with local authorities according to a system of allocation; (ii) internally generated resources, comprising taxes collected locally and income from municipal services; (iii) operations and investment grants and transfers provided by the central government; (iv) borrowings/loans from the central government; and (v) funding from development partners.

Total Municipal Revenues

Local governments in Côte d'Ivoire have two distinct characteristics. First, they remain highly dependent on shared revenues and on grants and transfers from the central government. Second, their investment budget for development remains small and insufficient for their needs, which is a greater challenge for urban areas with higher infrastructure requirements.

The failure to fully transfer financial resources is seen in limited financing for capital and operational spending and insufficient mobilization of own resources, even in larger cities. Local governments remain highly dependent on shared revenues as well as on grants and transfers from central government. Their investment budget for development is too small for their needs, which is challenging for Global and Regional Connector cities. For example, total revenues directly assigned to the 197 municipalities between 2007 and 2013 amounted to CFAF 374.6 billion (about US$750 million; figure 4.1), an average of only 0.44 percent of gross domestic product (GDP) (in Ghana, total revenues amounted to about 0.9 percent of GDP in 2012).

Cumulative total revenues for all 197 communes between 2007 and 2013 came to less than US$1 billion. They amounted to CFAF 374.6 billion (roughly US$750 million), representing a minimal share of the country's total revenue. Commune revenue as a share of GDP is practically insignificant, varying between 0.30 and 0.54 percent, with an average of 0.44 percent over 2007–13.

Figure 4.1 Local Government Revenues, 2007–13

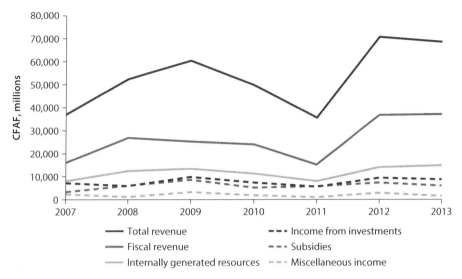

Source: Direction de la Comptabilité Parapublique.

Figure 4.2 Trends in Commune Revenue, 2007–13

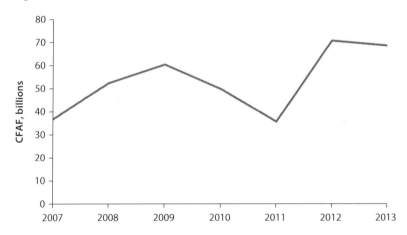

Source: World Bank calculations based on data from Direction de la Comptabilité Parapublique and data collected for this report in May–June 2014.

On average, communes register total revenues of CFAF 53.5 billion (US$107 million) each. The general trend shows average annual growth of 11 percent. Overall, however, total commune revenue has fluctuated in line with the political and economic situation: it fell between 2009 and 2011 before increasing by 99 percent in 2012 (figure 4.2).

Total revenue of municipalities remains marginal relative to service delivery needs. Between 2007 and 2013, the average fiscal revenue per capita was

CFAF 896, or less than US$2, marked by a deteriorating trend due to population growth and little increase in municipalities' total revenue. Municipalities' fiscal revenue (the largest component of their total revenue) comes from property taxes, licenses and permits, flat rate income tax, and other taxes. Over the period, property tax and licenses and permits represented the bulk of municipalities' fiscal revenue, at 37.9 percent and 36.5 percent, respectively. They were followed by the flat rate income tax (11.4 percent), with other taxes covering the remaining 14.2 percent.

Resources generated by municipalities include locally collected taxes and fees for some services. The authority of municipal authorities to collect taxes is governed by Law No. 2003–489 of December 26, 2003.[11] The laws on decentralization identify taxes to be collected directly by municipalities, including taxes on small traders, escrow taxes, market fees, transport fees, slaughterhouse fees, and so forth. The municipality also derives fees from some of the services it provides, and from activities in the area under its jurisdiction. Such services include legal and certification services, house leases, and rental of cultural centers. Local authorities generally have more room to maneuver with these taxes and fees and can determine the rates themselves.

The shared tax revenue received varies widely among the sampled municipalities. The three municipalities in Abidjan account for about 75 percent of the total fiscal revenue for the sample. This underscores the disparities in fiscal potential between municipalities inside and outside Abidjan—most economic activity is located within the economic capital. The picture is similar with own-source revenues: the three Abidjan municipalities account for 60 percent of the sample total. The issue of financial autonomy reveals how difficult it is for communes to mobilize resources locally. Key factors for this outcome include insufficient transfer of competences leading to conflicts between communes and certain line ministries, limited or no tax payer registration in local governments, and no associated technology for regular updates and management of revenue collection and administration.

The revenues and expenditures of communes appear to have the same characteristics. Generally, expenditure exceeds income; but, starting with the 2011 financial year, the situation appears to have improved. This augurs well for communes because they may be able to register financial surpluses and generate savings. It also reduces the risk of debt at the local government level. Starting from 2012, the ratio of income over expenditure was at least 1.2 (figure 4.3).[12]

Intergovernmental Fiscal Transfers

Local government fiscal resources consist mainly of transfers from shared revenues. This represents 50–60 percent of total financing. These shared revenues are administered and collected by the DGI and subsequently passed on to decentralized entities. The December 2012 finance law defined the revenue resources listed in table 4.2 as shared revenues in varying amounts (apart from the rent tax and the roads, hygiene, and sanitation tax). The shared revenue for all communes is about CFAF 26 billion (about US$52 million) per year. Shared revenue had

Figure 4.3 Comparison of Trends in Income and Expenditure of Communes

Legend: Total expenditure of communes — Total income of communes

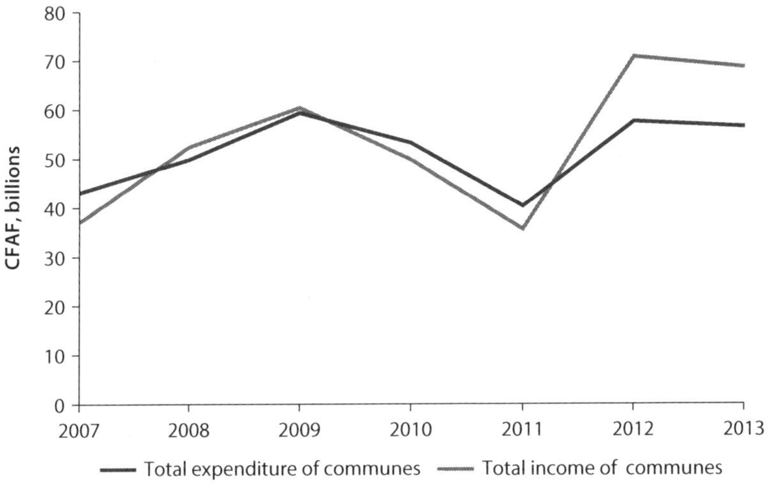

Source: World Bank calculations based on data from Direction de la Comptabilité Parapublique and data collected for this report in May–June 2014.

Table 4.2 Distribution Formulas for Shared Revenues

Tax	Municipalities (%)	Regions (%)	Road maintenance fund (%)	Sanitation and drainage unit (%)	Waste management unit (%)	National government (%)
Property tax	35	30	0	10	25	0
Farm tax	30	60	0	0	0	10
Special tax on motor vehicles	25	25	40	0	0	10
Licenses and permits	45	15	25	0	0	15
Flat-rate income tax	40	10	0	0	0	50
Housing tax	40	0	0	0	0	60
Rent tax	0	0	0	0	0	100
Roads, hygiene, and sanitation tax	0	0	0	0	0	100

Source: GoCI 2013.

fallen constantly from 2008 before recovering in 2012 with a catch-up effect. The strong growth after the postelectoral crisis led to annual average growth of 15 percent.

Shared tax revenue from central sources is allocated to municipalities by means of a transfer letter, but the transfer of these funds is most often neither timely nor predictable. The transfer of revenues to municipalities is carried out every two weeks and allows the accounts of each municipality to be credited rapidly as taxes are collected. But it does not guarantee that the actual cash is immediately available because the disbursement of funds is checked by the treasury accountant, often slowing the process if any basic documents are missing. Thus, revenue flows are not always on time or predictable. The collection of shared revenues is affected by difficulties in establishing a proper tax base because of the lack of a local information system and by the poor institutional capacity of the tax administration at a municipal level, which results from inadequate training and incentives.

Municipalities also receive support through central government transfers and grants. These include subsidies and miscellaneous grants for financing local government spending. The grants and subsidies include an overall General Financial Allocation (Dotation Globale Financière [DGF]), a general decentralization grant, an equalization grant/subsidy, and an investment grant for the implementation of development plans. The subsidies and contributions offset the costs imposed on local authorities and enhance balanced regional development through an allocation formula that benefits districts less endowed with resources. For example, DGF is allocated to local authorities each year, in accord with Decree No. 98–05 of January 14, 1998. It is calculated on the basis of 2 percent of the total revenue collected by the government two years previously. With this mechanism, the DGF allocated to local authorities each year is at least CFAF 30 billion (about US$60 million).

The model for allocation of the DGF includes a minimum grant and an additional grant. The aim of the minimum grant is to ensure that each community receives a minimum amount of resources per capita. This grant is equal to the amount of DGF received in 1996. The additional grant is meant to contribute to the operating costs of local authorities. This grant is allocated on the basis of several criteria: population, equity (based on poverty rates), and incentive, estimated at 20 percent, 50 percent, and 30 percent of the balance of the DGF after the minimum portion has been deducted.

In practice, however, the criteria for calculating and distributing the DGF are not strictly applied as they should be per Decree No. 98–05 of January 14, 1998. Each year, the Minister of the Economy and Finance sets an overall amount to be allocated to local authorities, based on the government budget. The allocation for each municipality is divided into a share for operations and a share for infrastructure and investment. The process of making these funds available to the local authorities is the responsibility of the Ministry of the Interior and Security (for the operational grant) and the line ministry involved in the sector (for investment operations). Local authorities thus have no control over these contributions, which are allocated unilaterally by the government according to impartial criteria; and they cannot use the amounts freely, as these funds are allocated for specific purposes (Kouadio and Assande 2014).

Given its current distribution formula, the DGF is essentially an equalization grant ensuring that rural, less-populated districts have higher funding per capita than urban districts. It stipulates no performance criteria for the municipalities. While this system helps address inequality between districts, it does not address the large infrastructure needs of urban areas, especially given the already high level of urbanization. The government may wish to look at other comparator countries in the region (Ghana, Senegal, Uganda, and so on) to see how they have developed grant systems that address urban infrastructure needs while targeting local revenue mobilization and enhancing greater discretion over use of the grants to local governments, in line with decentralization principles.

For 2014, the DGF is estimated at CFAF 45 billion (about US$93.8 million); CFAF 14 billion was allocated to the communes and CFAF 31 billion to the regions. The DGF breakdown for 2014 was:

- 55 percent for the operations grant, with CFAF 1 billion for Yamoussoukro (because of its status as administrative capital); 90 percent of the remaining amount was distributed in equal shares to the 187 communes (the 10 communes in Abidjan do not receive this endowment), with the remaining 10 percent being distributed proportionally, according to the number of inhabitants of each commune; and
- 45 percent allocated for investment/development, with 90 percent distributed in equal proportions among the 187 eligible communes, and 10 percent according to the population of the commune.

The share of national budget spending for local government grants has decreased over the last decade, and the allocation and disbursement of central transfers is not implemented in full accord with existing regulations. While the net amount of central government financing has more than doubled since 2003, the share of national budget spending on local government grants has decreased from 3.62 percent to 1.27 percent in 2014 (table 4.3). This seems to indicate a contradiction between the stated objectives of the government's decentralization policy and realization. It appears that the total amount of grants since 2008 has amounted to less than the required 2 percent in the national budget. And beyond changes in overall volume, financing to local governments is affected by the recurrent problem that the allocation and disbursement of government transfers are not made according to formal criteria. Implementation regulations of Law No. 2003–489 of December 26, 2003, to determine the details of the calculation and allocation of state transfers to local governments are not yet in place (World Bank 2014).

Local Revenues and Borrowing

Internally generated resources represent an average of 26 percent of total resources. Such resources have ranged between 24 and 28 percent over the period 2006–13, with a standard deviation of 1 percent. Communes are allowed to mobilize 25 percent of their resources on their own territory, the remaining 75 percent derived from government through fiscal revenue, subsidies, and income from investments. The average financial autonomy ratio for Ivorian communes is 22.5 percent. It has oscillated between a minimum of 17.8 percent in 2001 and a maximum of 33 percent in 2011. Miscellaneous revenues are not significant, with an average of 4 percent, while income from investments and subsidies make up 15 percent and 12 percent of total revenue, respectively. The amount of income from investments is a reflection of the rather poor investment capacity of communes.

Table 4.3 Percentage of Local Government Grants in the General National Budget

Year	National budget (CFAF billion)	Local government grants (CFAF billion)	LG grants as share of national budget (%)
2003	1,515	55	3.62
2004	1,986	57	2.87
2005	1,735	41	2.38
2006	1,966	40	2.02
2007	1,961	40	2.02
2008	2,129	41	1.94
2009	2,530	43	1.72
2010	2,482	43	1.74
2011	3,051	42	1.37
2012	3,161	43	1.35
2013	3,815	43	1.13
2014	4,248	54	1.27
Total	**30,577**	**542**	**1.77**

Source: Direction des Opérations des Collectivités Décentralisées.
Note: LG = local government.

Article 99 of the law establishing the local government financial, fiscal, and public property regime stipulates that local authorities may take out loans to cover expenditure under Title II of the budget (investments). The limits and conditions of such loans are established by decree of the Council of Ministers. The texts governing debt-financing options for communes limit the decision-making powers of local authorities because the latter are required to seek prior authorization from government or the regulatory ministry for any type of loan. These restrictions also apply to the use of the borrowed resources. The limits and conditions of such loans are established by a decree of the Council of Ministers. The January 1985 decree provides communes with the possibility of borrowing to finance investment operations.[13] Because access to loans remained quite difficult, the government established the Municipal Credit Fund (Fonds de Prêts aux Collectivités Locales [FPCL]) by decree dated August 30, 1989. In practice, however, loans are limited because of constraints in the fiscal capacity of local governments as well as the legal requirement for balanced budgets.

Ivorian local governments are increasing their debts: the short-term debt of Ivorian communes rose on average by 8 percent between 2007 and 2013. Most of this debt—about 80 percent—is owed to the private sector. A comparison of short-term debt with available financial resources plus short-term credit shows that communes are constantly faced with a cash flow deficit. By the end of the financial year 2013, the financial deficit stood at about CFAF 14 billion (about US$30 million).

Local authorities do not properly honor their commitments of loans. Local authorities borrow from the FPCL to finance income-generating projects. However, they do not adequately provide for the repayment of such loans.

Diversified Urbanization • http://dx.doi.org/10.1596/978-1-4648-0808-1

To date the FPCL has been funded mainly with debt financing from the financial market and by donors' contributions through specific projects. Since it started its activities, the FPCL has granted loans to the tune of CFAF 2.6 billion (about US$5.2 million) to 24 communes for the implementation of various projects (table 4.4). Priority is given to projects with the potential for generating revenue (about 85 percent). Infrastructure construction projects such as the construction of town halls, however, predominate. Because such investments are not profitable, especially in communes in the hinterland, it appears unlikely that the loans can be refunded. It is difficult for most communes to meet their commitments to the FPCL given their low fiscal capacity. As at September 30, 2013, the repayment rate was just 26 percent.

There are two main factors that limit access to FPCL loans. The first is the relatively high interest rate (11 percent) and the second is the low self-financing capacity of communes, because a contribution of 15–35 percent is required for each loan.

The restrictions on borrowing are also due to the government's institutional oversight over lending agencies. The government orients the activities of lending agencies by determining the conditions under which loans are granted to local authorities. As a result, the central government is the major distributor and regulator of loans granted to them. The current environment may, however, provide new opportunities for financing development in municipalities, in particular in Abidjan, with the opening of financial markets and the development of public and private financial instruments. Local authorities now have new opportunities available to them through the banking and financial markets, as well as specialized institutions. However, with the restrictions imposed by the law, it is not easy to use such means of financing. Additionally, given the existing fiscal space, the option for borrowing requires further analysis since most local governments have very limited savings, some even running with annual overspending due to high operational costs.

Inadequate Municipal Finances for Investment

Municipalities surveyed for this review confirm the reliance on shared fiscal revenues. The 14 municipalities surveyed for this review,[14] including main

Table 4.4 FPCL-Financed Municipal Investments, by Category

Project	Amount (CFAF thousands)	Percent
Market, bus station, slaughterhouse	2,203,737	84.7
Town hall	343,050	13.2
Dispensary	25,000	1.0
Hotel	14,150	0.5
Infrastructure	9,750	0.4
Mortuary	7,400	0.3
Total	**2,603,087**	**100**

Source: Study on the conditions for ensuring the sustainability of the FPCL.
Note: FPCL = Fonds de Prêts aux Collectivités Locales (Municipal Credit Fund).

Global and Regional Connectors, documented their reliance on shared fiscal revenues. Their total income was a cumulative CFAF 102.7 billion (about US$205 million) from 2007 to 2013, of which CFAF 52.8 billion (about US$106 million) was fiscal revenue (51.4 percent). Property taxes, licenses and permits, flat-rate income taxes, and other taxes represented CFAF 20.2 billion (about US$40 million), CFAF 19.5 billion (about US$39 million), CFAF 4.8 billion (about US$10 million), and CFAF 7.4 billion (about US$15 million), respectively. The average share of fiscal revenue in municipalities' total revenue fell between 2008 and 2011, from 62 to 41 percent, before starting to increase again in 2012 (47.7 percent) and 2013 (57.7 percent). Most municipalities do not make use of own resources to finance investment. The average own resource investment of Man and Bouaké was practically zero between 2007 and 2013 because of the crisis—all their own resources went to operations. In Korhogo, Soubré, and San-Pédro, the own resource contribution to infrastructure development was high, averaging more than 50 percent.

One of the major obstacles to funding investment is the difficulty in mobilizing own resources or central government resources and the high allocation for operational expenditures. For every dollar of municipal spending between 2007 and 2013, irrespective of location, 82 cents went for operations—with about 40 cents to staff costs—and only 18 cents to investment. Operational spending also covers facilities, supplies, and financial charges. Surprisingly, Regional and Domestic Connectors spend more on infrastructure than do the municipalities of Abidjan surveyed. Between 2007 and 2013, operating and investment expenditures were estimated at 83 percent and 17 percent for Regional and Domestic Connector municipalities, against 94 percent and 6 percent for municipalities in Abidjan, which undermines its role as a Global Connector. The average rate of income recovery from investments is 71.7 percent. The difficulty in mobilizing resources is one of the reasons for the gap between projections and actual infrastructure development. Donor assistance helps fill the gap. After years of crisis and a dearth of public funding, the government is now seeking to mobilize external resources to finance local infrastructure, including grants and soft loans.

Regional and Domestic Connectors spend more on salaries than Abidjan. From 2007 to 2013, the average percentages of operating budget used for staff expenditure, other charges, and financial charges were 60 percent, 39.8 percent, and 0.2 percent, respectively, for Regional and Domestic Connectors; and 39.9 percent, 59.9 percent, and 0.2 percent for municipalities in Abidjan. Bouaké (86.4 percent), Danané (76 percent), Korhogo (69.4 percent), Odienné (67.7 percent), Bondoukou (64.8 percent), Daloa (64.2 percent), and Man (64 percent)—all use most of their operating budget to pay staff. According to the authorities in Bouaké, their figure was exceptionally high because the youth involved as combatants during the crisis were later employed by the municipality.

Municipal investment expenditures cover a wide spectrum of infrastructure. They include electrification, road networks, land development, commercial and administrative facilities, cultural and leisure amenities, health, education, the environment, and water. The triennial investment plans and the management accounts of the sample show that municipalities generally give priority to three categories of investments: (a) community services, (b) sociocultural and human development, and (c) general services. Apart from Regional Connector Bouaké, Domestic Connector Bondoukou, and Global Connector San-Pédro, which allocate the bulk of their investments to general services, most other municipalities focus their efforts on roads, electricity and public lighting, public health and hygiene, water and water supply, and city planning and the environment.

Despite its small share of total investment spending, Abidjan accounts for nearly half of all investment in municipalities in Côte d'Ivoire. Abidjan spends CFAF 63.9 billion (about US$128 million), as against CFAF 68.2 billion (about US$136 million) for the other 187 municipalities. Investment across the country has always depended heavily on the political situation. With the signing of the peace agreement in 2007, investments increased sharply, but the 2010–11 postelection crisis caused investments to fall 23.6 percent to their lowest levels of the period under review.

The share of the national budget for local government grants has decreased over the last decade. The budget has been halved, and the financing allocation is affected because government transfers to local authorities repeatedly fail to follow official criteria—the regulations of Law No. 2003–489 of December 26, 2003, still not in place, for example (World Bank 2014).

Municipalities therefore have little capacity to finance infrastructure investments. The main reason for this is the limited level of own resources, fiscal revenue, and government assistance, along with problems in the legal, institutional, and intergovernmental fiscal framework. Further, the overall financial management standards at the municipality level are affected by poor financial and human capacity and lack of systematic oversight from central authorities, leading to little financial reporting, few systems, loans being updated without repayment, and other systemic issues, limiting the options for alternative financing mechanisms.

Municipalities are unable to generate large savings to enable borrowing. From 2001 to 2011, communes registered net savings, to the tune of CFAF 72.8 billion (about US$146 million) of which CFAF 24.4 billion (about US$49 million) was from communes in Abidjan and CFAF 48.1 billion (about US$96 million) from communes in the hinterland. Although communes in Abidjan contribute the most to total operating income, their real operating expenditure is also very high; therefore, their level of savings is lower than that of communes in the interior. The funding deficit is likely to be partly due to bottlenecks in the disbursement of government development subsidies. This represents the net debt flow of communes during the period and totals CFAF 48.4 billion (about US$97 million). According to the DGDDL, between 2003 and 2007, this gap fell to an average of CFAF 1.7 billion (about US$3 million). The gap is higher for communes in Abidjan than for those in the interior (table 4.5).

Table 4.5 Communes' Funding Capacity
CFAF million

	Former CNO zone communes	*Hinterland communes*	*Abidjan communes*	*All communes*
Real operating income	38,244	197,301	319,258	516,558
Real operating expenditure	36,395	149,221	294,536	443,756
Savings	1,849	48,080	24,722	72,802
Real income from investments	927	7,934	2,892	10,827
Investment capacity	2,776	56,014	27,614	83,629
Real investment expenditure	8,686	68,158	63,895	132,053
Funding gap or capacity	−5,910	−12,144	−36,281	−48,424

Source: DGDDL.

Strengthening the System for Municipal Finance and Expanding Financing Opportunities

The analysis of the financial situation of communes in Côte d'Ivoire reveals that they have little capacity to finance infrastructure investments. The main reason for this is the low level of internally generated resources, fiscal revenue, and government assistance combined with inconsistencies in the legal and institutional framework. In addition, the overall financial management standards at the commune level are affected by poor capacity and limited and systematic oversight from the central authorities, leading to prevalence of limited availability of financial reports, systems, the update of loans without repayment, and other systemic issues—hence limiting options for transitioning into alternative financing mechanisms.

The financing needs of cities have to be addressed within the context of devolved financial arrangements. Municipalities and regions are responsible for a wide range of public expenditures. Based on the principles of subsidiarity and least cost, municipalities are responsible for organizing community life and public participation in managing local affairs, for promoting and implementing local development, and for managing and maintaining public assets in their jurisdiction.[15]

The inconsistencies in the legal and institutional framework and its rollout—especially relative to the government's 2012 decentralization policy—need urgently to be reconciled. Devolution has not been accompanied by a transfer of financial and human resources. Law No. 2003–208 of July 7, 2003, on the transfer and distribution of responsibilities of the state to local authorities specifies 16 areas of expertise for transfer. But this division of powers is based on the old organization of local government with five levels of decentralization. Another impediment is that the implementation of the power transfer sometimes leads to conflicts of responsibility between decentralized entities and other public bodies.

The systemic gaps in financing across Global, Regional, and Domestic Connectors require immediate attention to address the issues of the regulatory framework, volume, and predictability of financing. Three sets of policy options need to be considered. First, address the inconsistencies between devolution and decentralization alignment so that delegated functions follow finance and so that minimum human resources capacity is in place. Second, strengthen municipal finance and revise the fiscal transfer systems in key areas, simplifying the number of transfers and supporting the expansion and improvement of own-source revenue collection. This entails registering all taxpayers, expanding street addressing and basic measures to consolidate the tax base and upgrading cadastral registers, and revising formulas for the allocation of shared revenues. Third, leverage collaboration among regions, municipalities, and utilities to generate economies of scale in infrastructure services delivery.

Complementing these interventions, the government should assess the efficiency of current transfer systems, consolidate administrative decentralization to enable improved performance at the commune level, and consider introducing new elements to incentivize performance. Steps could include (i) assess the performance of DGF and its efficiency in absorbing and using these resources; (ii) consider the introduction of other targeted development grants for urban areas with an emphasis on introducing conditions for performance (such as in revenue collection, budgeting, planning, and implementation, asset management, and financial management); (iii) introduce the use of a fixed percentage of national budget or national revenues as allocations for municipalities through DGF, to ensure predictable funding; (iv) review the performance of the FPCL and its relevance for the financing of local governments going forward, including addressing the issues of existing municipal debts; and (v) introduce minimum standards across all municipalities with an emphasis on large urban areas, focusing on human resources, audits, revenue collection, financial reporting, and budget and implementation.

In the medium to long term, government may explore the viability of additional new sources of financing. This would include (i) assessing the sustainability of the current municipal borrowing scheme to see whether or not it would be a credible instrument given the current low repayment rates; (ii) exploring to what extent municipalities in Abidjan could become sufficiently creditworthy to become eligible for subnational borrowing, including from the International Finance Corporation subnational financing window; (iii) exploring the opportunity to amend and update the public-private partnership (PPP) legislation to allow municipalities to further engage in PPPs[16] and strengthen their capacity to attract private sector investment in infrastructure and service delivery; (iv) investigating the opportunities for land-based financing, such as land value capture; and (v) expanding, deepening, and institutionalizing the existing mechanisms for intermunicipal collaboration (box 4.4). Of these potential new sources, (iii) and (v) will be the most promising options in the short to medium term.

Box 4.4 Mainstreaming Intermunicipal Collaboration

Intercommunal cooperation and development of municipal infrastructure are promising areas for municipal financing. One of the objectives of decentralization is to promote urban development and land planning. With the large number of municipalities and their disparities in population size, economic potential, and technical and human resources, it is hard to produce high-quality, affordable infrastructure and services that meet the expectations of individual users and the community as a whole. One solution is to promote groupings of municipalities to constitute another level of public policy. Their area would be in key local public services, including water distribution, sanitation, waste removal, and transport. Law No. 95–611 of August 3, 1995, defines the institutional framework for intermunicipal cooperation and is expected to be strengthened with a number of incentives to promote such cooperation.

Municipalities have already started to come together in this way. They have established an association, the Association of Cities and Communes of Côte d'Ivoire (Union des Villes et Communes de Côte d'Ivoire [UVICOCI]) and its various subgroups, as well as a few groupings of municipalities. UVICOCI also acts as a coordinator for the municipality subgroups. With the gradual development of municipal groupings, UVICOCI now has several regional and thematic groups to deal with issues in regions or homogeneous groups of municipalities. One of the purposes of grouping municipalities is to ensure that, within their territory, the responsibilities devolved from central government are fulfilled consistently, in a coordinated manner, and with effective use of resources (to avoid duplication).

Some groups have launched development projects, with partner assistance. These include building capacity, investing in infrastructure for municipalities, and managing forests and the environment. In the west, the European Development Fund has provided some towns with computerized systems and vehicles and has run pilot rural domestic water projects. Joint projects have been launched in health, agriculture, and education. Intermunicipal groupings have also been active in forest and environmental preservation.

Four sets of recommendations cover the key thematic areas described above.

Consolidate, Harmonize, and Enforce the Legal and Regulatory Framework for Municipal Financing

1. Establish an ad hoc committee to take over all draft and pending implementing legislation and propose corrections and additions to the existing text.
2. Refresh Act No. 2003–208 of July 7, 2003, on the transfer and distribution of competence of the state to local authorities to comply with the current organization of local government and to precisely define the powers transferred, taking into account the actual capacity of local communities.
3. Align the legal framework governing decentralization in Côte d'Ivoire with UEMOA directives, in particular the directive on the financial regime of decentralized bodies.
4. Ensure that municipal authorities and the regulatory authority alike strictly observe the regulatory deadlines for drafting and approving the triennial

program and the budget in line with the overall timetable set by Decree No. 31 of February 13, 1992.

5. Ensure effective enforcement of the Korhogo law, in particular those provisions that concern the salaries of municipal and regional workers, in order to avoid discouraging local government staff and to reduce staff losses.

Intervene to Strengthen the Intergovernmental Fiscal Framework

1. Adopt the Enforcement Decree of Act No. 2003–489 of December 26, 2003, to define the institutional framework and the method of calculation and allocation of the general operating grant and the general allocation of grants and transfers, making sure to take into account the umbrella organizations of the regions (Association des Régions et Districts de Côte d'Ivoire [ARDCI]) and communes (UVICOCI).

2. Revise the current procedure for provision of revenue sharing among the state, local authorities, and other agencies to take into account all taxes and state taxes allocated to local authorities. Ensure greater transparency regarding the modes of calculating shared fiscal revenue.

3. Make DGI systems adhere strictly to the time limit of 15 days for transferring the distribution tables of receipts to treasuries.

4. Develop disbursement plan transfers from the state to the local authorities in the beginning of each year, and adhere strictly to it. Quarterly transfers could be considered.

Strengthen the Local Revenue Base

1. Establish a mechanism for regulation limiting budget spending commitments with available resources to ensure the smooth implementation of the budget and avoid the accumulation of arrears.

2. Ensure that the regulatory deadlines for drafting and approving the three-year program and budget are complied with, both by municipal authorities and by the regulatory authority.

3. Encourage and support communes to formulate overall revenue enhancement plans, including exhaustive databases of taxpayers that can be updated regularly.

4. Modernize local tax collection procedures using geo-localization. A prerequisite is for the local cadastral register to be updated.

5. Build the capacity of municipalities and provide them with incentives to explore alternative financing mechanisms for infrastructure development in addition to continuing to enhance own-source revenue as a critical revenue source.

Follow Up on Specific New Areas for Municipal Financing

Asset and land management. Encourage communes to set up a database on communal land ownership, and establish a framework for consultation between the departments of the Ministry of Construction, Housing, Sanitation, and Urbanism and communes in order to supervise the attribution of land plots and ensure that municipal authorities are able to monitor such activities.

Public-private partnerships. Rectify decree No. 2012–1151 of December 19, 2012, to include specific reference to decentralized local authorities in particular communes, and undertake capacity-building interventions of selected communes for negotiating and managing PPPs.

Notes

1. This chapter is based on a desk review, including an analysis of financial data for local authorities, and on interviews with stakeholders including mayors and senior administrative officials from 14 communes.

2. Article 119 of the Constitution of August 1, 2000.

3. Including land use planning; development planning; urbanization and housing; communication; transport; health; public sanitation; environmental protection; urban security and civil defense; education, scientific research and professional and technical training; social, cultural, and human development activities; sports and leisure; promotion of economic development; promotion of tourism; communication; water, sanitation, and electricity; and social development areas, including support programs and safety nets for families, youth, women, children, the disabled, and the elderly.

4. See the review of the decentralization process conducted by the Ministry of the Interior and Security titled "Bilan de la decentralisation."

5. "Local authorities" is used for municipal and regional governments.

6. These are standard assumptions for decentralized service delivery models, but the study does not cover an analysis of service delivery costs between centralized and decentralized systems.

7. For example, in April 2014, after budgets had already been adopted, the ministry, unexpectedly, sent an official telegram to some municipalities, including Cocody, informing them of a 15 percent deduction from their regulatory 40 percent tax retrocession.

8. None of the 14 municipalities surveyed for this study has a strategic development plan.

9. Decree No. 31 of February 13, 1992, stipulates that the regulatory authority is granted 45 days from the date of submission, to approve the budget. Beyond this deadline, the municipal authority is allowed to begin executing the budget, even without approval. Officials stated, however, that in practice this deadline is never met, but the treasury accountant refuses to make payments until receiving notification of budget approval from the regulatory authority. Local authorities themselves are also sometimes to blame. When the mission carried out its tour in April, it noted that some municipalities' budgets had not yet been approved by the regulatory authority.

10. Article 17 of January 6, 1997, finance law No. 97–07 sets the amount, which is a percentage of overall revenue and varies according to the size of the population. The minimum percentage varies between 10 percent and 20 percent, and is inversely proportional to the size of the population. For communes whose population is below 20,000 inhabitants, the percentage is 20 percent, whereas, for communes with a population between 20,000 and 50,000, the proportion is 15 percent. Beyond 50,000 inhabitants the minimum proportion is 10 percent.

11. Article 109 of the law stipulates that "the tariffs and maximum rates of taxes collected by local authorities through assessment or as certificates of income shall be set by the

finance law." Article 110 states that "when the council of a local authority institutes a tax, it shall at the same session set the rate of such tax, bearing in mind the objective situation of its taxpayers."

12. This is due to the strong correlation between expenditure and resources and is, above all, a result of the budgetary rule that requires that the budget must show a balance between income and expenditure.

13. There are two stages in the loan process: (i) preparing the application and presenting it to the municipal council and (ii) reviewing and considering it in council. The result of the council's deliberations and the application are then transmitted to the Minister of the Interior and Security and the Minister of the Economy for joint approval.

14. Korogho and Odienné in the north; Yamoussoukro and Bouaké in the center; Daloa, Soubre, Man, and Danané in the west; San-Pédro in the southwest; Abengourou and Bondoukou in the east; and Yopougon, Adjamé, and Cocody in Abidjan.

15. Law No. 2003–208 of July 7, 2003, transferred specific responsibilities to municipalities on territorial development, development planning, urbanism and housing, roads and other communication networks, transport, health and hygiene, environment and natural resource management, security and civil protection, culture and social action, sport and leisure, economic development and employment, tourism, communication, water and sanitation, family, youth, and gender.

16. Local authorities are also increasingly turning to build–operate–transfer arrangements to make up for inadequate financing for income-generating infrastructure. This system has been used to construct markets, stalls, and kiosks. In Adjamé, a CFAF 12 billion market was built with financing provided entirely by the Société Ivoirienne de Concept et de Gestion, which will manage the market for 25 years and then turn it over to the municipality. Similar operations are in Treichville, Sinfra, and Daloa.

Bibliography

DGDDL (Direction Générale de la Décentralisation et du Développement Local), Côte d'Ivoire. *Bilan de la politique de décentralisation en Côte d'Ivoire de 2001–2011.* DGDDL.

GoCI (Government of Côte d'Ivoire). 2013. "Annex Fiscale." *Journal Officiel de la République de Côte d'Ivoire* (January 9).

Kouadio, Hugues, and Assande, Paul. 2014. "Côte d'Ivoire Urbanization Review: Work on Municipal Financing." Background paper for the Côte d'Ivoire Urbanization Review. Preliminary report. World Bank, Washington, DC.

Liu, Lilli, and Juan Pradelli. 2012. "Financing Infrastructure and Monitoring Fiscal Risks at the Subnational Level." Policy Research Working Paper WPS6069, World Bank.

Ministry of the Interior and Security, Côte d'Ivoire. 2006. "Bilan de la decentralization."

World Bank. 2014. "Mission d'évaluation des procédures de la Gestion des Finances Publiques locales."

Environmental Benefits Statement

The World Bank Group is committed to reducing its environmental footprint. In support of this commitment, World Bank Publications leverages electronic publishing options and print-on-demand technology, which is located in regional hubs worldwide. Together, these initiatives enable print runs to be lowered and shipping distances decreased, resulting in reduced paper consumption, chemical use, greenhouse gas emissions, and waste.

World Bank Publications follows the recommended standards for paper use set by the Green Press Initiative. The majority of our books are printed on Forest Stewardship Council (FSC)–certified paper, with nearly all containing 50–100 percent recycled content. The recycled fiber in our book paper is either unbleached or bleached using totally chlorine-free (TCF), processed chlorine-free (PCF), or enhanced elemental chlorine-free (EECF) processes.

More information about the Bank's environmental philosophy can be found at http://www.worldbank.org/corporateresponsibility.